CISKEI

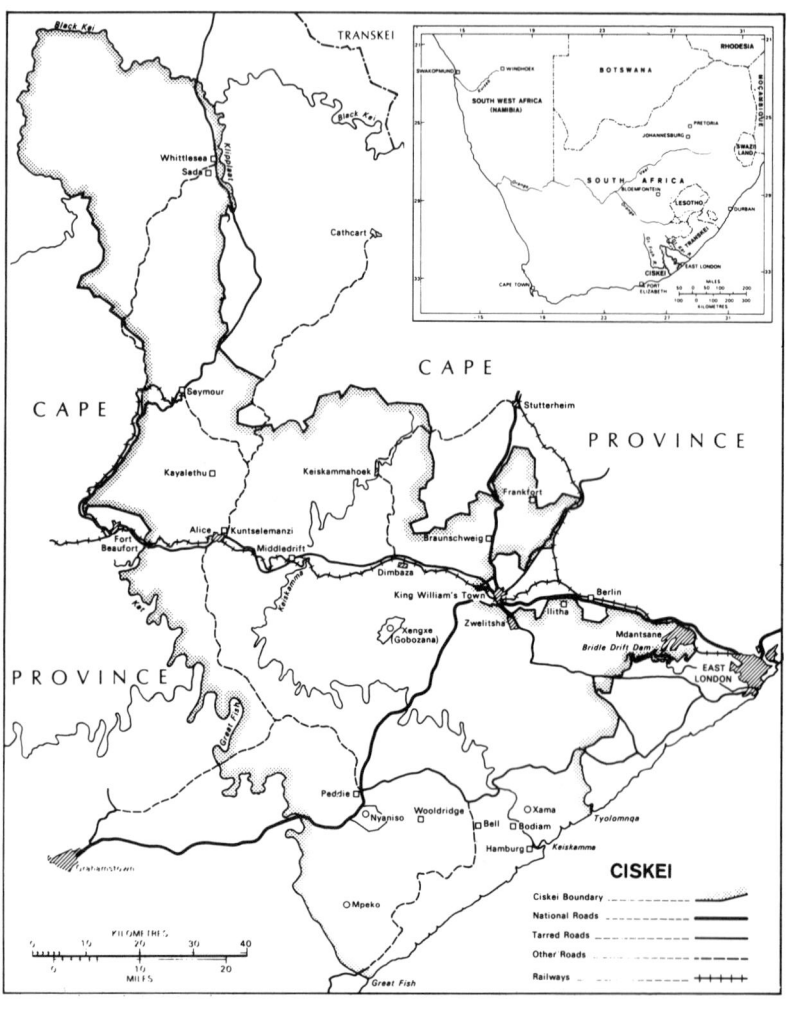

CISKEI

ECONOMICS AND POLITICS OF
DEPENDENCE IN A SOUTH AFRICAN HOMELAND

EDITED BY NANCY CHARTON

©1980 Croom Helm Ltd
Croom Helm Ltd, 2-10 St John's Road, London SW11

British Library Cataloguing in Publication Data
Ciskei
   1. Ciskeian Territory — Social conditions
   I. Charton, Nancy
   309.1'68'7   HN801.T/
ISBN 0-7099-0332-4

Printed and bound in Great Britain by
Redwood Burn Limited Trowbridge & Esher

CONTENTS

Acknowledgements
1. Introduction *Nancy Charton* — 9
2. Economic Development for the Ciskei *P.A. Black* — 16
3. Scattered Towns or an Urban System? *G.P. Cook* — 30
4. The Image of Agriculture in Two Ciskeian Rural Communities *J.B. McI. Daniel and N.L. Webb* — 48
5. The Ciskei Constitution *F.G. Richings* — 59
6. The Administrative System in the Ciskei *D.M. Groenewald* — 82
7. Ethnic Relations in the Ciskei *C.W. Manona* — 97
8. Ciskeian Political Parties *Nancy Charton and Gordon Renton kaTywakadi* — 122
9. The Legislature *Nancy Charton* — 149
10. Mass Communication in a Transitional Society *L.E. Switzer* — 185
11. Maqoma and Ciskeian Politics Today *M.G. Whisson and C.W. Manona* — 214
12. The Economics and Politics of Dependence *Nancy Charton* — 228

Bibliography — 235
Notes on Contributors — 246
Index — 248

ACKNOWLEDGEMENTS

We wish to acknowledge:
friendly co-operation and assistance from Chief L.L. Sebe and many government officials, opposition leaders and the people of the Ciskei;
financial support received from the Municipality of East London and the Human Sciences Research Council, who are not however responsible for opinions expressed;
the support and advice of three Directors of the Institute for Social and Economic Research, Rhodes University, Professors Denis Worrall, Michael Roberts and Jeffrey Opland;
statistical advice from Professor van der Watt, Department of Applied Mathematics, Rhodes University;
figures drawn by Oakley West, Geography Department, Rhodes University;
the secretarial services of Rene Vroom, Charmaine Riddin, Margaret Robinson, Celeste Herbert, Huibre Tomlinson and Jean Pote.

1 INTRODUCTION

Nancy Charton

1. Ciskei: A Socio-economic Profile

The area generally referred to as the Ciskei is situated on the eastern seaboard of South Africa between the Stormberg escarpment and the sea, the Great Kei river in the east and the Great Fish and Kat rivers in the west. It includes the black homeland created by the government of the Republic of South Africa in pursuit of its policy of 'separate development', as well as a white-owned corridor adjoining the Kei river. This latter strip of land separates the Ciskei homeland from the Transkei, now an independent state (see frontispiece).

The homeland, when ultimately consolidated, will consist of 800,000 hectares, of which approximately 13 per cent is classified as arable. Much of this land is overworked and badly eroded. The altitude varies from sea-level to some 1,200 metres on the inland plateau. The mean maximum temperatures vary from 30°C or less in July to 38°C and over in January while the mean minimum temperatures vary from below freezing-point in July on the higher ground to nearly 14°C along the coastal strip. Rainfall varies from 600 mm to 1,000 mm, the highest occurring in the vicinity of the escarpment. In spite of a relatively high rainfall for southern Africa the area is subject to periodic droughts. Few districts in the homeland have a potential for intensive agricultural development unless supported by irrigation. The region is used mainly for small stock and cattle farming, and small-scale crop production. Pineapples may be grown in coastal areas, and fruit and vegetable production is possible under irrigation. There are now three functioning irrigation schemes in the homeland and more are projected.

In the census of 1970 the black population permanently resident in the homeland was 526,000, some 20 per cent of which is urban.[1] The capital is at Alice, a small inland university town. The principal urban areas are Mdantsane, near East London, and Zwelitsha, the present administrative centre. The closeness of these urban black areas to centres of white economic development has meant that many could opt to become commuter labourers, rather than migrant labourers. The existence of job opportunities in contiguous white areas has stimulated the growth of the black towns. But in another sense it has inhibited their development. Black commercial enterprise and entrepreneurship have suffered from the proximity of white enterprises catering for a larger and wealthier market. Both Zwelitsha and Mdantsane are more like dormitory suburbs attached to the white urban areas, than fully fledged autonomous towns.

In both rural and urban Ciskei poverty is endemic. It is estimated that 14.4 per cent of the economically active men are absent in the 'white' areas earning their living.[2] Nearly 48 per cent of the population is under the age of 15, and population growth will thus continue to put pressure on the economic resources of the region. It is calculated that approximately 8,000 newcomers may be expected to enter the labour market each year between now and the turn of the century.

Geographers recognise four regions in the space economy of South Africa. The dominant region is centred on the southern Transvaal; it encompasses two-thirds of the national area, and contains all but three of its metropolitan nodes, it generates 75 per cent of the country's gross domestic product.[3] The remaining three regions are centred on Cape Town, Port Elizabeth and East London. The latter is the most poorly developed, due to its peripheral location in relation to Cape Town and the principal region, which includes Johannesburg and Durban, its hinterland lacks the mineral resources and the mining development characteristic of the principal region; it also lacks the agricultural development characteristic of the regions centred on Cape Town and Port Elizabeth. In South Africa regional inequalities are pronounced; the East London region is one of the poorest of all.

In the same way that the East London metropolitan region is peripheral to the principal region at the national level, Ciskei and Transkei are peripheral to East London at the regional level. The Ciskei relies heavily on subsistence agriculture; this accounted for from 19.5 per cent to 41.6 per cent of its GDP during the period from 1960 to 1971. The *per capita* income of the black inhabitants amounted to only R90.50.[4]

It is important to recognise that regional inequalities are not temporary features of the economy that will disappear with time. Myrdal for instance states that inequalities between regions are more likely to increase than decrease. The areas with inherent advantages will grow while those without special advantages will stagnate. The growing regions will attract flows of capital and labour; the lagging regions may lose population and even capital to the growing region which will further depress their economies. Upward and downward spirals of cumulative causation are likely to continue unless government action encourages economic activity in the stagnant region. These principals can be applied to both the Ciskei and to the region centred on East London. The Ciskei for instance exports labour both to East London and beyond, to the southern Transvaal. The East London region has been very slow to develop industrially, and has required outside stimulus to encourage investment. This has been provided by inducements offered to industrialists establishing factories in the area, in terms of the central government's 'border industries' policy, and in terms of the Physical Planning and Utilisation of Resources Act 1967. Even these stimuli have not promoted significant and sustained growth in the area.

2. Ciskei: Historical Perspective

The Ciskei has been the scene of conflict and interaction between black and white since the early eighteenth century. Both the white frontier farmers and the black Xhosa-speaking tribesmen desired access to the rich pasturage which exists in many areas. After more than a century of intermittent conflict the Ciskei was annexed by the British government in 1866 and incorporated into the Cape Colony. The Transkei was annexed during the following decade, but was always administered as a separate entity. Thus the history of colonial domination, and of the two different types of administration employed during that early period, account for the present distribution of the Xhosa-speaking people between two separate southern African territories, the Transkei and the Ciskei. This division is not strictly in accordance with the logic of the South African government's policy of separate development, in which the different 'peoples' of southern Africa furnish the bases for differentially constructed political institutions.

Because it was an integral part of the Cape Colony the black people of the Ciskei came to identify Cape Town as the focus of power, and the centre of government. Their educated elites became entitled to the limited franchise on the same basis as whites; thus from the end of the nineteenth century the political aspirations of the educated were focused on the central political institutions of the colony, and not on the traditional or local organs of government which were comparatively powerless.

Other factors consolidated the links between the Ciskei and the Cape Colony. Successive governors at the Cape pursued a policy of economic and cultural assimilation. The settlement pattern, which interspersed relatively small black and white farming areas, promoted integration at an economic level. There is evidence, for instance in the work of Colin Bundy,[5] that black farmers initially responded positively to the presence of a market for their produce. They even adopted new agricultural techniques, for example the use of the plough, although this ran counter to the traditional distribution of labour as between the sexes. Work opportunities on white farms were available to blacks who had been placed in areas soon made inadequate by a rapidly increasing population, and by techniques of agriculture related to periodic shifting, and to extensive use of pastures; individuation of land tenure often increased the pressure of population on land. The existence of growing commercial and industrial centres in East London, Queenstown and Port Elizabeth also provided urban employment opportunities close to home; large black residential townships grew up in these areas. White employers, whether rural or urban, were assured of a plentiful supply of cheap black labour. The blacks, because many of them retained a stake in the rural areas, were not obliged to supply the needs of their families from their urban employment; the rural allotments constituted a source of support for families, and security in the event of illness or old age.

The economic sphere was not the only field of integration. The Ciskei was an area of intense missionary endeavour, stemming initially from the English settlers. Schools, churches, hospitals, and ultimately a university, Fort Hare, grew up to play an important role in bringing European culture to the black population.

Thus many factors during the last century welded whites and blacks living between the Kei and the Fish rivers into mutually interdependent communities; and these same factors have tended to shape the institutions of both groups, economic, social and political. In particular they tended to mould the aspirations of educated blacks towards the acceptance of an integrated society, a white life-style and standard of living, and a polity in which they might share on the same basis as whites.

3. The Ciskei Research Project

The Ciskei Research Project was undertaken in 1974 in order to explore the interconnections between black and white in this area of South Africa at the present time. It was originally conceived by the late Professor D. Hobart Houghton as a desirable sequel to the Border Regional Survey carried out under his supervision in the early 1960s, and of the Keiskammahoek Rural Survey and urban research in East

Introduction

London undertaken by the Institute of Social and Economic Research of Rhodes University between 1947 and 1951. The latter surveys resulted in the publication of six volumes of reports. The rapidly changing political and economic situation suggested that another investigation was called for which would reassess urban and rural conditions, as well as political development in the regional, rather than the local context. This had not been examined before. The East London Municipality gave the plan for a new investigation its support, and application was made to the Human Sciences Research Council for the necessary funds. This application succeeded, and work began in 1974.

The project involved members of six departments of Rhodes University, the Departments of Anthropology, Economics, Geography, Journalism, Law and Political Studies. It was conceived as a unit with a single focus: the interrelationship of the Ciskei homeland with its environment, geographical, economic and political. It was jointly planned by the principal participants, but of necessity had to be multidisciplinary rather than interdisciplinary. Initially it was agreed that economic and political institutions would be studied functioning in their particular contexts, and that empirical material would be gathered from both rural and urban areas.

Methodologically speaking, the survey has not been geared to any particular theory or theories of economic and political development. Each participant has been free to devise his own methodology, and to adopt the approach with which he felt most comfortable. In each case where a theoretical framework has been used, it is made explicit in the text.

Many different methods were employed to gather the necessary data. Questionnnaires elicited information from the black employees of a selected sample of factories in the East London area, to determine the sex and age structure of the work force, their wages, level of education, rate of job turnover and living conditions. Forty-four members of the Ciskei Legislative Assembly were interviewed in order to determine their relationship with the electorate and to evaluate the channels of communication which connect the people with the legislature. Two township elections in 1974 in Mdantsane and Zwelitsha were observed and all participants interviewed informally. All voluntary associations in the townships were identified and office bearers were informally interviewed. The objective in this case was to evaluate voluntary associations as channels of communication in the political process.

Several surveys were made in Mdantsane. An economic survey of 300 randomly selected households sought to establish occupations, incomes and patterns of consumption in 1975. The political attitudes of another 300 randomly selected households were recorded in 1976. In this case the member of the household interviewed was selected in order to obtain a sample stratified for age and sex. Later in that year a mass-media survey covered 270 heads of households.

In the rural areas two villages were chosen for their contrasting lifestyles, the one relatively 'progressive', the other relatively 'traditional'. Both are Mfengu communities, one part of an Mfengu chiefdom, the other part of a Xhosa chiefdom. This contrast proved very valuable in studying ethnic groups in a minority situation at local level, within the chiefdom, and at regional level, within the context of the Xhosa-dominated Ciskei itself. The ethnic factor was also observed in a third area, this time a Xhosa minority in an Mfengu chiefdom. We are indebted to Professor Philip Mayer for permitting us to use this information gathered for another project under his supervision. At Nyaniso near Peddie and Gobozana near Middledrift (see frontispiece map) 50 heads of homesteads randomly selected in each of the villages were interviewed with a view to establishing patterns of social change, attitudes towards agriculture, and towards the mass media, and with a view to learning about the dissemination of information.

The technique of participant observation was used in both rural and urban areas. Research workers spent six weeks in each village, attending all social gatherings, talking with and interviewing villagers informally, and recording their impressions of the social and political process. The township elections in Zwelitsha and Mdantsane were also observed and our research worker sat in on the 1975 session of the Ciskei Legislative Assembly.

Other sources of empirical data were the verbatim records of debates in the Legislature from 1971 to 1976, the legislation passed and official Ciskei government reports. At local level the minutes of councils were examined when available, and also the records of the local labour bureaux, which direct migrant labourers to jobs in the 'white' urban areas. Press cuttings from all the English and Afrikaans newspapers culled by a cutting service from January 1974 to June 1977 were examined, using content analysis techniques when appropriate. The local Xhosa paper, *Imvo Zabantsundu*, was examined by a black journalist in order to assess its political news.

Finally in May 1977 a workshop was held in Grahamstown under the auspices of the Institute of Social and Economic Research where all participants were able to share their preliminary findings with members of the Ciskeian government, leading members of the Ciskeian opposition, the heads of Ciskeian government departments and a number of academics from other universities.

Work commenced on the project in January 1974. By the end of 1976 data gathering was complete. This book therefore represents developments in the Ciskei up until December 1976; however material has been reviewed and revised by most contributors up to July 1979.

Some difficulties were initially encountered. For instance, in 1974 legislators refused to answer questions of a socio-economic nature. The questionnaire was redesigned in the light of their objections, and was administered in 1975. The survey of political attitudes in Mdantsane also encountered opposition from the Township Council which saw the questionnaire as placing too much emphasis on tribalism. Here again offending questions had to be removed. In East London the paucity of information available about industries in that city made sampling a problem; resistance was also encountered from certain industrialists. In the rural areas our white research workers were unable to sleep in the village which they were investigating, although permits had been issued to them to work in the areas in question. Such regulations make the task of anthropologists very difficult.

However, in the three years of data gathering all research workers experienced more courtesy and co-operation than rejection. And it is notable that in the field none of the many surveys encountered any resistance, except the initial one in the Legislature.

Notes

1. Benbo, *Ciskei Economic Review* (Bureau for Economic Research re Bantu Development, Pretoria, 1975), p. 25. (Our estimates are somewhat higher, see p. 46).
2. Benbo, *Black Development in South Africa* (Perskor, Johannesburg, 1976), p. 31.
3. C. Board, R.J. Davies and T.J.D. Fair, 'The Structure of the South African Space Economy: An Integrated Approach', *Regional Studies*, 4 (1970), p. 383.
4. Benbo, *Ciskei Economic Review*, p. 36.
5. C. Bundy, 'The Emergence and Decline of a South African Peasantry', *African Affairs*, 71 (1972).

2 ECONOMIC DEVELOPMENT FOR THE CISKEI

P.A. Black

In the literature on economic development much attention has been given to the problem of income distribution. This is because economic development has been accompanied by an extremely unequal distribution of resources in general, and of income in particular. In most developing countries it is only a relatively small number of people who own land and capital, earn high incomes and who are reasonably healthy and well educated. Lipton puts it succinctly: 'the problem of poverty is a problem of the distribution of income, jobs and land'.[1]

Inequality is largely the outcome of the particular way in which the limited economic resources of developing countries have been allocated: most economists agree that these resources have not always been used in an economically efficient way. It is within this context that this chapter approaches the problem of the economic development of the Ciskei. The chapter consists of four main sections: in Section one we explain the process of economic development as seen by three schools of thought, namely the neo-classical, neo-Marxist and structuralist schools; Section two looks at the nature and extent of the economic problem as it exists in the Ciskei today; Section three deals with some general policy implications, and Section four with the role of the informal sector in the development of the Ciskei.

1. The Process of Economic Development

Neo-classical theories of development generally distinguish between two sectors of economic activity, namely a traditional agricultural sector in which incomes are generally low because of a supposedly unlimited supply of labour relative to capital; and a modern industrial sector where incomes are high due to a relative abundance of capital.[2] The respective marginal productivities and factor prices are therefore different between the two sectors: the price of capital is higher in the agricultural sector while that of labour is again higher in the industrial sector. Accordingly, capital may be expected to flow to the agricultural sector and labour to the industrial sector, until the differences in factor prices and incomes are completely eliminated, and with it the problem of underdevelopment too. To the neo-classical economists underdevelopment represents a temporary deviation from an equilibrium state, which is automatically redressed by the 'incentive-providing mechanisms of the market'.

To say that the predictions of the neo-classical theory have not come true is to state the obvious. There is enough evidence to show that the development problem has become progressively worse over the years. Capital has not flowed to the agricultural sector to any significant extent, and although it is true that many people have migrated to the industrial sector, only a relatively small number has managed to obtain adequate employment. In the industrial sector capital has been used relatively extensively and labour relatively sparsely, notwithstanding the fact that capital has been the scarce and labour the abundant factor of production. The reason for these inefficiencies lies in the generally imperfect nature of the market as it exists in developing countries, for example, imperfect substitutability and the indivisibility and immobility of the factors of production.

The *neo-Marxist* approach to development is based on the economic theories of Karl Marx.[3] According to the neo-Marxists, underdevelopment is an inevitable consequence of the system of international capitalism. Through various forms of imperialism, the capitalist system brings into effect a so-called dependency relationship between different countries, and between different groups of people within a country; the relationship is one in which a 'metropolis' or 'centre' exerts a dominating influence upon its 'satellite' or 'periphery'. The metropolis is dependent for its development on the underdevelopment of the satellite: it needs to destroy the traditional, precapitalist structures of the satellite in order to pave the way for the expropriation and appropriation of surplus value. In a recent attack on the dependency thesis, Kay showed that, *ceteris paribus*, the amount of surplus value appropriable by the metropolis depends, not on the underdevelopment of the satellite, but on its continued development:[4] 'In principle there is no counter to the argument that development increases the potential for exploitation'. However, since the development of the satellite may lead to the emergence there of new dominant groups capable of appropriating the surplus for themselves, there is an obvious need for the metropolis to determine the 'optimum' rate of development of its satellite: whereas too little development limits the amount of surplus value produced in the satellite, too much of it may threaten the dominant position of the metropolis altogether.[5]

The latter notion ties in well with the neo-Marxist interpretation of

South Africa's homelands policy.[6] As the Marxists see it, the development of the homelands is an attempt to counteract the declining productive capacity of the black reserve areas. This means in essence that industrial wages have to compensate for the lack of a subsistence basis. The purpose of the policy is to provide subsistence to migrant families in the homelands, which acts as a supplement to the low wages earned by migrants working in the white-controlled parts of the country. Not only does this enable white capitalists to maintain their rate of surplus value intact, but it also makes possible the reproduction of labour-power in the homelands. Moreover, the success of the policy is seen to depend on the ability of the system to maintain production in the reserves at a level sufficient to enable families to subsist, but not at a level sufficiently high as to discourage migration.

There are good reasons why both the classical and structuralist schools prefer to explain the phenomenon of underdevelopment in non-Marxist terms. Chief among these reasons is the spuriousness of the labour theory of value which, it is alleged, severely limits the predictive power of the general Marxist model.[7] For similar reasons, however, the *structuralists* either reject or adjust the neo-classical model in their attempt to 'identify specific rigidities, lags and other characteristics of the structure of developing economies'.[8] The structuralist school incorporates the writings of Myint, Myrdal, Prebisch, Singer and many others,[9] and it differs from the neo-classical and neo-Marxist schools in its particular methodological approach to economic development: 'The neo-Marxist policy recommendations suffer from the same defects as the neo-classical in that they are implicit in the initial assumptions rather than being derived from an analysis based on empirical estimates of the underlying structural relations.'[10]

Within a structuralist context, it is possible to distinguish between two basic demand relationships, namely the foreign demand and the demand of the domestic rich for the goods produced in developing countries. The foreign demand is usually met by firms which are able to import capital and technology cheaply from the economically advanced countries. This is made possible by the existence of overvalued exchange rates, artificially low interest rates and internal terms of trade which favour the industrial sector.[11] It is for these reasons that exporting firms generally tend to use techniques of production which are relatively capital- and skill-intensive. Moreover, the increased demand for skilled labour leads to wage increases which further encourage the use of labour-saving production techniques. The second demand relationship follows directly from the first. The increase in the incomes of skilled workers raises the demand for precisely those goods which are either imported or locally produced by means of capital-intensive techniques;[12] and in both cases the effect is to slow down the rate of growth of employment. Jolly sums up the total effect as follows: 'Slow growth in employment is in large part an example of the costs to the low-income countries of being dependent on the techniques of the rich.'[13]

The technological dependence of developing countries has generally led to considerable increases in the rural-urban wage differential and in the rate of rural-urban migration. Todaro has shown that the decision to migrate depends not only on the prevailing wage differential, but also on the probability of finding a remunerative job in the urban industrial sector: a person may be prepared to be unemployed or underemployed in the urban areas if he has a more than even chance of ultimately getting a job which pays him more than twice the amount that he can earn in the rural areas.[14] In the meantime, however, such migrants do have to earn a living somehow and this they are able to do by becoming self-employed in the so-called informal sector of the economy. The latter sector has received much attention recently, and since it is further explored in Section four below, suffice it to mention here that the sector consists of a wide variety of low-income activities all of which are characterised by self-employment, small scale of operation and illegal status.[15]

How do the homelands, and particularly the Ciskei, fit into this picture? It seems reasonable to argue that the economic development of South Africa has followed a general pattern similar to the one outlined above: the role of western or western orientated ideas, tastes and techniques in the development of South Africa is widely recognised; so, too, are the inequalities among the South African population. The underdevelopment of the Ciskei is one of the inevitable consequences of this overall pattern of development. It is indeed possible to argue that the policy to develop the Ciskei has generally arisen from a realisation of the basic untenability of a system which is based on inequalities between individuals, regions and nations.

2. The Economic Problem of the Ciskei

Owing to a lack of data it has become customary to define and measure the economic problem in developing countries in terms of the number of people who are unemployed and underemployed. It should be realised, however, that employment, or the lack of it, represents only one part of the general problem of underdevelopment; the provision of adequate employment opportunities will not by itself satisfy the widely divergent demands of the people. There is also a need for higher incomes, more and better health, education and training facilities, adequate transport services and other social amenities.[16] A similar approach is also reflected in the following statement by the Chief Minister of the Ciskei: 'The basic objectives of man, and therefore of all societies whether developing or developed, can be summarized in one phrase: to improve the quality of life.'[17]

The Ciskei is a land of extreme poverty. A survey of 1,000 rural households completed during the mid-sixties revealed that most workers were unemployed or underemployed, or else simply under-utilised in the sense of not being able to work at their most productive level.[18] This general underutilisation of labour largely explained the extreme and widespread poverty of the people: whereas the average household income was equal to only 38 per cent of the estimated corresponding Poverty Datum Line (PDL), no less than 91 per cent of all households received an income that was less than the PDL. If one looks at the rural underdevelopment of the Ciskei from the viewpoint of the socio-historical development of South Africa as a whole, it would appear that the main 'contributory' factors are the high rate of population growth, the lack of land and physical and human capital and, indirectly, the restrictions placed on the spatial and occupational mobility of Ciskeian workers.[19]

Turning to the urban areas, it appears that the black population of the combined East London-King William's Town region increased at the average annual rate of 4.8 per cent between 1960 and 1970.[20] Since this rate was partly attributable to the resettlement and continuous migration of work-seekers to towns like Mdantsane and Zwelitsha, it follows that the number of persons of working age may well have increased by more than 4.8 per cent per year. Against this, the number of local job opportunities for blacks grew at the lower rate of 4.2 per cent per year during the same period. The net effect of this discrepancy between supply and demand was that the non-working black population increased by 5.1 per cent annually, which suggests that unemployment in Mdantsane and Zwelitsha probably rose quite substantially between 1960 and 1970. Moreover, the trend seems to have continued in the seventies. In a survey of 300 Mdantsane households conducted in 1975, 217 persons reported that they were seeking work, but unable to find any. Of these, 47 persons earned an income from part-time work in both the formal and informal sectors of East London and Mdantsane. This left 170 unemployed persons, which is equivalent to an unemployment rate of 23 per cent, the corresponding rates for males and females being 16 per cent and 29 per cent respectively. These rates are much higher than most other comparable estimates of black urban unemployment in South Africa.[21]

In the Mdantsane survey the average household income was found to be R174 per month, the income per earner R82 and the income per head of population R31. More than 75 per cent of all households earned less than the average income of R174. The median income was estimated at R107, which means that 50 per cent of all households earned less than R107 per month, and 50 per cent therefore more. The difference between the average and median income figures is indicative of a highly unequal pattern of income distribution: whereas the earnings of a small number of households were well above the average income level, those of the great majority of households fell below it. One only begins to grasp the magnitude and extent of the prevailing poverty in Mdantsane when the above figures are compared with the corresponding PDL; for all its shortcomings, the PDL is still the only available measure of absolute poverty in South Africa. In 1975 the Institute for Planning Research at the University of Port Elizabeth estimated the PDL for East London at R105 per month for a family consisting of six persons.[22] If our sample is taken to be representative of Mdantsane as a whole, it therefore follows that in 1975 approximately 40 to 50 per cent of all households in Mdantsane earned less than the estimated minimum subsistence level of income.

As may be expected, income size appears to be positively related to the degree of skill and standard of education of earners. People on high incomes are mostly skilled and semi-skilled production workers, salesmen, administrative clerks and teachers, whilst those on low incomes tend to be service workers in the formal and informal sectors. The significance of the informal sector is reflected in the fact that 90 persons, or 14 per cent of all earners, were totally dependent on informal sources of income. A further 127 full-time earners, or 20 per cent of the total, received additional income from informal sources. These sources included needlework, knitting, carpentry, the buying and selling of meat, vegetables and beer, taxi services, money-lending, divining and board and lodging. As far as the relationship between income and education is concerned, it was found that people with low incomes were generally poorly educated insofar as very few of them had reached the higher secondary level of education. At the lower secondary and primary levels, however, the correlation was not very strong. This, together with the fact that there were many workers attending school part time and also many pupils performing part-time work, may point to the emergence of a class of 'educated' poor: an increasing number of people seem to be seeking education with a view to preparing themselves for jobs which they expect (or hope) will become available in the future.

The problem of Mdantsane is really a consequence of the fact that the industrial sector has consistently grown faster than the agricultural sector of the Ciskei. This left the growing population of the Ciskei with little or no alternative but to seek a livelihood in East London and in the other urban areas of South Africa. At the same time the demand for labour has not grown as rapidly as the labour supply: for reasons already discussed, the economy of East London has simply not been able to keep pace with the rising employment needs of the market, so that a growing number of people have been left unemployed, inadequately educated and trained and generally poor. The solution to these problems would seem to depend largely on the extent to which new employment opportunities can be created both in Mdantsane and in the rural areas of the Ciskei. Accordingly, while not denying the need to provide health, education and other social services in the Ciskei — a need which has already been recognised by the private and public sectors alike — the remainder of this chapter is devoted to an analysis of the employment potential of the Ciskei.

3. General Policy Implications

It has been shown that the Ciskei and its border areas have a comparative cost advantage in the production of such basic consumer goods as food, clothing, footwear, furniture and domestic dwellings, the reason being that production depends mostly on local materials and unskilled labour.[23] These are also the goods for which there is a potentially large and growing demand in the Ciskei. In the survey, for example, it appeared that approximately 63 per cent of any given increase in the income of Mdantsane residents is likely to be spent on basic consumer goods. What is required, therefore, is that local suppliers should create their own demand by means of a greater utilisation of the local market: an increase in the output of a good X not only provides more income to those who are engaged in its production, but it also raises the demand for X simultaneously by virtue of the new purchasing power created in this way.

Labour-intensive industries may be promoted either by direct action or indirectly, by changes in the relative prices of capital and labour. A good example of the latter is the use of labour subsidies which may be implemented in different ways. If the subsidy is based on the number of workers employed, rather than on the cost of labour, it may well involve some sacrifice in the growth of output. In some cases capital-intensive techniques may be more efficient than labour-intensive techniques in the sense that they use less capital per unit of output.[24] However, to the extent that productivity is measured in terms of the given market prices of capital and labour, any such difference in productivity between capital- and labour-intensive techniques may turn out quite meaningless. The reason for this is that market prices do not necessarily reflect the social opportunity costs of employing labour and capital in developing countries: labour is usually overvalued and capital undervalued because of various market imperfections.[25] It is in this sense that strategies which promote employment at the expense of output are often regarded as socially desirable — 'It is worth sacrificing production to reduce this evil' (of unemployment).[26]

Alternatively, if the subsidy is based on the cost of labour, its effect on employment is likely to be limited by technological conditions of factor productivity and substitutability; that is, it may favour those firms that use relatively capital- and skill-intensive production techniques.[27] This seems to be true of the decentralisation policy in South Africa where the subsidy is based on the cost of black labour. The policy has been relatively unsuccessful in terms of the number of job opportunities created by firms in the border areas of the homelands.[28] It is also true, however, that these firms use more capital per unit of labour than the firms which have been established inside the homelands themselves, the reason being that whereas firms in the interior tend to produce for the local markets of the homelands, border industries are geared to the non-homeland and external markets.[29]

There are numerous ways in which it would be possible to raise the overall performance of the Ciskeian economy. Firstly, there is an urgent need to redirect resources to the agricultural sector of the Ciskei. Past efforts to develop agriculture consisted largely of land-intensive (as opposed to capital- and labour-intensive) methods of production, for example, fencing and soil conservation by means of planting grass and building contour banks. These measures have yielded very modest results: although large parts of the Ciskei have already been developed on a land-intensive basis, the average grain yield per unit of land has remained practically unchanged for decades.[30] This is notwithstanding the great potential for agricultural development in the Ciskei. Brand, Lipton and others have shown that the existing level of output can be increased significantly by the use of such labour- (and capital-) intensive measures as the application of irrigation, seed, fertiliser and pesticides, as well as the promotion of credit and marketing facilities.[31] Given the shortage of land and an abundant supply of labour, 'the obvious strategy is to go for a labour-intensive agriculture'.[32] There can be little doubt that such measures would raise the number of people that can be supported by agriculture, and reduce the rate of rural-urban migration within the Ciskei.

Secondly, a strong case can be made for an increase in the existing financial concessions which apply to the various growth points in and around the Ciskei. Such an increase may well serve to attract industries that would otherwise have been discouraged by the relatively adverse spatial location of the Ciskei.[33] Another possibility is the introduction of differential financial concessions giving preference to labour-intensive industries. This may be achieved, for example, if the existing tax concession were made to vary either according to the size of the total cost of black labour, or with the number of black workers employed by decentralising firms. On the regional front, the various white and black local authorities might consider the creation of a fund which would enable them to provide additional financial assistance to prospective industrialists on a selective basis.

Finally, the Ciskei National Development Corporation could promote more small-scale manufacturing and service industries in the Ciskei, and particularly in Mdantsane and Zwelitsha. The effect of this would be to raise the labour content of investment in the area, insofar as these industries use less capital relative to labour than industries in the border areas of East London and King William's Town. Moreover, it would reduce the proportion of total income spent in the white areas, and hence redirect the otherwise dissipated spread effects to the Ciskei itself;[34] to this extent it would lessen the Ciskei's dependence on the white sector of the economy.

4. The Informal Sector

Although the existence of an informal as against a formal sector is generally recognised today, its role in development is a cause for much debate. Some regard it as a 'dependent' sector whose sole purpose is to provide cheap goods and services to the workers in the formal sector, thus enabling employers to maintain a given 'subsistence' or 'poverty' wage level. In this view, the informal sector is seen as 'part of the whole range of low-return activities which generate surplus for appropriation by the owners of foreign capital and by the compradors'.[35] Others see it as a potentially viable sector which is capable of performing the functions of the formal sector in a socially and economically more efficient way; that is, it supplies the goods and services not provided by the formal sector, or supplies them at a lower cost and it uses less foreign exchange and more labour per unit of output.[36] The reason why it is said to be relatively 'backward' is that it is constantly being discriminated against by the authorities: its illegal nature prevents it from competing with the formal sector on an equal footing, so that it is destined to remain small and poor relative to the formal sector. More generally, the interrelationship between the formal and informal sectors is largely an empirical question, and possibly also a normative issue which depends on one's particular viewpoint. What is more certain, however, is that the urban informal sector provides income-earning opportunities to a great many people who would otherwise have been worse off in the rural areas. The family system of self-employment could be said to have transferred from the rural to the urban areas.

Recent ILO reports on Kenya and Colombia[37] have come out strongly in favour of the adoption of measures which would raise the productivity of informal-sector activities. Such measures include a review of the existing health and housing standards, the total or partial abolition of the licensing system, a greater availability of loan capital, increased government purchasing of goods and services from the informal sector and the initiation of technical research into the type of products especially suitable for production by the informal sector. Most of these measures would also seem to be directly applicable to the Ciskei. For example, there may well be a need to relax some of the licensing policies which exist in towns like Mdantsane, Zwelitsha and Dimbaza. Licensing is in many ways a western invention the only purpose of which is to maintain western standards of health and business practice. Such standards are maintained by the artificial creation of monopolistic or oligopolistic markets, where the distribution of goods and services is placed in the hands of those who are capable of meeting the specific conditions of the licensing system. The result is that a relatively small volume of output is produced at relatively high prices. It is against such a background that informal businesses operate, and although they may be illegal and subjected to various forms of harassment, they are capable of, and often succeed in, providing a more equitable service than the formal sector.

It may also be possible to use the lending policy of the official development corporation as a means to promote informal-sector activities in the Ciskei. In the past the Bantu Investment and Xhosa Development Corporations have been severely criticised for supplying too few loans at too high interest rates. Interest was charged at the same rates as those applicable to similar institutions in the white areas of South Africa. The corporations also insist on obtaining some form of tangible security from prospective borrowers. Furthermore, it appears that loan facilities are sometimes subject to certain rather severe conditions pertaining to the management abilities of prospective borrowers. This point is worth stressing in greater detail:

> The method used in evaluating the requests for assistance is to weigh the personal factors pertaining to the applicant against the demands and potential of the business. Each applicant's age, training, previous experience, specific business knowledge and acumen and training potential are considered. Assets and liabilities are examined and the buying power on which the business concerned will be able to rely, in order to ensure economic success is surveyed.[38]

These practices largely explain why so few applications for loans have been successful in the past: by the end of 1972 the development corporations had approved only 16 per cent of the total number of loan applications received by them. The loans actually granted were mostly in respect of such relatively large-scale formal-sector services as general dealers, liquor stores, garages, restaurants, cafés and hotels.[39]

There is clearly an urgent need to abolish the various restrictions which inhibit the growth of the informal sector. Such a step would strengthen its competitive position vis-à-vis the formal sector, and enable the economy to provide more employment opportunities, lower the prices of goods and services and reduce the travelling costs of the consumer. Even if development along these lines might ultimately bring about a so-called 'formalisation' of the informal sector — for example, the emergence of employer-employee relations and various forms of quality control — this would not in any way undo its positive contributions in providing new jobs and incomes to the people of the Ciskei.

5. Summary

The present chapter adopted a so-called structuralist approach to the economic development of the Ciskei; that is, underdevelopment is seen as the outcome of certain structural rigidities which prevent the market from performing its normal allocative function. There is enough evidence to show that the market has failed extensively in its task of providing adequate job opportunities to the growing population of the Ciskei. This failure is further borne out by the large inequalities which exist among the people with respect to income, occupation, skill and education. The solution to these problems would seem to lie in the provision of such services as health, education and training, and in the promotion of labour-intensive industries in both the formal and informal sectors of the Ciskeian economy. Such a strategy would be consistent with the local economy's ability to produce labour-intensive consumer goods relatively cheaply. An increase in the supply of these goods not only provides more jobs to more people, but it also creates new incomes which are likely to be spent on the very goods in question: supply will create its own demand locally if it is regulated in accordance with the needs of the people.

Notes

1. M. Lipton, 'The International Diffusion of Technology' in D. Seers and L. Joy (eds.), *Development in a Divided World* (Penguin, Harmondsworth, 1971), p. 62.
2. G.H. Borts and J.L. Stein, *Economic Growth in a Free Market* (Columbia University Press, New York, 1964); J.C. Fei and G. Ranis, 'A Theory of Economic Development', *American Economic Review*, 51 (1961); D.W. Jorgensen, 'Surplus Agricultural Labour and the Development of a Dual Economy', *Oxford Economic Papers*, 19 (1967).
3. P. Baran, *The Political Economy of Growth* (Monthly Review Press, New York, 1957); A.G. Frank, *Latin America: Underdevelopment or Revolution* (Monthly Review Press, New York, 1969); T. Dos Santos, 'The Structure of Dependence', *American Economic Review*, 60 (1970).
4. G. Kay, *Development and Underdevelopment: A Marxist Analysis* (Macmillan, London, 1975).
5. P. Le Roux, 'An Analytical Approach to the Poor White Phenomenon in South Africa', paper read at conference of the Economic Society of SA, Pretoria (1977).
6. F.A. Johnstone, 'White Prosperity and White Supremacy in South Africa Today', *African Affairs*, 69 (1970); M. Legassick, 'Legislation, Ideology and Economy in post 1948 South Africa', *Journal of Southern African Studies*, 1 (1974).
7. B.S. Kantor and H.F. Kenny, 'The Poverty of Neo-Marxism: the case of

South Africa', *Journal of Southern African Studies*, 3 (1976).

8. H.B. Chenery, 'The Structuralist Approach to Development Policy', *American Economic Review*, 65 (1975).

9. H. Myint, *Economic Theory and Underdeveloped Countries* (Oxford University Press, London, 1973); G. Myrdal, *Economic Theory and Underdeveloped Regions* (Methuen, London, 1957); R. Prebisch, *The Economic Development of Latin America and its Principal Problems* (UN Department of Economic Affairs, New York, 1950); H.W. Singer, 'Dualism Revisited: A New Approach', *Journal of Development Studies*, 7 (1970-1).

10. H.B. Chenery, 'The Structuralist Approach to Development Policy'.

11. D. Seers, 'Rich Countries and Poor' in Seers and Joy (eds.), *Development in a Divided World*; G. Ranis, 'Unemployment and Factor Price Distortions' in R. Jolly, E. De Kadt *et al.* (eds.), *Third World Employment* (Penguin, Harmondsworth, 1973).

12. T. Weisskopf, 'Capitalism, Underdevelopment and the Future of Poor Countries', *Review of Radical Political Economics* (1972).

13. R. Jolly, 'Manpower and Education' in Seers and Joy (eds.), *Development in a Divided World*, p. 255.

14. M. Todaro, 'A Model of Labour Migration and Urban Unemployment in Less Developed Countries', *American Economic Review*, 60, (1969-70).

15. ILO, *Employment Incomes and Equity: A Strategy for Increasing Productive Employment in Kenya* (International Labour Office, Geneva, 1972).

16. Seers, 'Rich Countries and Poor'.

17. L.L. Sebe, 'Potential Problems and Priorities of the Ciskei', *AIESEC Journal*, vol. 1 (1975).

18. J. Maree and P.J. De Vos, *Underemployment, Poverty and Migrant Labour in the Transkei and Ciskei* (SA Institute of Race Relations, Johannesburg, 1975).

19. Ibid., pp. 6-8.

20. B.D. Phillips and V. Renders, *Industrial Change in the East London/King William's Town and Port Elizabeth/Uitenhage Metropolitan Regions: 1960-70* (Institute for Planning Research, University of Port Elizabeth, Port Elizabeth, 1976), p. 29.

21. University of Natal, 'Workshop on Unemployment and Labour Reallocation in South Africa', unpublished papers, Pietermaritzburg, 1977.

22. J.F. Potgieter, *The Household Subsistence Level in the Major Urban Centres of the Republic of South Africa* (Institute for Planning Research, University of Port Elizabeth, Port Elizabeth, 1975).

23. P. Black, 'An Analysis of Consumer Potential in Mdantsane', in N. Charton (ed.), 'A Socio-Economic Survey of the Border and Ciskei Regions', unpublished report, Institute of Social and Economic Research, Rhodes University, Grahamstown, 1978, p. 57ff.

24. F. Stewart and P.P. Streeton, 'Conflicts between Output and Employment Objectives' in Jolly, De Kadt *et al.* (eds.), *Third World Employment*.

25. ILO, *Employment and Economic Growth* (International Labour Office, Geneva, 1964); I.M.D. Little and J. Mirrlees, *Manual of Industrial Project Analysis in Developing Countries*, vol. 2, Social Cost Benefit Analysis (OECD, New York, 1969).

26. Stewart and Streeton, 'Conflicts Between Output and Employment Objectives'.

27. M.S. Ahluwalia, 'The Scope for Policy Intervention' in H. Chenery and M.S. Ahluwalia *et al.*, *Growth with Redistribution* (Oxford University Press, London, 1974).

28. T. Bell, 'Some Aspects of Industrial Decentralisation in South Africa', in *South African Journal of Economics*, 41 (1973).

29. N.J. Rhoodie et al., *Homelands: The Role of the Corporations* (Chris van Rensburg Publications, Johannesburg, 1974).

30. Benbo, *Black Development in South Africa*, pp. 80-3; S. Brand, 'Agricultural and Economic Development in Southern Africa' in J. Barratt et al. (eds.), *Accelerated Development in Southern Africa* (Macmillan, London, 1974).

31. M. Lipton, 'The South African Census and the Bantustan Policy', *World Today*, 28 (1972).

32. Ibid., p. 264.

33. Phillips and Renders, *Industrial Change in the East London . . . Regions*.

34. P.A. Black, 'Regional Development Strategy and the Black Homelands' in M.L. Truu (ed.), *Public Policy and the South African Economy* (Oxford University Press, Cape Town, 1976).

35. C. Leys, 'Interpreting African Underdevelopment: Reflections on the ILO Report on Employment, Incomes and Equality in Kenya', *African Affairs*, 72 (1973), p. 426.

36. ILO, *Employment Incomes and Equity*: J. Weeks, 'Policies for Expanding Employment in the Informal Urban Sector of Developing Economies', *International Labour Review*, 111 (1975).

37. ILO, *Towards Full Employment: A Programme for Colombia* (International Labour Office, Geneva, 1970); ILO, *Employment Incomes and Equity*.

38. Rhoodie, *Homelands*.

39. T. Malan and P.S. Hattingh (eds.), *Swart Tuislande in Suid-Afrika* (Africa Institute, Pretoria, 1975), p. 52.

3 SCATTERED TOWNS OR AN URBAN SYSTEM?

G.P. Cook

In order to provide the perspective for towns in the Ciskei it is necessary to outline the development and characteristics of an urban system. There are two major components to an urban system viz. the nodes or towns themselves and the channels of communication that link them. Neither is static, nor can they be regarded as separate entities for their interrelationships are all important in the functioning of the whole. The variety of urban places that make up the system evolve through time and perform both complementary and competitive roles to provide for the needs of people distributed over an area. Although the scale may vary the overriding level of organisation is national and the system is open to change at any level.

The process of ubanisation involves the evolution of an urban system in the broadest sense. Towns come into being and they grow in size both physically and in terms of population numbers as more people move away from the rural areas to live in them and become involved in nonagricultural activities. There are however other changes related to urbanisation and possibly these are less obvious for they include adaptations in the values, behaviour and life-style of the people, which ultimately permeate to all levels of society living in both rural and urban environments. Simultaneously as organisations and institutions change and isolated centres are increasingly brought into interaction with each other, so the urban system is built up through states of equilibrium. In the process the whole nation ultimately becomes transformed and has characteristics associated with a modern state. Modernisation which involves both urbanisation and industrialisation implies the introduction and spread of innovations in those organisations that relate directly to productive processes. It is therefore essential that regional mobility and interaction should be encouraged. Preferably this should be done through adaptation and development of the incipient urban system coupled with expansion of the communication network.

Individual towns may come into existence for any number of different reasons and are usually spread over an area in a manner which reduces competition. Nevertheless they do not exist in isolation for each town reflects the concentration of activities and people in response to local demand. Neither should they be regarded as separate entities for together they serve the needs of a national economic system. Although the overall number, size, location and functions of towns cannot be expected to be optimal nevertheless the principle of comparative advantage suggests that, given the local factors of production viz. land, labour, capital and enterprise and the relative merits of each location in this regard, every town should provide those functions for which it is best suited.[1] Naturally there will be duplication of certain functions but towns of similar functional complexity can be expected to be more or less equally spaced from one another. Furthermore because towns act as collection and distribution points and the level of demand for services varies (often with their frequency of use) a hierarchical system of centres usually emerges. Higher-order places tend to supply a wider variety of goods and services to people in a larger area than lower-order places whose influence is more limited in nature and extent. In theory the higher-order places could be expected to be more functionally complex and larger in population size than the lower-order places.

The majority of towns therefore act as service or market centres. In an area where semi-subsistence activities predominate a demand for certain products (non-durable consumer goods, for example, salt, sugar, matches, cooking oil) may exist but the low buying power of individuals coupled with their restricted mobility means that frequently there is insufficient support for permanent retail outlets to be economically viable. This feature is further aggravated by the fact that seasonal variations in the agricultural cycle cause local demand patterns to fluctuate. As a result demand is latent and short term and itinerant trading patterns dominate even where rural settlements are sufficiently dense to have a quasi-urban appearance. Where permanent stores do exist both high- and low-order goods are stocked and the traders often have alternative means of employment to supplement their income. The local economic system that results is fragmented. As a result the associated urban system is not conducive to mobilising resources for internal markets; neither is the spatial structure orientated towards economic growth or nation-building — all important aspects in a newly emergent state.

In addition to acting as service centres towns are focal points of industrial activity. As such they may compete with each other to attract particular industries geared to the local, national or external market. The growth associated with such industrialisation distorts any regular size distribution pattern. In general though the largest centres tend to have a comparative advantage over smaller centres particularly with respect to capital and entrepreneurial resources. The net result of the process of industrialisation is that it tends to favour agglomeration and encourage the development of regional inequalities that may have been incipient in the system. The principle of cumulative causation leads the larger places to grow at an accelerating rate. As they become more attractive so they divert people and investment from other areas and draw increasingly from the resources of the rest of the system with the result that regional differences become more marked. Even positive decentralisation and anti-growth policies are not necessarily sufficient to reduce such disparities particularly in an emerging country.

Development of both the functional and industrial character of urban places however implies that there is some connectivity between the nodes and the rest of the economy. In this respect the importance of interregional transport and communication networks cannot be overestimated. Without a system of links movement (of people, money, ideas, goods, services) is hindered and interaction between towns is inhibited because of the distance between them. As a result towns together with their immediate hinterlands, remain self-contained, at a very low level of economic development. It is against this background that the Ciskei towns must be considered and their role evaluated.

Ciskei Towns — The Nodes

When considering the towns of the Ciskei it should be remembered that the country has been and at present still is an integral part of the Republic of South Africa. The towns that have emerged developed in response to existing settlement and activity patterns and are integrated in the South African space economy through East London. This city, the major metropolitan node, has acted as an important force in structuring the economic space of the whole region. It is within the constraints imposed by the existing structure that the Ciskei urban system must evolve. The characteristics of the towns that are located within the declared boundaries of the Ciskei reflect the white superstructure of the Eastern Cape and are largely alien to the traditional culture. The first and largest group of towns are those that were established by whites and which are essentially part of the South African urban system. The second group of towns includes those established and developed by whites for occupation by blacks only and which in most cases are also geared to the white external economy. However there

Scattered Towns or an Urban System? 33

remains a third group of places which is the largest in numerical terms and which for want of a better description are termed 'rural villages'. These places have developed through consolidation, encouraged by whites, of black rural settlements in the reserves. Despite their origin they are essentially Ciskei oriented in that they reflect a response to local demand of the predominantly traditional society in their immediate hinterland. Assuming therefore that the Ciskei embarks on a path which involves modernisation as well as a desire to work towards regional equity it is these three groups of settlements that will form the frame for development and the medium for change.

The first group of towns established and occupied by whites (Table 3.1) numbered eleven in 1960 when they were all defined as urban for census purposes.[2] Increasing mobility of whites coupled with a trend towards white rural depopulation meant that by 1970 only seven qualified as urban centres in the census. Nevertheless all eleven towns still retain at least a postal agency and therefore they are all included in the South African urban hierarchy.[3] This means that their relative position with regard to other South African towns can be established on the basis of the goods and services they provide for both their local and surrounding rural residents. Furthermore as the classification is an international one they can be directly equated with overseas examples of similar functional status. Situated along major Eastern Cape routeways and originally acting as service centres for white farmers in their hinterlands, while also adminstering nearby 'African reserves', they have all been affected by the transition from South African to Ciskei government. Their last official links with white South Africa have been broken for in October 1977 it was officially announced that their municipalities and village management boards would be taken over systematically by the Ciskeian Township Board in the near future.

In terms of layout the dominant characteristics of this first group of towns reflect white mores, demands and economic status. The space occupied by white residential areas is roughly twice that devoted to black housing. Shops, noteworthy buildings and developed recreational facilities are almost all located in the white parts of town. Residential areas without exception still reflect the implementation of the Group Areas Act and are completely separate. During the present period of change and with the out-migration of both urban and rural whites the majority of these places have tended to stagnate and there are empty houses and shops. However once the transfer to the Ciskei is complete and vacant properties become available on the open market presumably the operation of free market forces will lead to integration of all racial

Table 3.1: Towns Established and Occupied by Whites

	Population						Functions											
	1960			1970										Commercial				
	White	Bantu	Total	White	Bantu	Total	Total	Rank	Administrative	Professional	Financial	Educational	Provisions	General	Services	Accom.	Social	Utilities
Alice	748	2,489	4,221	793	3,345	4,752	72	2	15	2	7	8	9	15	7	2	7	7
Keishammahoek	263	1,487	2,232	186	2,110	2,910	27	5	6	2	2	2	1	11		1	2	7
Seymour	126	694	1,072	130	1,217	1,654	16	9	6	3	1	1	1	3		1		6
Braunschweig	182	127	573	202	690	1,111	4	13	2			1		1				1
Peddie	393	617	1,072	318	628	1,087	36	4	11	2	1		3	11		1	5	7
Whittlesea	86	512	641	75	113	245	19	8	8			1	1	5		1	4	6
Middledrift	65	63	175	82	80	243	14	10	5			2	1	4			2	3
Frankfort	287	1,298	1,575		?		8	11						4		1	1	6
Bell/Bodiam	27	970	997		?		5	12	2					1		1	2	
Hamburg	28	868	896		?		3	14	1		1			2		1		2
Wooldridge	13	370	386		?		3	14	2					1				
Total	2,218	9,495	13,040	1,786	8,183	12,002												

groups in what is presently white area only. As far as the 8,070 (1970) black residents of these towns are concerned their houses are concentrated in 'locations' adjacent to the white laid-out area. These essentially dormitory suburbs are largely agglomerations of individual huts, wood and iron shacks, simple brick houses and some municipal-built houses not far from the town limits. They seldom have more facilities than schools, clinics and a few general dealer stores and in each case the residents are almost wholly dependent on the white town for employment and goods.

Of the eleven Ciskei towns included in the South African urban hierarchy only Alice has some real claim to the name of a 'town'. It is ranked sixth in the eight possible levels of urban places and its status is such that it has shown little or no functional disintegration during the transition from South African to Ciskeian town. Alice has a well-defined business district and the presence of Fort Hare University on the outskirts of the town together with Lovedale Training College means that the population is greatly increased during term times. Library services are therefore available and the buying power is sufficient to support a wider range of goods than would normally be expected in a town of that size and order. Local regional administrative functions, particularly those associated with the organisation of the area by whites, are concentrated in the town. Peddie, although ranking rather low as a local service centre, is typical of the seventh order of places in the South African urban hierarchy. There is an incipient business district where half of the ten stores are located but the remainder are scattered throughout the built-up area.

The remaining nine towns have all been classified as order eight centres — the lowest category in an urban hierarchy. The most developed of these towns is Keiskammahoek followed by Whittlesea which provides minimal goods for a service area which is strictly limited in extent. Seymour, Middledrift and Frankfort, although also regarded as urban, for census purposes, have little functional complexity and the latter two places have no real focus to the settlement. On the other hand Hamburg, no longer regarded as 'urban' in the census, is essentially a holiday resort and the majority of the houses are second homes of white South Africans only occupied for two or three months annually. Not unexpectedly therefore it has few services other than those providing for the immediate needs of holidaymakers. The remaining four places viz. Wooldridge, Braunschweig, Bell and Bodiam are in fact dispersed settlements with a church, general dealer cum postal agency, and police station spread over an area of a few kilometres and serving rural residents only in their immediate vicinity. Clearly the white-established towns play a very limited role in acting as market centres for the majority of residents in the Ciskei. Except in the case of Alice and Keiskammahoek, which each have two small concerns, no industrial development of any sort has occurred. The towns originated and developed as an integral part of the South African urban system with both their situation and associated communication network being typical of a colonial spatial structure. Production is geared to external markets and regional self-containment of the local rural communities is encouraged.

The second group of towns are those established by whites for occupation by blacks. A total of seven places fall into this group (Table 3.2). The most obvious differences between them and the towns discussed in the previous section lie in the fact that they have always been occupied by blacks, that the residential areas are characterised by great uniformity, that no real focused business centre exists and only a small proportion of commercial sites are provided, that the functional development is very low considering their population (even taking into account the relatively lower purchasing power of the blacks and earlier constraints on their business activities) and finally that virtually no industrial development has occurred. In fact the four largest in the group can be said to be almost entirely externally orientated rather than homeland focused. Furthermore none is situated more than 15 km from a white town and four lie on the border of the Ciskei. Each of these characteristics may be attributed to their role in relation to the South African urban system.

The two largest towns in this group are Zwelitsha and Mdantsane. Zwelitsha the first town of its type in the Ciskei, was established outside King William's Town in 1949 primarily to house the employees of a nearby textile firm. Mdantsane, started in 1962 for a similar purpose, shelters an increasing proportion of the East London industrial labour force. In 1970 these two towns together were the home of nearly 130,000 people or 24.2 per cent of the *de facto* Ciskei population. Their growth has continued steadily and by 1977 Mdantsane had a population sufficiently large for one to expect the emergence of typically urban characteristics by world standards. Yet except in terms of population concentration its urban status is low. As far as provision of goods and services is concerned neither Zwelitsha nor Mdantsane are even remotely comparable with places of related size in an urban hierarchy. The historical background to the establishment of these two towns[4] coupled with policy decisions regarding the location of industry

Table 3.2: Towns Established by Whites for Blacks

	Population 1975	Total	Rank	Administrative	Professional	Financial	Educational	Provisions	General	Services	Accommodation	Social	Utilities
									Commercial				
Mdantsane	98,289	110	1	4	6	2	32	6	20	1	2	37	7
Zwelitsha	29,816	44	3	7	3	1	10	8	9	6	1	6	7
Sada	20,770	26	6	3			9		2	4		8	5
Dimbaza	8,813	24	7	3		Ag	6	3	4	1		7	6
Kayalethu	1,056												
Kuntselamanzi	—												
Ilitha	900												
Total	159,644												

in the Republic and their position so close to the white towns have markedly affected their status. Mdantsane remains tied to East London, the primary source of job opportunities in the vicinity, as evidenced by the journey to work patterns.[5] Despite the fact that Zwelitsha has been the seat of government, and thus the number of locally available job opportunities in administration in particular has increased, the majority of Zwelitsha residents are employed either in the adjacent South African factories or King William's Town. Therefore both places have merely dormitory town status and are essentially part of the South African urban system.

A further two towns in this group, Sada and Dimbaza, were established within three months of each other in 1969 in order to house persons displaced from the Midlands, Karroo and Western Cape. Within a year they had achieved the status of 'town' in terms of the census definition. Today both population density and town layout are typically urban and some utilities, for example, water and refuse removal, are provided but functionally their status is low (Table 3.2). Although now the home of almost 28,000 people (6 per cent of the *de facto* Ciskeian population) these two places remain artificial constructs hardly integrated with the local rural community. The industries attracted through the Ciskei Development Corporation are largely exploitive in the sense that they are geared to an external economy and multiplier effects are virtually nonexistent.

The remaining three towns established in the Ciskei on land released from white occupancy do not qualify as urban in terms of the census definition nor can they be equated with places in an urban hierarchy due to their functional inadequacy. Kayalethu, the second township to be proclaimed in the Ciskei (6 June 1958), is situated in the foothills of the Juanasberg approximately 10 km north of Alice. It comprises 157 erven on which approximately 1,000 people were originally settled from white farms. On 10 November 1972 Kuntselamanzi, located on land immediately adjacent to Fort Hare University, was proclaimed a township. At that time due to the Group Areas regulations black professional employees could not purchase land or buildings in the white part of Alice. By establishing this township it was hoped that the demand for privately developed black housing would be met and a high-status residential area would develop. As the site for Kuntselamanzi abuts a large squatter settlement on the north west, and Alice has been incorporated into the Ciskei, the need for a separate black town has fallen away. However, the land remains open for suburban development as an integral part of the Alice/Fort Hare complex. The most recently proclaimed townships are those of Ilitha (28 June 1974), located beyond the north-western edge of the Mdantsane magisterial district, and Glenmore on Bantu Trust land near Committees Drift on the Fish river. The towns, with 250 and 500 houses each have total populations of nearly 2,000 and 3,000 respectively. Some of the residents are engaged in subsistence production but there are few local employment opportunities and the towns cannot be expected to become more than low-order service centres at best. A similar lowly status is likely to accrue to Ntabatemba, a new town which is intended to be located at the headwaters of the Black Kei river some distance from Sada. This urban settlement, which is still on the drawing-boards, is planned to deal with the influx of migrants from Hershel and Glen Grey districts whose lack of rights to agricultural land has necessitated that a town should be artificially created for them.

There is a third group of places, that is, the rural villages which have developed through consolidation of the rural population into relatively concentrated settlements. These places are homogeneous and form the focus of local agricultural activities. However they do not act as market centres for they are merely the clustered homes of an essentially subsistence farming community. These rural villages are not externally orientated, are usually situated at the end of a single access road, may lie more than 5 km from existing secondary roads, and, being based on a predominantly pedestrian community, have not become structurally linked with each other. Yet although each centre is independent, to some extent it does organise and control the surrounding space which the residents use for agricultural and pastoral purposes.

Unfortunately in the past, services for the rural population have not been centralised in these rural villages; for instance postal agencies, schools, training colleges and hospitals are frequently located nearby or between a group of them. Possibly as a result and in contrast to other parts of Africa[6] neither these nor the trading stores which are often white owned and managed, have led to any form of urban development even though tracks converge on them from their hinterlands and they are extensively used by the local rural population. Little data are available for such rural villages but Xama and Mpeko are probably typical of the larger examples while Gobozana and Nyaniso may be regarded as smaller concentrations of the same type. Where private enterprise has developed it takes the form of trading stores and, in an informal manner, vehicle and bicycle repair is carried out together with some tailoring and occasional small-scale craft production. Clearly the entrepreneurial level is low for, although they are the home of 69.5 per cent of the Ciskei *de facto* population, in 1973 there were only 157 black-run commercial outlets in the whole Ciskei excluding those located in Zwelitsha and Mdantsane.[7] The fact that some black enterprises exist in these rural villages suggests the emergence of truly indigenous urban centres is possible.

In summary the towns of the Ciskei can be said to be essentially a product of the South African social, economic and political system with which they are still integrated. On the one hand there are the spatially concentrated, externally orientated and functionally dominant towns which are a direct heritage of and largely dependent on white settlement in the area. In this group clearly Alice, centrally located and at a route intersection coupled with its relative functional complexity associated with the Ciskei's major tertiary educational establishments, is the dominant centre. Although it is the Ciskei capital, its small size and other characteristics give it no more than rural town status by any international standards. Among the entirely black towns on the other hand, by size alone Mdantsane should exhibit truly urban characteristics, and would seem to be an obvious focus to an emerging system. Unfortunately the significance of its metropolitan satellite relationship with East London cannot be overlooked as it is so closely connected with and dependent on the economy of that South African city. In addition its lack of development and weak links with the Ciskei as a whole mean that it cannot and does not dominate its hinterland, except perhaps parasitically by attracting migrants — especially those seeking work beyond the borders of the Ciskei. Zwelitsha, despite the fact that it is the administrative centre, is in a similar position with regard to King William's Town.

In direct contrast to the two former groups of towns there are the independent rural villages, too small as yet to play any real part in the system, but they cannot be ignored, and as centres of their local community fields they constitute units of significant economic and political potential. In spite of the differences between the three groups of places they form the nodes around which an urban system may develop. However, their importance is largely dependent on the establishment of connecting links and their integration into a complex interacting whole.

Ciskei Links

The links in an urban system are not merely road and rail connections,

but involve all levels of communication from the intangible flow of
ideas and information to the measurable volume of goods or people
transported from one point to another. Of particular importance too is
the nature of the two-way action and the facility with which it can
occur. Analysis of these patterns is a time-consuming task and, just as
the nodes can be discussed in a simplistic manner, so the transport network can provide an indication of probable interaction through its
geometry. Volume, frequency and intensity of interaction have been
found to be closely related to and conditioned by the arrangement and
nature of the channels in a network.

Table 3.3 indicates the number of road links that connect each town
in the Ciskei with other places. In addition a single railway line links
Alice, Middledrift and Dimbaza with the two main lines to Johannesburg from East London and Port Elizabeth respectively. The existence
of a transport net in the Ciskei as a whole is constrained by the fact
that the mountainous edge of the escarpment effectively cuts off the
northern third of the country from the remainder. This has meant that
north-south links are very limited. Reflecting the earlier white pattern
of farmland and production flows, the northern route system is
organised around Queenstown and then along the Ciskei border to East
London while the southern part is trisected by a national road and a
rail/road route focused on King William's Town and then directly on to
East London. Flows are therefore externally orientated and except for
links between the white towns no network can be said to exist at the
primary level. Even at the secondary level links are limited to connections between main roads and are also externally focused. Finally there
is a branching system of tertiary roads linked only indirectly to the
secondary roads and the majority of consolidated rural settlements in
particular are located at the ends of each branch. Clearly the road and
rail links are merely entry and dispatch routes rather than an inter-
locking service system.

Growth and the Ciskei Urban System

As yet, although there are towns in the Ciskei, no urban system can be
said to have evolved and the internal space economy remains largely
unstructured. Little more could be expected when it is remembered
that the consolidation proposals are not as yet implemented and establishment of a new boundary cannot normally reorientate flows
immediately. Thus the Ciskei at present remains an integral part of the

Table 3.3: Ciskei Links

Towns in order of population size	No. of exits/entrances	
	Tarred	Untarred
Mdantsane	2	
Zwelitsha	1	
Sada		1
Dimbaza		1
Alice	2	3
Keiskammahoek		4
Seymour		3
Braunschweig		1
Peddie	2	2
Kayalethu		1
Ilitha		1
Whittlesea	2	3
Middledrift		1
Frankfort		4
Bell		1
Bodiam		2
Hamburg		1
Wooldridge		2
Kuntselamanzi		1
Glenmore		1
Rural villages:		
Xama		2
Mpeko		2
Gobozana		1
Nyaniso		2

South African space economy, though the towns in particular are reflecting the effects of the transitional status and the disruption associated with the migration of various population groups. If the decision is taken for the Ciskei to continue within a capitalist economic system and retain the boundaries as delimited there appear to be at least three options open if the towns are to be integrated into a single urban system.

The first alternative is to maintain the status quo by retaining more or less unchanged the existing towns and the links between them. In this way the Ciskei would remain essentially tied to the South African economy in a largely passive and dependent supply role. Increasing pressure on the land resulting from rapid population growth will inevitably lead to further out-migration if the present trend is allowed to continue. Arrangements can be made for wages of migrant workers to be paid in the Ciskei, thus developing local banking facilities, making capital available and ensuring that a larger proportion of the earnings is spent locally. However this would not reduce the level of competition with already established firms in South Africa nor does it mean that the destructive social change associated with migrant labour is in any way ameliorated. Of course it is possible that a larger proportion of the potential migrants could be deflected to the East London metropolitan area and by living in Mdantsane or Potsdam, remain *de facto* residents of the Ciskei. Again although industries in the East London metropolitan area would probably benefit, this strategy would be unlikely to assist the Ciskei to any marked degree. Rural depopulation would continue and the Ciskei would be faced with the problem of providing sufficient housing to cope with the influx to Mdantsane already more than three times as large as the next biggest centre, Zwelitsha. Associated with a pattern of rural depopulation and the parasitic growth of a single centre the functional character of the existing towns could be expected to show further signs of disintegration resulting from declining purchasing power in the hinterlands. Little attraction would be offered by the urban places. This coupled with the externally orientated communication system would lead to further relative declines. It would seem therefore that a more positive urban planning policy is required if an integrated Ciskei-focused urban system is to develop.

The second alternative urban strategy that may cope with natural increase while reducing migration and also attracting skilled workers back to the Ciskei involves the introduction of industrial activities to selected centres. However, industrialisation requires skilled labour which must be paid, and an infrastructure which must be built up. Both therefore use up a developing country's scarce resource — capital. This problem is aggravated when, as in the Ciskei, raw materials are not available locally and skilled labour has to be attracted to the area concerned in direct competition with existing concerns outside the national borders. In fact as Logan[8] points out such industrialisation policies 'when superimposed on a colonial spatial structure . . . increase regional differences in economic development'. In the case of the Ciskei this warning is particularly appropriate, for the present towns are geared towards an external market and regional inequalities already exist. Furthermore, although the national account may show increasing evidence of secondary industrial growth, the localised nature of industrial activity when coupled with the lack of spread effects may reduce the chance of any real change for the country as a whole. There may be an increase in the number and size of certain towns while their functional nature will not develop in a concomitant manner. Even when industrialisation policies are combined with an approach which tries to build up existing small markets in peripheral areas success may be limited. Without very strong countermeasures industrialisation tends to encourage further internal migration and may lead to a regional overconcentration of population which is as undesirable as primacy if the aim is to develop an urban system and bring about an overall improvement in quality of life for both rural and urban areas.

The third alternative is to take a macroscopic view. Building on the existing pattern it is possible for the urban places and their interconnections to be organised in a manner that will result in a well structured urban system.[9] This in turn will provide the medium through which modernisation can take place and within which increasing numbers of people can be supported. Basic to this approach is the idea that an area which is to develop requires a combination of towns of various types and sizes in which a wide variety of different functions can be carried out. These towns may then be expected to form 'centres of modernisation which act as catalysts for economic growth ... and from which the benefits of modernisation flow outwards'[10] so revitalising the stagnant economic system. An essential component of the strategy is a positive and directed policy to encourage all types of economic activity (business, marketing and small-scale industry) to develop and locate in those existing towns where the effects can be expected to benefit the largest area. Thus in order to bring about sustained regional development throughout the Ciskei, activities that can function successfully at a variety of different places need to be encouraged and deliberately established in lagging areas. In this regard restructuring of the urban pattern is unnecessary. By grafting tertiary functions onto towns at each level of the existing hierarchy it would be possible to get greater economic efficiency which will lead to better spatial integration of the whole area.

To achieve this aim large-scale capital outlay is not essential, for a decentralised pattern of investment which encourages black entrepreneurs and professionals to provide services in existing towns should stimulate urban growth and attract progressive Ciskeians back to the homeland. As closer links between these places and the rural areas develop they may act as centres from which social change radiates. Expansion and functional development of these towns also would provide intervening opportunities for rural migrants and may help to stabilise population flows.

It is possible to capitalise on the existing system still further and obtain effective results by manipulating the very lowest level of settlements as well. Coupled with a policy which emphasises agricultural growth in an effort to achieve interregional equity should be one which concentrates on existing rural villages and agricultural settlements. An articulated pattern of rural centres is essential to provide local foci and in turn to support and be supported by the regional towns. The framework exists in which demand can be created and also met in the local area and these existing places should be used to provide the necessary services while disseminating new ideas to the farmers. They should also act as market centres and collection points with sites for storage, transport and processing which will be required as agricultural production develops. Grouping of business enterprises in these places should make them true market towns and thus will help to stimulate greater agricultural productivity in their immediate hinterlands. Provision of small-scale convenience outlets will assist in developing local entrepreneurial skills by focusing the potential evident in the existing informal retail sectors. The status of these rural villages can be expected to increase in response to population growth and while they could develop into important local foci they should be carefully selected for investment with due regard to the maintenance of efficient resource allocation. The problem of identifying such growth centres among the rural villages can be solved by making use of straightforward mathematical techniques[11] which will select the most central places taking into account the particular configuration of the Ciskei boundaries. Planning to include them with an integrated system of towns should be coupled with an awareness of changes in local demand and supply conditions that will occur as the system evolves.[12]

A key component to a development plan based on integration of an urban system is the transport net that links all the urban places. It is therefore essential that detailed analysis of the existing infrastructure should be carried out and that the present inadequate mesh be adapted to serve the whole of the Ciskei in an efficient manner. By concentrating on the internal links which already have a national focus and selecting the appropriate nodes to stimulate modernisation, capital investment will have immediate and far-reaching effects. As regional economic health depends largely on the degree of accessibility to centres of production and consumption[13] internal migration may be reduced if access to social and economic services is made more or less even throughout the country. In addition the transport net and related towns will provide the means through which political, institutional and social change can be funnelled.[14]

Conclusion

A pattern of rapid urbanisation and steadily increasing interregional inequality is already evident in the Ciskei and without active countermeasures the inertia of the existing pattern will help perpetuate the imbalances and result in further economic and social polarisation. In addition the longer the present externally orientated spatial organisation persists the more difficult it will be to alter and the greater the cost to the emerging state. This is particularly the case if communal land tenure gives way to individual ownership and if high concentrations of people are resettled on released land without the means of integration into the system. At present half the Ciskei population live outside the boundaries of the country and 30 per cent of the *de facto* residents are urban. If world trends are followed almost 50 per cent of the population will be living in urban centres by the turn of the century and that proportion will double in the following two decades. In the light of this projection, and if Ciskei nationals are to be attracted back to the country and normal population growth catered for, change in all sectors and at all levels will be essential. Such change can most realistically be accommodated through the development of a fully integrated urban system comprising functional nodes linked by efficient communications and serving the whole country. Innovations relevant to the Ciskei would be encouraged in a truly urban environment and new ideas may be readily communicated through an urban system and made accessible to all members of society. Naturally the changes in economic, social, administrative and political structure that will occur as the Ciskei evolves are bound to have repercussions on the spatial organisation of the country. However by taking into account the total system of settlements and their interactions it is possible to modify plans and adapt to change. Only a development strategy that considers regional peculiarities and evaluates relative urban locational patterns can achieve the optimal utilisation of agricultural, mineral and energy resources. An approach that considers both nodes and their links will work towards evening out levels of living throughout the system. The provision of modern services in smaller places should enable the increasing population to find jobs in the framework of the region as a whole. Furthermore by retaining local structure a smoother transfer to new ways of economic activity and behaviour should be achieved.

Notes

1. R.J. Johnson, *Spatial Structure* (Methuen, London, 1973).
2. Population census 1970 Report 02-05 – 10 states: 'Urban' can be described as follows:
   (a) All cities and towns with some form of local management
   (b) Areas of an urban nature, i.e. areas with urban amenities (water, electricity, etc.) but without some other form of local management.
3. R.J. Davies and G.P. Cook, 'Re-appraisal of the South African Urban Hierarchy' in *South African Geographical Journal*, 50 (1968), pp. 116-32.
4. T.J. Gordon, 'The Evolution of Mdantsane' in G.P. Cook and J. Opland (eds.), *Mdantsane* (Institute for Social and Economic Research, Rhodes University, Grahamstown, forthcoming).
5. D.R. Matravers, 'It's All in the Day's Work' in Cook and Opland, *Mdantsane*.
6. J. Vincent, 'The Changing Role of Small Towns in the Agrarian Structure of East Africa', *Journal of Commonwealth and Comparative Politics*, 12 (1974), pp. 261-75.
7. Benbo, *Ciskei Economic Review*.
8. M.I. Logan, 'The Spatial System and Planning Strategies in Developing Countries', *Geographical Review*, 62 (1972), p. 237.
9. E. Brutzkus, 'Centralised vs. Decentralised Pattern of Urbanisation in Developing Countries', *Tijdschrift voor Economische Sociale Geographie*, 64 (1973), pp. 11-23.
10. T. McGee, *The Urbanisation Process in the Third World* (Bell, London, 1971).
11. M E. Harvey and M.S. Hung, 'The Application of a p-Median algorithm to the identification of nodal hierarchies and growth centres', *Economic Geography* 50, 3 (1974), pp. 187-202.
12. El Shaks, 'Planning for systems of settlement in emerging nations', *Town Planning Review*, 47, 2 (1976), pp. 127-38.
13. T.J.D. Fair, 'Some Spatial Aspects of black homeland development in South Africa', Occasional Paper 6, URRU, University of Witwatersrand, Johannesburg, 1975.
14. J.B. Riddell, *The Spatial Dynamics of Modernization in Sierra Leone*, (Northwestern University Press, Evanston, Ill., 1970).

4 THE IMAGE OF AGRICULTURE IN TWO CISKEIAN RURAL COMMUNITIES

J.B. McI. Daniel and N.L. Webb

Chief Minister L.L. Sebe[1] highlighted the economic problems of the homelands in general and the Ciskei in particular when he stated that

> the really big problem is the limited potential and limited capital for industrial development. Several homelands possess mineral resources, it is true, but for the most part the basis of the economy in all the homelands for years to come will be agriculture and the industries springing therefrom. Only a spectacular increase in agricultural production and industrial development will make it possible for the inhabitants of the homelands to be fed adequately and provided with sufficient job opportunities.

With approximately 80 per cent of its *de facto* black population classified as rural, and with 48.5 per cent under the age of 15,[2] the Ciskei must give serious attention to agricultural development in order to provide food for an expanding population, to create employment opportunities, and to assist in the transition to a modern economy.

The concept of the family economic unit proposed in the Tomlinson Commission Report[3] became, in part, the basis for planning the rural areas in the homelands. A major aim was to encourage the emergence of a group of full-time farmers. Two aspects of the policy related to the rehabilitation of the land and the resettlement of the inhabitants. Over large areas limited rehabilitation has taken place insofar as the arable areas have been consolidated; grazing and residential areas have been demarcated; and basic soil conservation measures have been introduced. Resettlement has brought about a change in the pattern of homestead location but not in land use. The training of large numbers of farmers has not occurred nor has a class of full-time farmers emerged. The Commission concluded that a gross income of R120 per annum, at prices prevailing in the fifties, was adequate to attract blacks to full-time farming in areas where both crop and animal husbandry could be practised. In referring to planning in the King William's Town district, Houghton[4] states that full economic units ... are usually somewhere between 6 morgen of arable plus grazing for 14 cattle units and 9 morgen of arable plus grazing for 10 cattle units ... in all cases the combined holding is designed to yield R120 per annum under existing farming practice. The average combined holding of arable and grazing will work out at 40 morgen per family ... Indeed, at present, owing to the desire not to dispossess any present landholder only a small minority get the full unit.

The same story is told in virtually all areas. Sebe[5] confirms the failure of resettlement:

According to the annual report for the Department of Agriculture and Forestry 78% of the Ciskei has been planned. By this is meant 'physical planning'. It means in effect that people have been moved into villages, arable areas set aside and grazing areas fenced off into camps. As phase I — the foundation for production planning, this is excellent — but unfortunately this is where the matter seems to have ended ... To only about 10 per cent of the families in the Ciskei was it possible to allocate such an economic unit — the majority of the rural people eke out an existence on 1 morgen and even less. (One morgen = 0.857 ha.)

The economic unit did not prove to be the cornerstone of resettlement even though it formed the basis of planning.

Evidence that the Tomlinson Commission concept of the economic unit has failed to transform farming in the Ciskei is provided by the following sets of statistics:

1. In 1971/2 the subsistence sector contributed 31.3 per cent to the GDP of the Ciskei. The contributions of the private and public sectors were 19.4 per cent and 49.3 per cent respectively.[6]

2. In 1973/4 the gross value of plant production, animal production and forestry was R1,881,000, R2,734,000 and R66,000 respectively, giving a total of R4,681,000.[7] Using the 1970 population data to calculate the per capita earning from farming (that is, plant and animal production and forestry) it is found that for the total population the figure is R9.15 per capita and for the rural population alone R11.40. In fact, this calculation makes no allowance for any population increase since 1970. Consequently the real per capita value of production is likely to be lower than that reflected above. If it is assumed that the

average family consisted of six people, the per capita earnings per family from farming and forestry were R55 for the total population and R68 for the rural population.

3. In 1973 income from migrant workers and daily commuters working in white areas accounted for over 70 per cent of the total income of *de facto* black residents.[8]

4. The survey results in the two Ciskeian communities of Gobozana and Nyaniso revealed that 40 per cent of the households failed to produce sufficient food for their own requirements.

To what can this failure to make farming enterprises more productive be attributed? Land tenure, the dualistic structure of the economy, the need for incentive and mental attitudes, are some of the reasons that have been examined to explain this state of affairs. Many of these approaches are fraught with controversy. Not all scholars would agree with Daniel when he discusses land tenure in Swaziland, stating that the attitude of the Swazi towards land will not change simply through the introduction of freehold tenure,[9] nor will all agree with Holleman when he maintains that the crux of the problem is to be found in the dual structure of the economy of the rural population.[10] Fisk and Shand[11] examine the incentive factor and develop a model in which 'the utility of money in the group can be expressed in terms of indifference curves plotting income against leisure'.

The purpose of this chapter is to explore the contribution that an environmental perception study may be able to make to the improvement of agriculture in two semi-subsistence Ciskeian communities — Gobozana and Nyaniso. In South Africa little attention has been paid to the attitudes of rural inhabitants to farming and to agriculture in particular, especially among the blacks, yet ultimately it is the people on the land who determine whether or not a policy is executed as planned. It is therefore important to understand attitudes both within groups and between groups.

The attitudes of the people towards agriculture were investigated in three spheres: the preference for agriculture in relation to other sociocultural activities and options open to them, namely religion, social occasions, local-level politics, the importance of cattle and employment in town; the perception of how production could be increased; and the perceived adequacy of field size.

In all three spheres the investigation focused on the image of agriculture held by the people because people do not come to decisions on the basis of the real environment but on a simplified, often distorted image of it.[12] Downs makes this more explicit when he states that 'spatial behaviour is a function of the image, where the image represents man's link with the environment'.[13] The conceptual scheme for research into geographic space perception put forward by Downs shows how information taken from the real world becomes part of the image held by the individual. In turn the image influences decisions and consequently behaviour. Man as a decision-maker is therefore influenced by the image of the real world. In examining the implications of the model of a man-environment system which he has proposed, Brookfield[14] claims that 'the perceived environment may change independently of the real environment, and is particularly responsive to short-term changes in the real environment'. If the statement is accepted and if it is possible to understand farming as the people on the land perceive it, it may be possible to change the pattern of behaviour, where necessary, by changing the image of agriculture. In other words, if information can be fed into the system as a result of the understanding of the image based on perception, suggested changes are more likely to be successfully introduced. Since the mental image is conceived as reality by the individual and is therefore the key to behaviour, changing patterns of behaviour by changing the image should be possible. In practical terms a study of the image of agriculture could reveal what approaches should be adopted by extension officers or persons interested in raising the standard of production. The analysis below is based on information obtained from a questionnaire administered personally by fieldworkers to 50 households in each of the two communities.

The study was confined to two rural areas in the Ciskei,[15] Gobozana and Nyaniso. Gobozana, located over 20 km from King William's Town, is not served by a network of roads and is characterised by a more traditional life-style than Nyaniso which is situated less than 7 km from Peddie, but more important, is adjacent to the national road joining East London and Grahamstown. In Nyaniso the greater influence of western ideas finds expression in the type of dwellings, brick and mortar being common, and dress styles. The two areas were chosen primarily because of these contrasts. In both communities residential, arable and grazing land had been consolidated in accordance with the Tomlinson Commission formula but it had not been possible to give each homestead an economic holding. Only 6 per cent of the homesteads had plots near the size advocated by the Tomlinson Commission while 90 per cent had between one-third and one-sixth of the recommended size or no arable land at all. Both areas lack industrial development, are located in a zone where mixed farming is possible and are characterised by a semi-subsistence economy. The intrusive element of wage employment outside the areas means that the people are no longer entirely dependent on the land for their needs.

In an attempt to determine the relationship between agriculture and socio-cultural factors the household heads in the Gobozana and Nyaniso communities were asked to rate the importance of agriculture against religion, social occasions, local-level politics, employment in town and animal husbandry (cattle). Both preliminary fieldwork and relevant literature suggested that these could be regarded as the most important considerations that could influence the image of agriculture. Agriculture is defined as the cultivation of the land; religion as church attendance and the practice of traditional rituals; social occasions as beer and other parties; and local-level politics as meetings with leaders in the community such as the headman and the chief. The responses obtained are summarised in Table 4.1.

Table 4.1: Perceived Importance of Agriculture

Socio-cultural factors	Communities					
	Gobozana		Nyaniso		Total	
	n	%	n	%	n	%
(a) Agriculture	31	63	15	38	46	52
Religion	11	22	10	26	21	24
Social occasions	—	—	11	28	11	13
Local-level politics	7	14	3	8	10	11
	49	99	39	100	88	100
(b) Agriculture	16	32	23	49	39	40
Cattle	9	18	15	32	24	25
Both	25	50	9	19	34	35
	50	100	47	100	97	100
(c) Agriculture	45	92	35	76	80	84
Employment in town	4	8	11	24	15	16
	49	100	46	100	95	100

In relation to the criteria selected in Table 4.1, column a, the contrasts between the communities of Gobozana and Nyaniso are both greater and more important than the similarities. In comparing the two communities there is some similarity in the percentage of persons ranking religion first (22 per cent and 26 per cent) and to a lesser extent a similarity in the percentage of persons ranking local-level politics first. In the less traditional society of Nyaniso local-level politics appear to be less important than in Gobozana. The contrasts are noticeable in the ranking of social occasions and agriculture. In Gobozana no one regarded social occasions as being his most important concern but in Nyaniso social occasions (28 per cent) were ranked after agriculture (38 per cent). In both communities a higher percentage of persons ranked agriculture above the socio-cultural elements of religion, social occasions and local-level politics but in the more traditional community of Gobozana nearly two out of three heads of households regarded agriculture as more important in contrast to only two out of five in Nyaniso.

Respondents were asked to give reasons for their decisions and where relevant these reasons, as well as other information about the respondents that had been collected during the survey, were used in an attempt to explain the above patterns of ranking. In both communities the group who perceived religion (the church) as the most important cultural institution had the highest average level of education (standard three). In view of the fact that 48 per cent of the household heads had received no formal education it is submitted that a difference of educational achievement of one or two standards can be significant. Those who regarded local politics as the most important factor felt obliged to attend the political functions and enjoyed doing so. It is not possible to generalise about the persons participating in local-level politics because of the small numbers involved. Nevertheless a trend that deserves closer study is the apparent decrease in the interest generated by local-level politics as a community loosens its traditional bonds. The preference for social occasions was influenced by age and the lack of education. The average age of the persons making this choice was 70 and not one had received any formal education. Age and infirmity precluded the members in this group from taking an active role in cultivation and it can be understood why social occasions were important to them. It could also be significant that in the more traditional society of Gobozana no one regarded social occasions as being of prime importance. In the two communities taken together, a slender overall majority ranked agriculture first, yet only two out of the 46 claimed that agriculture was a desirable way of life. The remaining 44 regarded agriculture as basic to physical survival. Agriculture was not seen as a source of income but rather only as a source of food. Table 4.1, column a, reflects the most important factor in the lives of the people while the dominant reasons for that choice as well as the similarities and especially the contrasts between Gobozana and Nyaniso shed some light on the question of perception. What then are the implications of these findings for extension services and the development of these areas?

In looking at the socio-cultural aspects as a whole and relating the responses to the problems associated with agriculture, the following considerations deserve serious thought:

1. Only 52 per cent of the total number of people interviewed in both communities regarded agriculture as the most important aspect in the socio-cultural sphere of their lives. Any agricultural extension work therefore must acknowledge and make allowance for the fact that agriculture is not given top priority by a large number of household heads. If an alternative form of physical survival could be found, presumably many would feel less strongly about the relative importance of agriculture. That only two respondents regarded agriculture as a desirable way of life indicates, at least partially, why little progress has been made in improving existing levels of production. The attitude of the majority reveals that agriculture is a necessity, a case of survival rather than a way in which money can be made especially if commercial methods of farming were introduced. Change this attitude and it is possible that the value of cash crop farming may be realised, an appreciation which could lead to higher levels of production.

2. There is some indication that age and standard of education of the heads of households influence attitudes towards the church and social occasions, thus indirectly decreasing the number of people who regard agriculture as being of primary importance. The better educated show a clear allegiance to the church though no cause and effect relationship is necessarily implied. The older group prefers the social occasion to the hard work of cultivation and as the trend is for younger people to migrate to the city of East London and other work centres there could be a lessening of interest in the cultivation of the land. Those remaining, representing an older generation, become less and less interested in agriculture; as the average age of a community increases, the level of production decreases, thereby encouraging more people to leave the rural homestead. As this movement gains momentum the progressively older groups, not previously attracted to the towns, may leave, thus increasing the average age of those remaining and causing a further decrease in productivity. If the feedback from the migrants is positive, the rate and tempo of migration could speed up the whole process outlined above.

3. The contrasts between the communities of Gobozana and Nyaniso

could well be indicative of contrasts throughout the Ciskei, that is, that attitudes are not the same in all settlement areas or localities. Failure to recognise that such differences exist could have been an inhibiting factor in the sphere of extension work. The task of encouraging agriculture in the less traditional areas may have been underestimated because it was not understood that less dependence was placed on agriculture for survival (Table 4.1, column a) and that therefore many household heads did not regard agriculture as being of fundamental importance. Conversely, agriculture in the more traditional areas might stand a better chance of success because of the greater dependence on agriculture for survival and the greater number of household heads who regard agriculture as fundamentally important. Too frequently perhaps there is the temptation to have one policy for all areas. Did the failure to ascertain what people felt about resettlement schemes contribute to the failure of the policy put forward by the Tomlinson Commission? Indeed the failure of many development projects may have been due to the fact that the people for whom they were designed were not consulted, and that what they perceived about the projects was never determined.

Evidence from the present study suggests that a pilot survey to test attitudes or perceptions could reveal where problems in relation to greater productivity lie before so-called improvements are proposed and introduced. In the more traditional area of Gobozana nearly two-thirds of the household heads regarded agriculture of prime importance, but in the less traditional area of Nyaniso it was found that interests were more evenly distributed between agriculture, church and social functions. Planning must take cognizance of these contrasts. Clearly a greater effort will be required to improve agriculture in Nyaniso than in Gobozana. It can therefore be suggested that the prevailing perception of agriculture should be taken into account and should directly influence the approach adopted in agricultural extension services.

4. Cattle usually play a more important role than agriculture in the functional system of the Xhosa-speakers, including the Mfengu. The responses to the relative importance of agriculture, or cattle, or both are recorded in Table 4.1, column b. In the more traditional society of Gobozana approximately 1 in 5 ranked cattle first, 1 in 3 agriculture and 1 in 2 appreciated the importance of both. In the more westernised community of Nyaniso approximately 1 in 2 ranked agriculture first, 1 in 3 cattle first and 1 in 5 both agriculture and cattle. The reasons for these differences are hard to determine. They may be due to the fact that many household heads were women or they may repre-

sent ideas held by members of a community in transition, especially as so many from Nyaniso attached importance to agriculture. Research may reveal other reasons. Leaving speculation aside, the contrast between the two communities could be important. That nearly one-third of the respondents in Nyaniso ranked cattle first compared with 18 per cent in Gobozana, could indicate that there is still a strong traditional attitude towards stock in spite of cultural changes that may have occurred in Nyaniso. In fact the chances of introducing mixed farming seem to be greater in the traditional area than in the more westernised community. On the other hand, the latter community may be less dependent on cattle for ploughing. The acquisition of tractors would influence the image of a homestead's dependence on both cattle and cultivation.

5. In analysing how more food could be produced (Table 4.2) attention is focused on the degree to which the farmers perceive the solution to lie in the realm of their own endeavours (good tilling and correct ploughing), acquisition of external aids (fertiliser and machinery), or a combination of these categories. A category reflecting negative responses is also included. The most striking feature of Table 4.2 is that 66 per cent of the responses in Nyaniso fall in the negative category, again implying that extension work would experience greater difficulties here compared with Gobozana where household heads appreciate the role which they and members of their families will have to play in raising the level of production. The contrast between the two communities is again evident.

Table 4.2: Perception of Ways of Increasing Agricultural Production

Ways of increasing production	Gobozana		Nyaniso		Total
	n	%	n	%	n
Positive Response					
Good tilling	12	25	5	10	17
Correct ploughing	8	16	–	–	8
Fertiliser	2	4	2	4	4
Machinery	1	2	3	6	4
Good tilling and fertiliser	8	16	3	6	11
Correct ploughing and fertiliser	5	10	–	–	5
Miscellaneous	12	24	4	8	16
Negative Response					
Don't know	–	–	11	22	11
Nil response and Miscellaneous	1	2	22	44	23
Total	49	100	50	100	99

6. An important finding illustrated in Table 4.1, column c is the fact that in both communities the majority of those interviewed preferred cultivating the land to wage employment in town. This is relatively less important when it is realised that the survey undertaken would not incorporate the persons who had chosen to work in urban areas. Those remaining would, in large measure, represent the group who did not want to work away from the homestead.[16] Even so, in the more westernised community fewer people (76 per cent) ranked agriculture above wage employment compared with Gobozana (92 per cent). If nearly a quarter of the people in an area would prefer to work in a town for wages, there is a good chance that they would be less likely to be interested in learning about ways and means of increasing agricultural yields.

7. Earlier it was stated that in the two communities only 6 per cent of the surveyed homesteads had been granted arable land near the sizes advocated by the Tomlinson Commission for an economic unit. Table 4.3 underlines how the image can differ from real world conditions. The surprising feature of Table 4.3 is the number of respondents who regarded the size of their fields as adequate in view of the situation outlined above.

Table 4.3 Perceived Adequacy of Field Size

	Gobozana		Nyaniso		Total	
	n	%	n	%	n	%
Adequate	21	46	14	42	35	44
Inadequate	25	54	19	58	44	56
Total	46	100	33	100	79	100

Differences in the perception of agriculture have been noted between the communities of Gobozana and Nyaniso. Further research could attempt to explain these differences in detail but it is the recognition of these differences that could assist extension work in the rural areas. While the similarity of the two communities studied is noticeable in the low levels of productivity and education, the differences in the image of agriculture are too persistent to be ignored as decisions and behaviour are influenced by the image, and understanding of the image is perhaps a prerequisite for successful extension work. If behaviour is leading to low productivity and poor agricultural practices, a change in the image could lead to a change in behaviour. The recognition that images vary from place to place even in an apparently homogeneous territory indicates clearly that common policies applied to all areas are likely to fail. A preliminary survey to ascertain what attitudes are held by the people and what their image of agriculture is, would appear to be a prerequisite for any development project. In this way an agricultural development policy can be related to the people who will be responsible for making it work.

Notes

1. L.L. Sebe, 'The Role of the Scientists in the Development of the Homelands', unpublished paper read at 72nd Annual Congress of South African Association for the Advancement of Science, Grahamstown, 1974, pp. 3-4.
2. Benbo, *Ciskei Economic Review*, p. 20.
3. Tomlinson Commission Report, Union of South Africa, Department of Native Affairs, Verslag van die Kommissie vir die socio-ekonomiese ontwikkeling van die Bantoe gebiede binne die Unie Van Suid Afrika (Government Printer, Pretoria, 1956).
4. D.H. Houghton, *The South African Economy* (Oxford University Press, Cape Town, 1964), p. 75.
5. Sebe, 'The Role of the Scientists', pp. 5-6.
6. Benbo, *Ciskei Economic Review*, Table 6.3, p. 34.
7. Ibid., p. 38.
8. Ibid., p. 36.
9. J.B. McI. Daniel, 'The Swazi Rural Economy: Some Thoughts on the Problems of Land Tenure', SA Geographical Society, Jubilee Conference Proceedings, 1967.
10. J.F. Holleman, *Experiment in Swaziland* (Oxford University Press, Cape Town, 1964).
11. E.K. Fisk and R.T. Shand, 'Early Stages of Development in a Primitive Economy: The Evolution from Subsistence to Trade and Specialization' in C.R. Wharton (ed.), *Subsistence Agriculture and Economic Development* (Frank Cass, London, 1970), p. 265.
12. D. Lowenthal, 'Geography, Experience and Imagination: Toward a Geographical Epistomology', *Annals Association of American Geographers*, 51 (1961); H.C. Brookfield, 'On the Environment as Perceived', *Progress in Geography*, 1 (1969); P.M. Downs, 'Geographic Space Perception: Past Approaches and Future Prospects' *Progress in Geography*, 2 (1970); H.C. Prince, 'Real, Imagined and Abstract Worlds of the Past', *Progress in Geography*, 3 (1971) and D.C.D. Pocock, 'Environmental, Perception Process and Product', *Tijdschrift voor Economische en Sociale Geografie*, 64 (1973).
13. Downs, 'Geographic Space Perceptors', p. 70.
14. Brookfield, 'On the Environment', p. 64.
15. See frontispiece for map.
16. J.B. McI. Daniel and R.W. Waxmonsky, 'East London: Study of Black Industrial Employees in Relation to Migration Characteristics' in N. Charton (ed.) 'A Socio-Economic Survey of the Border and Ciskei Region', Unpublished Report, Institute for Social and Economic Research, Rhodes University, Grahamstown (1978).

5 THE CISKEI CONSTITUTION

F. G. Richings

1. Introduction

The purpose of this chapter is to set out, in a form intelligible to laymen (that is, those with no legal training) the salient features of the Ciskei Constitution and something of its background. At the outset, two points must be stressed.

Firstly, what follows is an outline only. A whole chapter, even a monograph, could be devoted to such topics as the development of the constitution, electoral law in the Ciskei, or the procedure in the Legislative Assembly. If the writer has dwelt in some detail on the powers of the legislative assemblies of the self-governing territories, this is because their nature and extent is not always appreciated — yet they form the very basis of the concept of self-government.

Secondly, the whole question of the establishment of self-governing black territories within the borders of the Republic is a highly contentious one in terms of South African — and international — politics. It is, for example, well-known that with negligible exceptions, international recognition has been refused to both Transkei and Bophuthatswana, over which South Africa relinquished control on 26 October 1976 and 5 December 1977 respectively.[1] Should the Ciskei ultimately request, and attain, 'independence' there is no reason to believe that the attitude of the international community towards it will differ. While this chapter is not concerned with the wider issues of domestic or internatinal politics, these should not be lost sight of, in order fully to understand the motives behind, and implications of, the South African Government's so-called 'Black Homelands'[2] policy.

What follows, then, is a lawyer's viewpoint of the Ciskei constitution. As such it cannot hope to satisfy all readers, many of whom will no doubt wish more emphasis had been placed on certain aspects and less on others. The writer hopes, however, that it will succeed in its main aim, namely, to provide a framework within which the other contributions to this book may be more easily understood.

The law stated is as at 1 July 1979.

2. The Background to the Constitution

The passing of the Bantu Authorities Act, 1951, effected a radical change in the structure of local government in that part of South Africa colloquially known as the Ciskei. The system of local governmental institutions on the English model developed during the previous half-century was to be swept away and supplanted by three new local adminstrative bodies known as tribal, regional and territorial authorities. In all three of these bodies a strong emphasis was placed on appointment in accordance with custom, as opposed to election by taxpayers and landowners, which had been a hallmark of the defunct council system.[3] Several features of the present Ciskei constitution may be traced back to this new policy regarding the government of the black population of the Republic, taken in 1951.

The next important step in the administration of the Ciskei (and of the black population of South Africa generally) occurred in 1959 when the Promotion of Bantu Self-government Act was passed. According to its long title, the Act's purpose was 'to provide for the gradual development of self-governing Bantu national units and for direct consultation between the Government . . . and the said national units in regard to matters affecting the [ir] interests'. Eight 'national units' were designated by section 2(1) of the Act,[4] which also made provision for the appointment of Commissioners-General. The function of these commissioners was to serve as a link between the central government and the national unit (or units) to which they were accredited, as well as to give 'guidance and advice' on admnistrative, social, educational and economic matters and to 'enlighten the population in regard to Government policy and legislation' (Section 3).

Four years later, the self-government envisaged by the 1959 Act was granted to the Transkei.[5] Its constitution made provision for a variety of legislative, judicial and administrative matters, including a unicameral legislative assembly with wide powers of repealing South African legislation, including Acts of Parliament, in force within the territory.[6]

The Bantu Homelands Constitution Act 1971, facilitated the creation of further self-governing black territories within the Republic. This Act, however, differed from the Transkei Constitution Act in two important respects. In the first place, the Act was merely an enabling one, in that it did not itself bring self-governing territories into existence but empowered the State President to do so by proclamation in the *Gazette*. This procedure was adopted to avoid a multiplicity of virtually identical constitution Acts on the statute book, each of which, moreover, would have required the cumbersome and time-consuming procedure of an amending Act for its alteration. The Act thus merely provided the framework around which each individual constitution was to be constructed, with due regard to the characteristics of the territory in question.

In the second place, unlike the Transkei, self-government was to be effected in two stages. In terms of Chapter One of the Act, the State President was empowered to establish a legislative assembly for each of the seven areas (exclusive of the Transkei) in which designated black ethnic groups were situated. Such an assembly would have the right to legislate on a number of specific topics, but its powers were to be more limited than those of its Transkeian counterpart, in that ability to amend or repeal an Act of the South African Parliament was expressly withheld. Provision was also made for the establishment of an Executive Council, as well as an administrative infrastructure on the Transkeian pattern.

In terms of Chapter Two of the Act, the State President was empowered to advance the status of a legislative assembly by declaring the area for which it was established to be a 'self-governing territory within the Republic'. Such a territory would then become entitled to its own flag and national anthem; the Executive Council would be replaced by a Cabinet and the powers of the Legislative Assembly extended to include amendment or repeal of an Act of Parliament.

A 'first-stage' Legislative Assembly was established for the Ciskei on 21 May 1971, to replace the Ciskeian Territorial Authority.[7] (The membership of the latter body was transferred *en bloc* to the newly-established Assembly.) Fourteen months later on 1 August 1972, the territory was declared 'self-governing' in terms of Chapter Two of the Act.[8] The first elections were held during February 1973.[9] On 21 May, the reconstituted Assembly met for the first time.[10]

3. The Ciskei and its Citizenship

In terms of the Ciskei Constitution Proclamation 1972 (as amended) the self-governing territory of the Ciskei comprises all the black areas situated within the magisterial districts of Mdantsane, Zwelitsha, Hewu, Victoria East, Keiskammahoek, Peddie and Middledrift; the area of the Zibula tribal Authority in the magisterial district of Stutterheim; and certain farms in the magisterial district of Queenstown (Section 2 (2)). The result is that, in law, the Ciskei does not consist of the geographical area lying roughly between the Great Fish and the Kei rivers, and colloquially known as the Ciskei, but of the black areas only. (A 'black' area is one referred to in Section 25(1) of the Bantu Administration Act, 1927 read with Section 21(1) of the Bantu Trust Land Act, 1936.)

In terms of the Bantu Homelands Constitution Act, the State President is empowered, after consultation with the Legislative Assembly and Cabinet concerned, to modify the boundaries of a self-governing territory (Section 1(2) read with Section 26(1)).

Acting in terms of this provision, the magisterial districts of Herschel and Glen Grey were excised from the Ciskei in 1975 (thus reducing its land area by 18.7 per cent) and added to the Transkei.[11] In turn, the South African government undertook to purchase white-owned farms adjoining the Ciskei in order to consolidate the latter's territory. At present this consists of five large and thirteen smaller blocs of land, covering 523,377 ha. Although a portion borders on the coast, it does not include territorial waters.[12]

'Citizenship' of the territory is provided for by the Bantu Homelands Citizenship Act 1970. In terms of this Act, every black person in the Republic 'shall be' a citizen of one of the areas for which a territorial authority has been established (this term including an area possessing a legislative assembly) (Section 2(2)). A citizen exercises franchise rights in the area concerned, and enjoys all others rights, privileges and benefits and becomes subject to the duties and obligations of the citizenship, as are accorded or imposed upon him in terms of law (Section 2(3)).

How, then, is citizenship determined? According to the Bantu Homelands Citizenship Act, the following are the criteria:

(a) birth within the area, provided at least one parent is a citizen at the time, or
(b) the speaking of a language (including any dialect) used by the black population of the area, or
(c) relationship to any member of the black population of the area, or identification with any part of such population, or association with any such part 'by virtue of . . . cultural or racial background'.

A further way in which citizenship of an area may be acquired, is on application after domicile for a period of five years (Section 3).

Acquisition of such citizenship, however, does not involve forfeiture of South African citizenship. In this regard s.2(4) of the Act provides:

> A citizen ... shall not be regarded as an alien in the Republic and shall, by virtue of his citizenship of a territory forming part of the Republic, remain for all purposes a citizen of the Republic and shall be accorded full protection according to international law.

Internationally, therefore, citizens of self-governing territories remain South Africans, and travel on South African passports.

In view of this fact, is it juridically correct to speak of 'citizenship' of a self-governing territory? Certain writers have attempted to defend this use of the term by pointing to the distinction in law between 'citizens' and 'nationals' of a state — the former being endowed with full political rights, the latter being mere subjects who enjoy the state's protection without possessing the rights of citizens. Thus, until 1946 for example (when the Philippines became independent) Filipinos were American nationals without being United States citizens. On this analogy, a distinction should be drawn between for example, Ciskeian 'citizens' who are, however, at the same time South African 'nationals'.[13] The fatal flaw in this otherwise attractive argument is that South African law draws no distinction between citizenship and nationality. The South African Citizenship Act, 1949, speaks only of citizens and aliens — there is no intermediate category. The correct position appears to be that 'citizens' of self-governing black territories are South African citizens, with certain rights and duties vis-à-vis their 'homelands'. To group these rights and duties under the term 'citizenship', it is submitted, is misleading.

The real reason for the use of this term seems to have been political — 'to denote a new and stronger tie of allegiance'[14] to the territories in question. In furtherance of this aim, Sections 27 and 28 of the Bantu Homelands Constitution Act make provision for a flag and national anthem for each territory. In addition, an amendment to the South African Constitution provides for the recognition of additional official languages within a territory.[15] In terms of the Ciskei Constitution Proclamation, Xhosa has been recognised as an additional official language of the Ciskei alongside English and Afrikaans and in addition Sesotho may be used for 'governmental, legislative, judicial and administrative purposes' (Section 33).

4. The Legislature

The legislature of the territory is termed the Ciskeian Legislative

Assembly and consists of 57 members; 35 official and 22 elected[16] (Section 3). The official members consist of the Paramount Chief of the Ama-Rharhabe (who may, however, act through a representative in the Assembly: Section 4) and 33 chiefs of tribes in respect of which tribal authorities have been established. The remaining 22 members are elected in nine electoral divisions. The number of members to be elected in respect of each electoral division is determined by the Ciskeian Cabinet, proportionate to the number of registered voters in each, with the proviso that each division be allotted at least one member (Section 5). This provision does away with the necessity for periodic delimitations as in the Republic, and furnishes a simpler — if more rough and ready — method of apportioning the members amongst the voters.

The legislature is thus both unicameral and hybrid in nature. An alternative method of incorporating the chiefly element would have been to create a bicameral legislature on the South African pattern, with the chiefs constituting the upper house, and the elected members, the lower. This scheme, however, was not adopted because firstly, the size and population of the territory did not warrant it, and more importantly, it might have led to a deadlock between a 'conservative' official upper house and a popularly elected lower one.[17]

The vote is given to every Ciskeian 'citizen' who has attained the age of 18 years. Registration is necessary and in addition such citizen must not be subject to any disqualification (Section 6(1)). Disqualifications (which are similar to those for the Republican franchise) include conviction for treason or murder; conviction of a corrupt or illegal election practice coupled with an order that the accused be declared incapable of voting; and a declaration that the voter is mentally disordered in terms of statute (Section 7). A candidate for election to the Assembly, however, must have attained the age of 21 (Section 8(1) (a)).

The registration of voters and the conduct of elections are governed by Proclamation No. R 194 of 1972,[18] read with the Ciskei Constitution Proclamation. In terms of the former proclamation, the electoral division in which a citizen is entitled to be registered as a voter, is that in which he is domiciled (Section 9(a)). If the citizen is domiciled outside the Ciskei, his electoral division is that within which he was born. If he was born and is domiciled outside the territory, the division is that in which he claims he is entitled to be registered, by reason of his tribal affiliation with the residents of such division (Section 9(b)).

Voting at an election is by secret ballot (Section 38(4)). Each voter has as many votes as there are members to be elected in the division.

These must all be exercised (Section 38(6)), and not more than one vote may be recorded in respect of any one candidate (Section 6(1) of the Constitution). Provision is made for voters who are unable to vote in the prescribed manner, due to illiteracy or some physical incapacity. These have their ballot papers completed by the polling officer on their behalf, in the presence of two witnesses, after making their choice by word of mouth (Section 39). Despite the fact that the electoral divisions are multi-member, no system of proportional representation applies: those candidates, equal to the number of members to be returned who receive the greatest number of votes, are declared duly elected (Section 49(2)). If, due to an equality of votes, it is impossible to determine who the successful candidates are, this is resolved by drawing lots (Section 49(3)).

The Legislative Assembly is situated in Zwelitsha, near King William's Town, which is also the seat of government (Section 12(1) of the Constitution).[19] It has a life-span of five years, but the State President may, at the request of the Ciskeian Cabinet or the Assembly, dissolve it before the expiration of this period (Section 9(1)). Sessions must be held at least once a year so that a period of not more than twelve months intervenes between the last day of a session and the first day of the next (Section 12(3)). Meetings of the Assembly are presided over by a chairman (and, in his absence, a deputy chairman). These are elected from amongst the members by secret ballot, at the first sitting, and hold office for the duration of the life of the Assembly (Sections 27 and 28). The routine business of the Assembly is under the control of a secretary.[20]

Procedure in the Assembly, as with other legislatures in South Africa, is modelled on that of the House of Assembly in Cape Town. All questions are determined by a majority of votes of the members present, including the chairman. In the case of an equality of votes, the member presiding at the sitting also has a casting vote, which he must exercise.[21] The number of members constituting a quorum is surprisingly high: unlike the House of Assembly no definite figure is mentioned; instead, it is provided that a quorum shall be 'any number of members exceeding half' the membership of the Assembly (Section 13(2)). Proceedings of the Assembly are, in general, open to the public (Section 13(4)). There is freedom of speech and debate, in that no member is subject to any legal proceedings by virtue of anything he may have said or brought before it (Section 3A of the Bantu Homelands Constitution Act; Section 13(3) of the Constitution). Speeches may be delivered in English, Afrikaans, Xhosa or Sesotho and translated from the language of delivery into one or more of the other languages if the Chairman so directs (rule 51, Standing Rules). A *verbatim* record of the Assembly's proceedings is kept in Xhosa, and (in alternate years) in English and Afrikaans (Section 34(2) of the Constitution).[22]

A bill in the Legislative Assembly goes through the customary three readings, with a committee stage after the second reading. The procedure adopted is laid down by the Standing Rules.[23] Only public bill procedure is used, however — no provision is made in the Standing Rules for private or hybrid bills.

Once a bill has passed the Assembly, it is presented to the State President for his assent, via the office of the Commissioner-General of the Ciskei. The assent is signified by signing one copy of the bill in question (Section 31). After assent, the 'Law' (in the Ciskei, known as an 'Act') must be published by the Cabinet in the territory's *Gazette*, whereupon it has the force of law (Section 32).

Three copies of the Act — one in each official language — must be enrolled on record in the office of the Registrar of that division of the Supreme Court having jurisdiction in the area in which the legislative assembly buildings are situated. In the case of a conflict between the three versions, that signed by the State President prevails (Section 33).

5. The Assembly's Legislative Powers

The legislative powers of the assemblies of self-governing territories are laid down by s.30 of the Bantu Homelands Constitution Act 1971. As these powers comprise the keystone of the concept of, and justification for, self-government, they will be dealt with in some detail.

In terms of s.30(1) (a), each assembly has the power to make 'laws' on all matters referred to in the First Schedule to the Act. At present these are, broadly,

(a) the administration and control of government departments and the employment of officers
(b) education for blacks (excluding University education)
(c) the provision of welfare and health services for blacks
(d) the control of business undertakings and the planning and establishment of industrial, mining and financial ventures
(e) agriculture, fish and game preservation, the conservation of flora and fauna and the destruction of vermin

(f) public works, and the erection of government buildings

(g) the establishment and control of lower courts and the administration of justice in respect of blacks, the appointment of justices of the peace and commissioners of oaths, the control and administration of such part of the police force as may have been transferred to the government of the territory; prisons for blacks; and legal aid

(h) roads (but not national roads), the regulation and control of road traffic and motor carrier transportation

(i) direct taxation on citizens of the territory (whether resident within or outside it) and on property situate therein

(j) municipal and other local institutions and tribal and regional authorities

(k) births, deaths, marriages and customary unions and the execution of wills and administration of deceased estates, in respect of citizens

(l) the raising of loans and the collection of all revenues and fees which accrue to the Government

(m) the establishment of public holidays; the licensing and control of places of amusement and recreation and the regulation of horse-racing and the licensing of totalisators

(n) the establishment of libraries and library services in respect of blacks, the establishment of parks, museums, art galleries and botanic gardens, and the reservation of places of historical or scientific interest

(o) the protection of life, persons and property

(p) the conclusion or ratification of treaties and agreements with the South African Government

(q) the division and amalgamation of existing tribes, the constitution of new tribes and the appointment, conditions of service, retirement and dismissal of paramount chiefs, chiefs and headmen (provided that the tribal or community authority concerned has first been consulted) and

(r) the imposition of penalties for the contravention of any law made by a legislative assembly

According to s.30(1)(b) any 'law' passed by an assembly may provide for 'the amendment or repeal of any law, including any act of Parliament, in so far as it relates to any [scheduled] matter and applies in the area or to any citizen of the area whether such citizen is resident within or outside the area . . . '

Conversely, in terms of s.30(3):

no law made after the date on which an area is . . . declared a self-governing territory (including any Act of Parliament, but excluding a law made by the State President or the legislative assembly concerned) which relates to any [scheduled] matter . . . shall apply in that area or in relation to any citizen of that area in respect of whom that legislative assembly is empowered to make laws . . .

Finally, a number of matters 'are reserved from legislation' by the assemblies. These include military matters; the establishment and control of factories for the manufacture of arms, ammunition and explosives, foreign relations; postal, telegraph, telephone, radio and television services, railways, harbours, national roads and civil aviation; immigration, banking and currency; customs and excise duties; and the 'amendment, repeal or substitution' of the Act itself (Section 4). (Although at first sight this particular section appears unnecessary in view of the restriction of the assemblies' legislative powers 'scheduled' matters only, it does achieve the effect of limiting the 'protection of life, persons and property' provision, which might otherwise have seemed too wide.)

In regard to the above provisions, a number of further points may be made, and conclusions drawn, concerning the nature of the 'self-government' accorded by the Act:

(a) The matter upon which the assemblies are competent to legislate are not static, but may be expanded by the addition of further items to the Schedule. Until 1978 this had to be accomplished by means of the somewhat cumbersome procedure of an amending Act. From 1971 to 1978 the Schedule was amended on six occasions: once in 1972, once in 1973, twice in 1974, once in 1977 and once in 1978.[24] In the latter year, however, the Bantu Homelands Constitution Act was amended by the insertion of s.37A, which permits the State President to 'amend' the Schedule merely by proclamation in the *Gazette* and also to amend any other provision of the Act by the same means, for the purpose of giving effect to the amendment. Such an amendment, however, will only come into operation on a date determined by the Minister of Plural Relations and Development and then only in the area (or areas) determined by him. Although this section apparently bestows the power to 'amend' (Afrikaans 'wysig') the Schedule only, it clearly also envisages extension of the powers of assemblies by the addition of further items.[25]

(b) The powers bestowed by the Act on the legislatures of the self-

The Ciskei Constitution

governing territories are considerably more extensive than those enjoyed by Provincial Councils. Thus, the topics upon which the former are competent to legislate are far wider, embracing matters such as the control of lower courts and prisons, police, legal aid, tourism and intoxicating liquor, which are withheld from the latter.[26] Furthermore, Provincial Councils are prohibited from amending or repealing an Act of Parliament whereas the legislature of a self-governing territory may do so.[27] In addition, unlike Provincial Councils,[28] the legislative assemblies have the power to legislate with extra-territorial effect on certain matters — but on a 'personality' basis only. In this regard s.30(2) of the Act states:

> Where in terms of the said Schedule a legislative assembly is empowered to make laws applicable in any area outside the area for which it has been established or in relation to citizens of the last-mentioned area who are or are resident elsewhere than in the said last-mentioned area but within the Republic, any such law shall have effect and may contain provisions for the due enforcement thereof in any such first-mentioned area or, as the case may be, in relation to any such citizen in any place within the Republic wherever such citizen may be, or may be resident.

(It should be noted too that this 'personality'principle applies even within the self-governing territories in some respects, in that legislation on certain matters applies to 'citizens' only.)[29]

(c) Although wide powers have been accorded the legislatures of the self-governing territories, it should however be stressed that these remain very much part of the Republic, whose unitary nature remains unimpaired. Thus, despite the wording of section 30(3) it is clear that Parliament is entitled to legislate for such a territory on any matter, even one falling within the ambit of the Schedule. (The courts would, however, not lightly presume that this was Parliament's intention.) Parliament could if it chose even take the extreme step of abolishing the self-governing territories without their consent, and reincorporating them into the provincial system.

In addition, the State President (in effect, the South African Cabinet) has the power — equal to that of Parliament[30] — in terms of s.25(1) of the Bantu Administration Act, 1927, of legislating by proclamation on *all* topics for all the black areas of the Republic. In 1977 this power was used to extend the Criminal Procedure Act 1977 to the Ciskei and five other self-governing territories.[31] The Cabinet also exercises absolute control over the legislation of the self-governing territories, in that it may advise the State President (which advice he must take)[32] to withhold his assent to any law passed by an Assembly (Section 31(2) (a)). No Ciskeian Acts, however, have been vetoed thus far.

(d) Finally, what is the role of the courts in regard to the self-governing territories? More important, what attitude have they adopted towards them? Here, two matters fall to be considered.

Firstly, s.19 of the Bantu Homelands Constitution Act provides:

> Any provincial or local division of the Supreme Court of South Africa having jurisdiction in any area or portion of any area for which a legislative assembly has been established . . . shall be competent to pronounce upon the validity of a law of that legislative assembly.

This section gives the Supreme Court the so-called 'testing right' in regard to such legislation. As, however, the latter would appear to be orginal and not delegated (and thus fall into the category of statutes as opposed to mere by-laws),[33] the grounds upon which the Court could declare a law to be invalid are extremely limited. The most usual instance would be where an assembly purports to legislate on an 'unscheduled' topic.

Secondly, since the granting of self-government to the Transkei in 1963, the Courts, on numerous occasions, have been called upon to determine to what extent Acts of Parliament and Provincial Ordinances apply within the various territories. This is due to s.30 of the Act, whose practical effect is to freeze what might loosely be termed 'South African legislation' on the scheduled topics, as at the date of establishment of a self-governing territory.[34] Whilst such legislation continues to apply within the particular territory until amended or repealed by the legislative assembly, it remains unaffected by any subsequent repeal of, or amendment to it by its legislative progenitor.

To take a straightforward example: in S v. Dlanga 1968 (1) SA 5 (E) it was held that the Cape Road Traffic Ordinance of 1966 was not applicable in the Transkei, as it had been passed after the granting of self-government (that is, 30 May 1963) and the 'regulation and control of road traffic' was one of the matters upon which the Transkeian Legislative Assembly was competent to legislate. The former Cape Road Traffic Ordinance of 1955 thus remained in force in the Transkei, despite its repeal by the Cape Provincial Council.

In *Dlanga*'s case the 'South African legislation' under consideration fell foursquare within one of the scheduled topics. Where this was not the case, the views of the various divisions of the Supreme Court as to the applicability of such legislation were not harmonious. In general, two approaches could be discerned: certain divisions placed a restrictive interpretation upon the powers of the legislative assemblies, whereas others placed a more liberal construction upon these powers.

The two approaches are well illustrated by the following example: in 1972 the South African Parliament amended the Stock Theft Act, 1959, by abolishing the mandatory compensatory fine (payable to the owner of unrecovered stolen stock) imposed upon persons convicted under it. While there was no doubt that the Stock Theft Act itself applied within the various self-governing territories, did the amendment apply as well? Put in another way, after the granting of self-government, who was the competent legislative authority in regard to such a matter — the South African Parliament or the legislative assemblies? (Stock theft *per se* was not one of the scheduled topics.)

In *S* v. *Moagaesi* 1974 (1) SA 137 (NC) the Northern Cape Division held that compensatory fines for stock theft still applied in Bophuthatswana on the ground that this concerned 'the protection of life, persons and property' — one of the scheduled matters. The competent legislature was thus the legislative assembly of the territory and not the South African Parliament. This decision was followed by the Orange Free State Provincial Division in *S* v. *Xhaba* 1975 (1) SA 632 (O) and again by the Northern Cape Division in *S* v. *Sion* 1975 (2) SA 184 (NC).

In the unreported cases of *S* v. *Ngobeni* (TPD 27 August 1973) and *S* v. *Letlhake* (TPD 12 December 1973) however, the Transvaal Provincial Division held the exact opposite — the amending Act did apply within Bophuthatswana and thus compensatory fines for stock theft had been abolished there; the Eastern Cape Division came to the same conclusion with regard to the Ciskei in *S* v. *Quma* 1974 (3) SA 722 (E). These decisions were arrived at on the basis that although the legislative assemblies had the power to legislate for 'the protection of life, persons and property' they could only impose sanctions for the breach of their own laws on this topic.[35] This led to the absurd result that while the legislature of a territory had no power to alter penal sanctions in a South African Act on, say, intoxicating liquor, it had the power to sweep away such an Act in its entirety — penal sanctions and all! (Intoxicating liquor is one of the topics on which an assembly may legislate: item 19 of the Schedule.)

The result of these differing approaches was that where a self-governing territory straddled more than one division of the Supreme Court (as did Bophuthatswana) South African legislation on a particular topic might be held both to apply and yet not to apply; clearly an anomalous position.

This conflict was resolved by the Appellate Division in *S* v. *Heavyside* 1976 (1) SA 584 (AD), in which a liberal construction of the assemblies' powers, and more in keeping with the spirit of the Bantu Homelands Constitution Act, was adopted.[36]

6. The Executive

The executive government of the Ciskei is vested in a Cabinet, consisting of a chief minister and six (until 1975, five) other ministers.[37] These are responsible for the control and administration of the various departments. At present these consist of the departments of the Chief Minister and of Finance; the Interior; Works; Education; Agriculture and Forestry; Justice; and Health and Welfare. Allocation of portfolios is made by the chief minister (Section 25(3) of the Constitution Proclamation).

As there is no formal head of the territory (such as the governor in a colony) to make cabinet appointments, an alternative method has had to be devised. Until 1975 this was election by secret ballot by the members of the Legislative Assembly from amongst their ranks, at the first session after a general election.[38] The merit of this scheme was that it provided for an executive of the 'best man' type, but with the rise of clearly defined political parties in the Ciskei it might have become unworkable in practice, and have led to dissension both within the Cabinet Room and outside it. In 1975, therefore, the Constitution was altered.[39] The chief minister is now elected by the Assembly, and the remaining members of the Cabinet appointed by him, within a peiod of seven days (Sections 17 and 18(1) of the Constitution).

Until 1975 removal of either the whole cabinet, or an individual minister, from office was effected by the State President (that is, the South African Cabinet) after a petititon 'for sound and cogent reasons' by the Legislative Assembly. Since this date, only the chief minister may be thus removed; other ministers are now removed by notice in writing by the chief minister.[40] There is, however, no convention that the State President must accede to a request for removal and thus at present cabinet responsibility in the strict sense of the word does not exist.

Apart from the foregoing, a member of the Cabinet vacates office on losing his seat in the Assembly or by resigning (Section 23).

Meetings of the cabinet are presided over by the chief minister (Section 25(1)).[41] The Constitution specifically provides that all questions arising are to be determined by a majority of votes of the members present, and in the case of an equality of votes, the chief minister has a casting vote (Section 26(1)). Now that appointments to the Cabinet are made by the chief minister (presumably from amongst his supporters in the Assembly) and no longer by the Assembly itself, this particular provision would appear to be redundant. Meetings may be attended by the Commissioner-General of the Ciskei and also by the Departmental secretaries (all of whom are at present whites, seconded from the Department of Plural Relations and Development) if the Cabinet permits (Section 26(4)).

Ministerial salaries are laid down by the Ciskei Payment and Privileges of Members of the Legislative Assembly Act 1973 (as amended in 1977). The chief minister receives R13,680 per annum; other ministers R11,160. Ministers are assisted in the discharge of their functions by a staff of civil servants. Their appointments, conditions of employment, discipline, retirement and discharge are regulated by the Ciskeian Public Service Act 1972.

7. The Administration of Justice

This topic is not dealt with by the Ciskei Constitution Proclamation, but by the Bantu Homelands Constitution Act. In terms of s.14(1) of this Act, the establishment of a legislative assembly for a black area does not affect existing courts of law. These continue to function as before 'until altered or disestablished by the authority having power to do so'.

Who, then, is the competent authority? To all intents and purposes this is now the minister of justice of the area concerned, in whom is vested the power to establish or disestablish such courts (Section 14(1A)). This power is, however, subject to a number of qualifications. Firstly, it relates to lower courts only, and not to that division of the Supreme Court of South Africa having jurisdiction within the area. Furthermore, the jurisdiction, powers, duties and functions of such courts may not exceed those of a magistrate's court under the Magistrate's Courts Act, 1944 (Section 15(1) (a)). Secondly, no court may be established or disestablished, or any judicial officer appointed, with jurisdiction over persons who are not blacks, without the approval of the South African Minister of Plural Relations and Development (Section 14(1) (a)). Conversely, this personage retains his power to establish or disestablish a magistrate's court within the area to hear cases in which any of the accused or parties is not a citizen (Section 14(3)). Thirdly, although the Act does not say so specifically, the control of prosecutions remains vested in the Attorney-General who is subject to the control of the South African Minister of Justice.[42]

The Act also makes provision for the transfer of any existing magistrate's court to the government of an area for which a legislative assembly has been established. This is accomplished by the State President, by proclamation in the *Gazette* (Section 14(2)). To date a number of magistrates' courts have been thus transferred, including those at Mdantsane and Zwelitsha, and black magistrates and prosecutors appointed. A regional court for the territory has also been recently established.[43]

On the proclamation of an area as self-governing, the State President may constitute a High Court for the territory, and make regulations as to its constitution and jurisdiction (Section 34). Although the Act is silent on the matter, if the model of the Transkei High Court (now the Transkei Supreme Court) is followed,[44] such a court will have the same status and powers as a division of the Supreme Court of South Africa, whose jurisdiction within the territory it will replace. It is probable that the jurisdiction of the present (Bantu) Divorce Court and Appeal Court for Commissioners' Courts will also be transferred to it. Appeals from a decision of the High Court will lie to the Appellate Division in Bloemfontein.

As yet, no High Court has been constituted for the Ciskei, as the volume of work does not warrant it and the Eastern Cape Division of the Supreme Court exercises jurisdiction there.

8. Finance

In terms of s.6 of the Bantu Homelands Constitution Act, all revenues accruing to the government of a self-governing territory are to be paid into a Revenue Fund. Such revenue is derived from

(a) taxes, levies and rates imposed on citizens in terms of certain Acts of the South African Parliament as well as any law of the legislative assembly concerned; income tax payable in terms of any Act of Parliament or Provincial Ordinance by any private company managed and controlled in the territory concerned and in which blacks have a controlling interest; and estate or succession duty payable in terms of any Act of Parliament in respect of the estate of any citizen of the territory who was ordinarily resident there at the time of his death

(b) all income deriving from those matters in respect of which the legislative assembly is competent to legislate (for example, animal taxes, licence fees, rent etc)

(c) an annual grant from the State Revenue Fund representing the saving made by the transference of certain administrative matters to the Government of the territory concerned, and

(d) such additional grant as may be made by the South African Parliament.

The annual estimates of revenue and expenditure are prepared by the cabinet of the territory. After submission to the Minister of Plural Relations and Development to determine the contribution to be made by the South African Parliament these are submitted to the legislative assembly for appropriation (Section 9). The Act provides that no monies may be withdrawn from the Revenue Fund except in terms of a law of the assembly (Section 8). In addition, a legislative assembly may not originate or pass any rate, resolution motion or bill for the appropriation of taxes unless the Cabinet has made recommendation to this effect (Section 7). As is the case with the South African Parliament, the Standing Rules of the Ciskeian Legislative Assembly lay down a special procedure regarding financial measures (see Para. XIII).

The accounts of a self-governing territory are audited by the South African Auditor-General, until the legislative assembly in question provides otherwise. (No such provision has yet been made in the Ciskei.) The administration and control of the Revenue Fund is governed by the South African Exchequer and Audit Act 1975, and the regulations framed in terms of it (Section 35).

9. Future Constitutional Development

Although the declared purpose of the Bantu Homelands Constitution Act, as set forth in the preamble, is 'to provide for the development of Bantu nations to self-government and independence' certain self-governing black territories have indicated that they will not be seeking the latter status in the immediate future. Amongst these are KwaZulu and Qwa-Qwa. The main reason would appear to be the present fragmentary nature and economic non-viability of these territories.[45] It is probable, too, that the non-recognition of Transkei and Bophuthatswana by the international community — and with it, the eclipse of visions of United Nations membership and embassies abroad — has had a somewhat chilling effect. In 1977 the South African Government accordingly brought a Bill before Parliament[46] which provided for a third phase in self-rule — that of an 'internally autonomous country'.

In terms of the Bill, declaration of a self-governing territory as internally autonomous (effected by the State President by proclamation, with the approval of the Senate and the House of Assembly) would have brought about two important changes in its constitution. Firstly, provision was made for the 'designation or election of a person as head of the executive government'. The details of this office, including the holder's powers and duties, his (or her) title, the manner of designation or election, and the terms of office and conditions of service were to be supplied by law of the legislative assembly in question. Also, the power of assenting to the territory's legislation was to be transferred from the State President to this personage. Secondly, the powers of the territory's legislative assembly were to be extended still further, in that (subject to the provisions of the Act, including any limitations contained in the Schedule) it would be able to legislate 'in respect of all matters . . . in so far as it may be necessary for the internal peace, order and good government of its country'.

However, despite an explanatory statement by the then Minister of Bantu Administration and Development that the Bill would make a self-governing territory 'fully autonomous as far as its internal operations (*sic*) were concerned' in that it would have 'legislative authority over all its internal affairs so that only foreign relations were excluded',[47] the Bill still withheld from the legislature of an 'internally autonomous country' competence on a wide variety of matters that are normally considered 'internal'. These included postal, telegraph, telephone, radio and television services; railways, harbours and national roads and currency, banking and control of stock exchange (see s.4 of the Bantu Homelands Constitution Act). In addition, the limitations on legislative competence contained in the First Schedule were to continue to apply; these, in general, imposed a sort of legislative *apartheid* through use of the terms 'black' and (more discreetly) 'citizen'.

More important, even though the power to assent to legislation was to vest in the head of the executive of the territory, the South African Cabinet still retained its former control. Here, the amending Bill provided:

Every bill passed by a legislative assembly of an internally autonomous country, shall, before being assented to by the head of the executive government, be submitted to the Minister [of Bantu Administration and Development] and the Minster may, within twenty-one days after receipt of such bill by him, notify the head of the executive government that the bill will, by reason of its implications for the Republic, be submitted by him to the State President for his consideration . . .

The Bill further provided that no bill could be assented to before the elapse of 21 days, or, where a bill had been submitted to the State President (that is, the South African Cabinet) for consideration, until any recommendations (that is, alterations) made by him had been given effect to.

Finally, declaration of a territory as 'internally autonomous' was in no way to affect the unitary nature of the South African constitution. 'Citizens' of such territories were to remain South African citizens and Acts of Parliament on non-scheduled topics were to continue automatically to apply there. The practical effect of the amending Bill, in short, was to extend still further the powers of the various black assemblies.

This Bill, however, after its first reading in the Assembly during the 1977 session of Parliament, was not proceeded with, nor was it reintroduced in 1978. The indications in fact are that it has been shelved indefinitely. The reason would appear to be fear on the part of the South African Government that certain 'homelands', especially Bophuthatswana and the Ciskei, would opt for this third phase of self-rule, rather than complete 'independence' which is the Government's ultimate aim. In consequence of the Bill's withdrawal, Bophuthatswana's 'independence' was accomplished late in 1977.

What then, of the Ciskei? In August 1978, a commission was appointed by the Ciskeian Government to enquire into and report upon the feasiblity of independence for the Ciskei.[48] Special attention was to be given to the following matters:

(a) the prospects or otherwise of obtaining international recognition
(b) the prospects of obtaining consolidation of Ciskeian territory
(c) what changes in the present Westminster-type of constitution would be desirable
(d) what arrangements should be made with the South African

Government concerning citizenship of an independent Ciskei, and
(e) the prospects regarding the future economic development of the Ciskei and the attainment of economic independence.

The report of this commission is not expected before 1980, and if independence is to come at all, it is unlikely to occur before 1981.

Notes

1. Status of Transkei Act 1976; Status of Bophuthatswana Act 1977. (The boundaries of Bophuthatswana were extended by the Bophuthatswana Border Extension Act 1978.) For accounts of the present Transkei Constitution, see I. Rautenbach, 'The Constitution of the Transkei', *Tydskrif vir die Suid Afrikaanse Reg*, 1 (1977), pp. 199-209; J.C. Bekker, 'The Judicial System of Transkei', *Comparative and International Law Journal of Southern Africa*, 11 (1978), pp. 27-46; and W.H.B. Dean, 'A Citizen of Transkei', *Comparative and International Law Journal of Southern Africa*, 11 (1978), pp. 57-67.

2. The official terminology for the black population of South Africa has had a somewhat chequered history. Originally referred to as 'Natives' in Acts of Parliament and official documents, in the early 1950s the term 'Bantu' gained favour; see, for example, the Bantu Authorities Act, 1951. The terminology was accordingly altered by s.16 of the Native Laws Amendment Act, 1962 and s.100 of the Bantu Laws Amendment Act 1964: The Department of Native Affairs, for example, now became the 'Department of Bantu Administration and Development' and a 'Native', a 'Bantu'. (All along, however, educated blacks preferred the term 'African'.) In the 1970s the term 'black' came to be preferred, both by the blacks themselves and by South African officialdom. As far as the former were concerned, this coincided with the 'Black Power' movement in America (and later, South Africa). As regards the latter, there was always the awkward problem of what to call blacks from outside South Africa. According to official dogma, they were not 'Bantu'; calling them 'Africans' (Afrikaans: 'Afrikaane') was a trifle embarrassing. In 1978, in terms of s.17 of the Second Bantu Laws Amendment Act, the terminology was changed, yet again. The term 'Bantu' was either to be deleted from the statute-book altogether, or substituted by the term 'Black'. The Department of Bantu Administration and Development became the 'Department of Plural Relations and Development', and the Minister's title changed accordingly. 'Black Homelands' are now (misleadingly) 'Black States'. 'Bantu beer' – always colloquially called 'Kaffir beer' – is now 'sorghum beer'. It appears as though the titles of Acts of Parliament have also been altered retrospectively, the Bantu Authorities Act, 1951 becoming the 'Black Authorities Act' and the Bantu Homelands Constitution Act 1971 the 'Black States Constitution Act', but this is not clear from the wording of the section. In this chapter, the pre-1978 terminology for Acts of Parliament has been adhered to.

3. For a discussion of the Bantu Authorities Act and its implementation, see D.M. Groenewald, 'Die Administratiewe Funksionering van Bewindsinstellings in die Ciskei met besondere verwysing na plaaslike bestuur', unpublished MA thesis, Rhodes University, Grahamstown, 1976, pp. 130-66; *Annual Survey of South African Law* (Juta and Co., Cape Town, 1951), pp. 16-19 and Lord Hailey, *An African Survey Revised 1956* (Oxford University Press, London, 1957), pp. 429-31.

The Ciskei Constitution

4. The North Sotho, the South Sotho, the Swazi, the Tsonga, the Tswana, the Venda, the Xhosa and the Zulu.
5. Transkei Constitution Act 1963, which came into operation on 30 May 1963.
6. See, in general, *Annual Survey of South African Law* (Juta and Co., Cape Town, 1963), pp. 56-70.
7. Proclamation R 118, Government Gazette 3110 of 21 May 1971.
8. Proclamation R 187, Government Gazette 3622 of 28 July 1972 (The 'Ciskei Constitution Proclamation').
9. Groenewald, 'Die Administratiewe Funksionering van Bewindsinstellings'.
10. M. Horrell and D. Horner (eds.), *A Survey of Race Relations in South Africa, 1973* (South African Institute of Race Relations, Johannesburg, 1974), p.160.
11. Proclamation R 95, Government Gazette 4682 of 25 April 1975. The excision took effect as from 1 November: Proclamation R 238, Government Gazette 4874 of 17 October 1975.
12. This follows from the definition of the territory, as laid down in the Ciskei Constitution Proclamation.
13. See J.F. Heyne, 'A Transkeian Citizen of South African Nationality?', *Tydskrif vir Hedendaagse Romeins-Hollandse Reg*, 26 (1963), pp. 44-9, and F. Venter 'Bantoeburgerskap en Tuislandburgerskap', *Tydskrif vir Hedendaagse Romeins-Hollandse Reg*, 38 (1975), pp. 239-53.
14. Heyne, 'A Transkeian Citizen', p. 46.
15. Republic of South Africa Constitution Act, s. 103(3) (as amended in 1963 and 1971).
16. On its establishment in August 1972 there were 50 members: 30 official and 20 elected. In 1975 the numbers were decreased to 29 official and 15 elected, following upon the excision of the Herschel and Glen Grey districts (see page 62). In 1977, Proclamation R 304, Government Gazette 5790 of 28 October 1977 increased the membership to 33 official and 22 elected. Two further official members were added in 1979 by Proclamation R 14, Government Gazette 6274 of 19 January 1979 and Proclamation R 64, Government Gazette 6409 of 20 April 1979.
17. In the election of February 1973, Mr (now Chief) Lennox Sebe's group won 13 of the 20 elective seats, but he was elected Chief Minister by the Assembly by 26 votes to 24. Thus, of the 30 official members, 17 were opposed to him: Horrell and Horner (eds.), *A Survey of Race Relations*, pp. 159-60.
18. Proclamation R 194, Government Gazette 3630 of 11 August 1972 as amended by Proclamation R 239 Government Gazette 5753 of 30 September 1977 and Proclamation R 54, Government Gazette 5936 of 17 March 1978.
19. This seat is temporary only; in time it will be moved to Alice, where the University of Fort Hare is situated.
20. Ciskeian Legislative Assembly: Standing Rules of Procedure, rule 52. Rule 53 somewhat oddly provides that officials of the Assembly 'fall under the Department of the Chief Minister and perform their duties under the general directions (*sic*) and control of the Secretary of the Chief Minister's Department'. (According to the usual parliamentary practice, these officials should be completely independent of the Executive.)
21. Section 13(1) of the Constitution Proclamation and rule 93 of the Standing Rules of Procedure. Initially, the Chairman had only a casting vote, but a deliberative vote was given to him through an amendment to s.13(1) of the Constitution, by Proclamation R 32, Government Gazette 4179 of 1 March 1974. The reason for the amendment was the small majority of the governing party in the Assembly, which might have led to a deadlock. (The writer has been

informed that the deliberative vote is not in fact used.)
22. In actual fact, only in 1974 were the debates in Xhosa – Afrikaans; since then they have all been in Xhosa – English.
23. These rules were made pursuant to the Ciskeian Standing Rules of Procedure Act 1972, promulgated as Government Notice R 1680, Government Gazette 3658 of 22 September 1972.
24. By s.12 of the Bantu Laws Amendment Act 1972; s.15(1) of the Bantu Laws Amendment Act 1973; s.24 of the Bantu Laws Amendment Act 1974; s.10(1) of the Second Bantu Laws Amendment Act 1974; ss.3 and 4 of the Second Bantu Laws Amendment Act 1977 and s.19 of the Bantu Laws Amendment Act 1978.
25. In 1973, however, Parliament indirectly *decreased* the powers of legislative assemblies by 'elucidating' the expression 'Bantu education' appearing in item 2. Originally the item referred to 'Bantu education' only, but by reason of the Bantu Laws Amendment Act 1973 this was qualified by the addition of the words 'excluding education provided by a university or a university college established by or in terms of any Act of Parliament'. In the long title of the amending Act this was described as an elucidation of the expression concerned, but in fact amounted to an indirect decrease of powers.
26. See s.84(1) of the Republic of South Africa Constitution Act, 1961.
27. For example, the Ciskeian Marketing Act 1976 repealed two Acts of the South African Parliament: the Marketing Act 1968 and the Egg Production Control Act 1970.
28. *Smithers* v. *C I R* 1928 CPD 242; *R* v. *Belman* 1940 TPD 169.
29. See, for example, items 7A, 15, 23 and 26 of the First Schedule.
30. *R* v. *Maharaj* 1950 (3) SA 187 AD at 194D.
31. Proclamation R 155, Government Gazette 5680 of 22 July 1977.
32. In terms of s. 16(1) of the Republic of South Africa Constitution Act, 1961, 'the executive government of the Republic . . . is vested in the State President, *acting on the advice of the Executive Council*' (emphasis added).
33. E. Kahn, 'Some Thoughts on the Competency of the Transkeian Legislative Assembly and the Sovereignity of the South African Parliament', *South African Law Journal*, 80 (1963), 473 at 476. (The main distinction between a statute and a by-law is that the latter may be declared invalid on the ground of unreasonableness, whereas the former may not.)
34. For a full discussion of this somewhat involved topic, see F.G. Richings, 'The applicability of South African legislation in the self-governing Bantu territories', *South African Law Journal*, 93 (1976), pp. 119-26 and D.H. van Wyk, 'Die posisie met betrekking tot wetgewing in die Bantoetuislande', *Tydskrif vir Romeins-Hollandse Reg*, 37 (1974), pp. 1-12.
35. The courts deduced this from item 32 of the First Schedule, which bestowed the power to impose penalties 'for a contravention of . . . any law made by the legislative assembly.'. The courts interpreted this to mean that penalties might *not* be imposed for contravention of a law *not* made by the legislative assembly. This was erroneous, as the power to legislate always includes the power to impose penalties, at least insofar as bodies exercising original powers are concerned.
36. See Richings, 'The Applicability of South African legislation', pp. 124-5.
37. The sixth department, that of Health and Welfare, was created in 1975 by Proclamation R 246, Government Gazette 4884 of 31 October 1975.
38. Section 16 of the Constitution. At the first meeting of the legislative assembly after the granting of self-government, Mr Lennox Sebe was elected Chief Minister. Thereupon, the opposition decided not to nominate candidates for the remaining Cabinet seats. Horrell and Horner (eds.), *A Survey of Race Relations*, p. 160.

39. Proclamation R 86, Government Gazette 4653 of 11 April 1975.
40. Section 22(1) as amended by Proclamation R 86 of 1975 (*supra*).
41. A circular cabinet room, designed along the lines of a tribal hut, was completed in 1977.
42. Section 3(5) of the Criminal Procedure Act 1977. The Attorney-General also has the power, in terms of the proviso to s.15(1) (a) of the Bantu Homelands Constitution Act, to remove cases from one court to another, whether such court be within or outside the territory. The reason for this proviso appears to be to avoid a white accused appearing before a black Magistrate — at least where the accused objects.
43. The way was cleared for its establishment by an amendment to ss.9 and 9 *bis* of the South African Magistrates' Courts Act, 1944 (dealing with the qualifications and appointment of regional Magistrates) by the Ciskeian Magistrates' Courts Amendment Act 1977.
44. Establishment by Proclamation R 173, Government Gazette 3981 of 20 July 1973.
45. See the interview with the Chief Minister of Qwa-Qwa, Mr T.K. Mopeli, in the *Sunday Tribune* of 2 October 1977, p. 10. He pointed out that the territory consisted of only 48,300 hectares, of which only a third was agriculturally viable and that independence would be 'totally ridiculous'.
46. Bantu Homelands Constitution Amendment Bill (B 91 — 1977).
47. *Eastern Province Herald*, 29 March 1977, p.2.
48. Government Notice 14, Ciskei Official Gazette 177 of 4 August 1978.

Acknowledgements

Professor J.C. Bekker, Director, Institute for Public Service Training and Administration, University of Zululand.
Mr F. Jansen, Chief Clerk, Department of the Chief Minister and Finance, Ciskei.
Mr G.D. Maytham, Secretary, Department of the Chief Minister and Finance, Ciskei.
Mr W.M. Myikana, Senior Information Officer, Ciskei.

6 THE ADMINISTRATIVE SYSTEM IN THE CISKEI

D.M. Groenewald

The present administrative structure in the Ciskei cannot be fully comprehended without paying some attention to its historical setting.

The structural pattern of the traditional authority system was composed of a three-tier hierarchy. The independent tribe was controlled by a chief (inkosi) who was in theory the senior member of the senior lineage of the royal clan. The dispersed settlement pattern of the population (they were pastoral farmers) necessitated decentralisation of control. To achieve this purpose the tribal territory was divided into districts (imihlaba) under the control of a sub-chief (inkosana). The latter was normally a close relative of the chief. The districts in turn were subdivided into wards (izithile) under the control of headmen (iziduna).

Authority in each of these tiers contained both judicial and administrative elements in that the particular leader could settle disputes and give orders or allocate goods to everyone living in his territory. Although authority was theoretically in the hands of one person, the decision-making process was spread throughout the whole group and the aim of all decisions was consensus. Government involved the participation of all the male members of a particular unit.

The whole concept of authority in the traditional system deviated from the classical Weberian authority of bureaucratic systems in the following ways: The authority role was not clearly divorced from other roles (for example, kinship); there was no formal training for office; and relations between ruler and ruled were diffuse and particularistic. It is very important to note that the authority of the chief was not unquestioned, but had to be recreated from time to time. The essence of this is that chiefs could not rule on their own, but had constantly to consult their councillors and people in order to obtain consensus.

The traditional system of government was influenced and changed through contact with European migrants and successive policy measures of both the Dutch and British governments who ruled the Cape colony. The first significant policy measure was taken in 1780 when the Fish river was designated as the eastern boundary of the white settlement. This constituted a policy of land demarcation. Ignorance of the traditional system is reflected in many policy measures. Thus Major-

General Dundas, as acting Governor at the turn of the eighteenth century, wished to end hostilities with the Xhosa-speaking tribes and tried to promote this 'by conciliatory means, by ambassadors, by presents, and by promises, to endeavour to impress the king or great chief of the Kaffir nation with confidence that the government wished to maintain peace'.[1]

Such a plan was repugnant to the other chiefs as each chief was an independent ruler and the relationship between them was a parallel one and not one of superordination or subordination.

In 1817 this mistake was repeated when Lord Charles Somerset acknowledged *Ngqika* as the supreme authority through whom internal control over the population could be established.[2] This direct and misplaced interference in internal affairs led to one of the numerous Frontier Wars (the Fifth).

The colonial policy followed by the British was influenced by two important factors, viz. the ideological and the economic. It was not the outflow of any preconceived plan; rather, as De Kiewiet puts it, it was the outcome and not the governor of events.[3]

During the Sixth Frontier War which started in 1834, Sir Benjamin D'Urban expelled the hostile Rharhabe chiefs from their own territory and allocated the land to *Mfengu* chiefs who had requested protection by the British. This constituted a classic case of ignorance because a very high premium was put on land and on territorial independence.

The first far-reaching administrative measures were introduced by Sir Benjamin D'Urban and comprised the following: government by the chiefs was to be controlled by agents who were also responsible for preliminary investigations into more serious criminal offences. Indigenous members were recruited as policemen to assist the agents. Both these measures seriously affected and undermined the authority of the chief and also deprived him of a source of income in the form of fines. For the first time a traditional community was placed under the direct control of a European power. D'Urban viewed traditional rule as an obstacle in the way of order and civilisation. He perceived the incompatibility of development and traditional society: dislocation does seem to be a necessary prerequisite to bring about change.[4]

Sir George Napier instituted an annual salary to be paid to chiefs which would make it worthwhile to control and disapprove of depradations. This salary was also connected with the removal of the judicial powers of the chief which had constituted an important source of revenue. It resulted in further weakening the status of the chief in the sense that he could no longer fulfil one of his traditional virtues, namely generosity.

Lieutenant-General Peregrine Maitland announced in November 1846 that, 'no chieftainship shall hereafter be recognized in British Kaffirland'.[5]

This measure was reaffirmed by Sir Harry Smith on 5 January 1848, when the chiefs had to vow not to recognise any chief except Her Majesty Queen Victoria, and her magistrates. This policy was changed by Sir George Cathcart when he negotiated the termination of the Eighth Frontier War. Tribes were to be governed by their own chiefs according to tribal rules and customs. The administrative and judicial authority of the magistrates was to be removed and they became political agents.

Sir George Grey (1854-61) made a further contribution to the oscillating policy when he formulated the future administration of British Kaffraria:

> The plan I propose . . . is to attempt to gain an influence over all tribes . . . by employing them upon public works . . . ; by establishing institutions for the education of their children, and the relief of their sick, by introducing among them institutions of a civil character suited to their present condition, and by these and other like means to attempt gradually to win them to civilization and Christianity, and thus to change . . . our foes into friends who may have common interests with ourselves.[6]

Grey's 'institutions of civil character' included the following measures: chiefs were to be paid an annual stipendium to ensure their independence; a system of magistrates was established 'to convince the natives that our laws were better than their own'.[7] The territory of each chief was divided into districts under headmen and sub-districts under sub-headmen who were also remunerated by the Crown.

Looking at Grey's measures in retrospect they constituted, in modern terminology, a rather comprehensive development plan. Grey clearly indicated his objectives and he also stipulated the measures necessary to achieve those objectives. His measures touched virtually every sub-system of society, namely the economic (by providing employment on public works), the social and cultural (through schools and hospitals), the administrative and political (through institutions of a civil character) as well as the judicial (through the magisterial system and legal reforms).

In 1883 the Cape Native Laws and Customs Commission recom-

The Administrative System in the Ciskei

mended that a council system be instituted. This led to the passing of the Glen Grey Act, No. 25, 1894. Section Seven of this Act provided for the establishment of location councils consisting of three members. They were given ordinary local government functions pertaining to their particular area. In practice these location councils did not prove successful. They did, however, fulfil an important function in the sense that they provided a forum for the inhabitants to voice their opinion. Section 38 of the Act also provided for the establishment of a district council consisting of twelve members plus the local magistrate as chairman and additional member. Six members were nominated by the Governor-General while the remaining six were nominated from the members of the constituent location councils. The district council proved to be an instant success as can be gathered by a report in 1896 which read:

> The council, formed as it has been of the leading advanced natives in the District, has secured the confidence of the people, its members have taken a keen interest in the welfare of the district, and have evinced a considerable grasp of work which at the beginning of the year was new to all of them.

In 1919 it was reported: 'As providing means for the expression of public opinion amongst the natives the institution is of a great service in the administration of Native Affairs in the district.'[8]

The importance of the district council was twofold: firstly, it provided a means of participation and expression in the vacuum created by the continued undermining of the traditional authority; and in the second place, it created an opportunity for the 'advanced' inhabitants to play a meaningful part in local administrative affairs. It was inevitable that the establishment of schools and the missionary effort in particular and the whole civilising policy in general should have led to the creation of an educated elite. Unfortunately, in traditional systems such people are not accommodated and often come into direct opposition with traditional leaders. The council system was therefore a promising foundation on which elected forms of administrative organisation could have been built.

After unification in 1910 the first administrative step of importance for the Ciskei was the passing of the Native Affairs Act, 1920 which provided for the establishment of local councils which were composed of not more than nine members. Section 6 of this Act empowered a local council to provide for the following within its area of jurisdiction:

(1) the construction and maintenance of roads, dams and channels and the prevention of soil erosion;
(2) the provision of a suitable system of water supply;
(3) the combating of livestock diseases;
(4) the eradication of weeds;
(5) an efficient system of sanitation;
(6) the establishment of hospitals;
(7) the improvement of agricultural methods;
(8) afforestation; and
(9) the provision of educational facilities.

The Bantu Affairs Commission[9] held consultative talks throughout the country in order to establish as many local councils as possible.

One of the problems was that the level of development in certain areas did not justify the establishment of local councils with their relatively wide range of functions. The following local councils were established in the Ciskei apart from the Glen Grey District Council which already existed.

(1) The Middledrift Local Council – Proclamation No. 3 of 1927.
(2) The Tamacha (King William's Town) Local Council – Proclamation No. 4 of 1927 amended in 1932.
(3) The Peddie Local Council – Proclamation No. 127 of 1927.
(4) The Victoria East Local Council – Proclamation No. 128 of 1927.
(5) The Keiskammahoek Local Council – Proclamation No. 34 of 1928.
(6) The Herschel Local Council – Proclamation No. 219 of 1930.
(7) The East London Local Council – Proclamation No. 77 of 1932.

The benefits of the Council system have been very quickly recognized by the Native people of this area. The local Councils, under the guidance of the Native Commissioners, have soon developed a sense of responsibility and a very proper desire to serve the interests of the people. The best men have nearly always been chosen as Councillors and a great deal of useful work has been accomplished.[10]

Act No. 23 of 1920 also provided for the establishment of General

Councils; however the Ciskeian General Council was only established in 1934.

A résumé of adminstrative measures before 1951 must emphasise the fact that all the chieftaincies which had been reorganised into a general bureaucratic structure did not become units of local administration because the administrative structure was based on districts and locations which seldom corresponded with tribal borders. District administration involved an interaction between the magistrate, the chief and the headman.[11] The headman was seen as an agent of the central administration and was expected to perform more and more functions, especially with regard to the conflict areas between the magistrate and the people which were inter alia, the collecting of taxes, soil rehabilitation (in particular stock reduction measures), the demarcation and maintenance of forest areas (which limited the gathering of firewood), and disputes about borders.

Prior to 1951 the emphasis was on stabilisation with no effort to bring about dynamic development. Ironically conditions for development, in retrospect, were ideal because of the relative dislocation of traditional structures of authority. In addition a system of direct rule was established in the Ciskei and African experience has shown that such a system, as followed by France in her colonies, could result in more rapid development than the system practised by the British in Northern Nigeria for example.

It would appear that development and a rigid maintenance of traditional structures are not reconcilable, that is, development is essentially a disruptive process in which the educated elite play a very important role. In the Ciskei these favourable conditions were created by, inter alia, the gradual undermining of the chief's traditional authority, the long period of contact with Western civilisation and economy, the creation of administrative structures which did not necessarily follow tribal lines, and the accommodation of advanced educated Africans in administrative structures like the Glen Grey district council and the other seven local councils created between 1927 and 1932.

In 1951, however, in an effort to introduce a uniform system of administration for the whole of South Africa, the so-called Bantu Authorities System was introduced. Points of criticism of the system which follow are not necessarily criticisms of the system *per se*, but of its mode of introduction and application in the Ciskei where a completely different set of circumstances, as compared to the rest of the country, was to be found.

This system had to comply with three requisites. In the first place it had to be truly representative of the whole community, as was the case traditionally. With reference to this point it will suffice to say that the Ciskei was no longer a purely traditional community and that traditional ways of representation tend to exclude the advanced element in such a community. The second requisite was that it should be a dynamic body able to influence all sections of the community towards progress. It has already been indicated that progress is not compatible with a maintenance of traditional forms and apart from this, these institutions can hardly be described as dynamic. Lastly such a body had to take the responsibility for the creation of a dynamic developing community.[12]

A brief look at some of the policy principles underlying the introduction of the new system reveals that Bantu Authorities were to be based on the traditional system of authority, because, it was reasoned, the chief and his councillors were the people most suited to revive the old customs and usages. In the Ciskei this amounted to a purposeful reconstruction of something which had to a large extent been destroyed. In other parts of South Africa this step merely meant the legalising of something which was still in existence.

In addition it must be noted that the introduction of the top two tiers of this system, that is, regional and territorial authorities, amounted to new 'creations' which were not necessarily based on traditional principles. In this respect it should be remembered that a strong criticism by the white government of the old council system was the fact that councils were foreign or new institutions. It seems to be an anomaly to criticise one institution and then to replace it with something to which the same objections may be raised.

Section 2(a) of the Bantu Authorities Act, No. 68, 1951, prescribes that a tribal authority be established in respect of a tribe or ethnic unit under a chief or headman and a community authority in respect of a community or communities and tribes. The councillors of a tribal authority are those members of the tribe who are acknowledged as councillors according to the customs of that tribe. But traditional principles are discarded when the councillors of a community authority are elected because this is done according to Western democratic principles. It should be kept in mind that the existence of such principles were sharply criticised when they were applied to the former council sytem.

Section 2(b) of the Act of 1951 provides for the establishment of a regional authority in respect of two or more tribal or community authorities. Such a regional authority is composed of the chief of each tribal authority, the chairman of each community authority, plus one representative appointed by each tribal or community authority. A regional authority must consist of at east eight members.

Proclamation No. R 496 of 1961 established a Territorial Authority for the Ciskei which was composed of 22 members. This upper tier of the Bantu Authority system was essentially a policy-making body and hence will not be discussed in detail.

Tribal and community authorities are empowered to fulfil a detailed and wide range of local government functions. At present 38 tribal authorities and three community authorities are in existence in the Ciskei. As local government bodies they are caught in the vicious circle which is evident in local government throughout the world, that is to say, the units are too small for meaningful local government performance and because they are too small, functions tend to be centralised. An example of this centralising tendency in the Ciskei is the fact that since 1969 the finances of tribal and community authorities have been handled by the Department of the Chief Minister and Finance. Another instance is the appointment of civil servants to all the posts of secretaries of the tribal authorities. Because the tribal authorities have not proved competent to carry out some of their functions, increased centralisation has resulted. There is an inevitable clash between development objectives (on the one hand) which are centrally determined and the desire for participation in local affairs, on the other.

It is ironic that while there is a world-wide concern about the limited population and revenue of local government units and a constant search for larger units, in 1969 it was thought necessary to remove all executive functions from the regional authorities in the Ciskei and to reduce them to mere advisory bodies. This is a strategy not unknown in Africa where there seems to be a tendency to move away from large administrative units because people lack a sense of loyalty to them.

The necessity for such intermediary bodies is emphasised by Jack Koteen;

> Local authorities are not able to mobilize needed planning talent, and yet are too far removed to depend upon planning efforts at the center ... There is a need for a continuing institutional framework within which local officials can come together with central officials, discuss common problems, and co-operate in planning to solve them. Some experts indicate the need for planning regions which lie between the central government and the local jurisdictions.[13]

In Tanzania, for example, the district councils dwindled in popularity as instruments of local government. In 1972, however, they were modified into district development councils. As far as the Ciskei is concerned this seems to be a possibility well worth examining. Such a body might be composed of the magistrate, technical representatives of central government departments and representatives from the tribal and community authorities within the district. A similar arrangement exists in Malawi where there are district development committees.[14]

The centralisation of local government functions is part of the complex relationship between a central government and its local authorities and this relationship is largely determined by financial grants to the local authorities. 'It can, in a sense, be said that the degree of local autonomy enjoyed by a council is invariably in inverse proportion to the amount of government assistance it receives.'[15]

Local government in developing countries has two basic aims: in the first place the development of social and technical services, and, secondly, the identification by the councillors with this development. With development as the chief aim it appears that there are four possibilities regarding the execution of functions:

(1) Local authorities can be regarded as the channel through which all development should take place. This will require larger units.

(2) Development must be undertaken by the central government through its technical departments. Under such a dispensation local authorities will be limited to less important functions such as sanitation, markets.

(3) A partnership in which the central government subsidises the local authority with money and personnel.

(4) A clear distinction between the functions of the central government and that of local authorities. This, in practice, will amount to the same situation envisaged under the second possibility.

The territorial authority, which was intended to be at the apex of the Bantu Authority system, is neither an administrative nor an executive body, but a 'political' one, in that it is a legislature (since 1972 it has in fact been called the Legislative Assembly). An important consequence of this is that decisions taken by the legislature concerning local aspects must in the end be implemented by the same men who took the decision. Thus, for example, the legislature may decide upon the desirability of a soil conservation measure. The implementation of such a measure must be undertaken at local level by the very chiefs, in their capacity as leaders of the tribal authority, who took the decision in the first place. There are advantages and disadvantages to such a system where there is no clear separation between the people making the decisions and the people implementing them.

An obvious advantage is that such a situation may be useful in facilitating communication between the governors and the governed, as the people who make the decisions are in an excellent position to explain them to their local supporters via the tribal authority. It can also be assumed that needs and demands at the local level can effectively be transformed into political inputs and people can identify themselves more easily with the political leadership.

The disadvantages are manifested in the fact that the political leaders of the Ciskei have committed themselves to a purposeful development strategy for the Ciskei. This commitment contains a great conflict potential since resistance can be expected when the innovating thrust of development programmes collides with rural traditions and customs. This will be particularly true of attempts to modernise farming practices and to raise agricultural output. Change is distrusted because it is considered to be disruptive of the complex network of relations which holds society together. In addition political loyalty is governed more by a sense of belonging to a concrete group than by identification with policy goals.

An area where the traditional power of the chief severely handicaps rural development, is that of land tenure. A chief may take land away from a man if he produces a surplus — this fact is sometimes attributed to witchcraft. Chiefs can also confiscate land which, in their opinion has been cultivated 'improperly'. This limits the application of new techniques. It is unheard of to appeal against such decisions. Even where the power of chiefs has been eroded and undermined, the prerogative of land allocation is usually the last to be taken away and this privilege can be expected to be guarded jealously.

The question immediately arises as to whom the chiefs, in their capacity as administrators in the tribal authority, are answerable in the implementation of policy decisions. It is indeed ironic that they are responsible to themselves, because they are also the policy-makers. This problem, however, is not limited to the Ciskei. 'In the non-Western political process there is a high degree of substitutability of roles ... Even within bureaucracies and governments, individuals may be formally called upon to perform several roles.'[16] The application of this to the Ciskei situation implies that the chiefs in their administrative capacity are not restricted to rule-application or other output functions as Almond envisaged it, but that they also perform input functions such as interest articulation and aggregation. This problem is more fully explored in Chapter 9.

The 'Central Administration' of the Ciskei consists of seven departments, viz. Department of the Chief Minister and of Finance, Department of the Interior, Department of Works, Department of Education, Department of Agriculture and Forestry, Department of Justice, and Department of Health and Welfare.

The importance of a competent government service becomes apparent when the following considerations are taken into account. The Ciskei is committed to a policy of rapid development which implies the implementation of social and economic measures. The functionally structured government service suddenly experienced an increase in the variety, quantity and complexity of its functions as a result of its dual role of entrepreneur and administrator — a situation where the administrative load was outpacing administrative capability. Finally, the rapidly expanding budget demanded a competent civil service. Table 6.1 reflects the increase in the budget between 1970 and 1976.

Table 6.1: Ciskei Budget 1970/1 — 1975/6

Year	Amount	Percentage increase on previous years
1970/1	R8,853,900	—
1971/2	R10,730,500	21
1972/3	R11,994,000	12
1973/4	R15,958,000	33
1974/5	R20,142,000	26
1975/6	R34,237,000	70

Source: Ciskei Government Reports of Auditor General.

These factors resulted in a fast-growing government service which involved a massive recruitment drive. Recruitment, however, could only satisfy demand for posts in the entry grades. The authorised establishment of the Ciskeian Government Service comprised 7,003 posts as at 31 December 1977. The schedule in Table 6.2 reflects the position as at the end of 1976 and 1977, and the very rapid growth in even one year.

Unfortunately, the Ciskei lacks indigenous experienced civil servants at senior and executive level. These levels are consequently staffed by officials seconded from the Republican administration, a situation analogous to that frequently found in the former British colonies. Two classic bureaucratic problems usually stem from such a situation. In

Table 6.2: Ciskei Public Service Establishment 1976/77[17]

Department	Establishment at 31.12.76	31.12.77	% Change
Chief Minister and Finance	150	198	32.0
Justice	227	252	11.0
Education	352	406	15.3
Interior	206	192	6.8
Agriculture and Forestry	878	988	12.5
Works	2001	1896	6.2
Health & Welfare	2694	3091*	14.7
Total	6508	7003	7.6

*This increase was due mainly to the fact that two hospitals were taken over.

the first place we find overcentralisation as a result of a lack of confidence in junior staff. 'The system is founded on belief in the infallibility of judgment if taken at sufficiently high levels no matter how far removed from the scene of action or the situational facts.'[18] Secondly, and related to the first, such a situation necessitates the rapid promotion of people through the ranks with the result that they have no time to adjust to each new position, or to acquire a broader perspective of the functions of their new position or of the department as a whole.

The Ciskei, however, is becoming less dependent on seconded officials. The percentage of seconded incumbency decreased from 25 per cent in 1969 to 11.35 per cent in 1973; 9.57 per cent in 1974; 5.9 per cent in 1975; 4.7 per cent in 1976; and 3.1 per cent in 1977. Table 6.3 shows how the fixed establishment was staffed as at 31 December 1977.

It is clear that the Ciskei is gradually Africanising the government service, which is commendable. Rapid and forced Africanisation could lead to a lowering in the standards of efficiency which would imply wastage of scarce resources. Under certain circumstances a decrease in standards is inevitable and might even be considered a realistic adaptation to changing conditions. Sometimes the complex standards of administration and the departmental structures and procedures evolved by seconded officials are not understood by local officials and this can unnecessarily delay the process of Africanisation.

On the whole, however, this process has proceeded quite satisfactorily in the Ciskei and is facilitated by the courses conducted by the training and efficiency divisions of the Ciskeian Public Service Commission. During 1977 a total of 747 civil servants attended informal (in-

Table 6.3: Ciskei Public Service Establishment at 31.12.77[19]

Department	Permanent Ciskeian Incumbents	Ciskeian officers out of adjustment*	Republican officers held against posts	Temporary Ciskeian employees	Vacancies	Total	Percentage seconded incumbency
Chief Minister and Finance	54	53	16	7	45	198	8.0
Justice	120	38	23	–	65	252	9.1
Education	196	32	7	153	16	406	1.7
Interior	98	20	11	18	40	192	5.7
Agriculture and Forestry	261	19	30	567	109	988	3.0
Works	206	29	55	1303	249	1876	2.9
Health and Welfare	1242	56	78	529	1157	3091	2.5

*Held out of adjustment against posts of higher or lower grading for various unavoidable reasons.

service) training courses ranging from 'Induction' to 'Hospital Stores'; 'Game Reserve'; 'Radio and Audio Visual' (attended in Great Britain); and 'Water Sewerage Purification'. A further 138 students attended universities and colleges with the purpose of obtaining qualifications.

The efficiency division handled, inter alia, the following major projects in 1977:

(i) Implementation of new filing systems in all departments
(ii) An investigation into the procedures in township offices
(iii) The creation of various posts in the various departments
(iv) Numerous requests for the supply of labour-saving devices

In conclusion, it should be stated that the problems described in this chapter are not peculiar to the Ciskei, but are in fact characteristic of most developing countries. If, however, the Ciskei is to pursue a meaningful policy of development, structural changes will have to be made. The history of development in most of the developing countries may be summarised as follows: 'The attitude of the political elite was characterised by ambivalence. They sought to work for modernisation, without giving up their love for tradition.'[20]

Notes

1. G.M. Theal, *History of South Africa Since the British Conquest* (Swan Sonnenschein, London, 1920), p. 52.
2. P. van Biljon, *Grensbakens Tussen Blank en Swart in Suid Afrika* (Juta & Co., Cape Town, 1947), p. 174.
3. C.F.J. Muller, *Die Britse Owerheid en die Groot Trek* (Juta & Co., Cape Town, 1948), p. 15.
4. Theal, *History of South Africa*, pp. 129-48.
5. van Biljon, *Grensbakens*, p. 205.
6. A.E. du Toit, 'The Cape Frontier: A Study of Native Policy with Special Reference to the Years 1847-1866', *Archives Yearbook for South African History*, vol. 17, Part 1 (1954).
7. K.N. Bell and W.P. Morrell, *Selected Documents on British Foreign Policy 1830-1860* (Clarendon Press, Oxford, 1928), p. 583.
8. E.M. Brookes, *The History of Native Policy in South Africa from 1830 to the Present Day* (Nasionale Pers, Pretoria, 1927), pp. 254-5.
9. This is an advisory body established by the Act of 1920 and consists of the Minister for Native Affairs as chairman or an alternative chairman with not less than three or more than five members who may be members of either House of Parliament. The present Commission differs in character from the body contemplated in the 1917 draft legislation which was intended to be independent, non-Parliamentary and therefore powerful. The present Commission is subordinate, parliamentary and its powers depend on whether the personality and resolution of its members can make it powerful.

10. Ciskeian General Council, Proceedings and Reports of Select Committees of the Session of 1934.
11. W.D. Hammond-Tooke, *Command or Consensus* (David Philip, Cape Town, 1975), p. 109.
12. Department of Bantu Administration and Development, Memorandum for the Guidance of Bantu Authorities, Government Printer, QD 53255331-1962-73-250, Pretoria.
13. K.J. Rothwell (ed.), *Administrative Issues in Developing Economies* (Lexington Books, Mass., 1972), pp. 63-4.
14. R.A. Miller, 'District Development Committees in Malawi', *Journal of Administration Overseas*, 9 (1970), pp. 129-45.
15. I.D. Cameron and B.K. Cooper, *The West African Councillor* (Oxford University Press, London, 1961), p. 211.
16. H.G. Kebschull, *Politics in Transitional Societies* (Appleton-Century-Crofts, New York, 1968), p. 65.
17. Ciskei Government, Annual Report of the Ciskeian Public Service Commission, 1977.
18. I. Swerdlow (ed.), *Development Administration Concepts and Problems* (Syracuse University Press, New York, 1963), p. 47.
19. Ciskei Government, Annual Report of The Ciskeian Public Service Commission, 1977.
20. J.L. Finkle and R.W. Gable, *Political Development and Social Change* (John Wiley & Sons, New York, 1971), p. 328.

7 ETHNIC RELATIONS IN THE CISKEI
C.W. Manona

The political developments of the 1970s in the Ciskei raise some interesting questions with regard to inter-ethnic relations. Using field data collected between 1975 and 1977 in two villages in the Ciskei this study examines the relations between the two main ethnic groups in the Ciskei, the Xhosa and the Mfengu. The two groups are historically distinct and, though they have been in close contact for a period of over a century, have remained largely apart and in the past opposed each other on numerous occasions. What we wish to illuminate here is the fact that in more recent years these traditional rivalries have been aggravated and particularly after the Ciskei attained self-rule in 1972 there has been more open hostility between the two groups. Ethnic antagonisms emerged quite clearly during the election campaign for the Ciskei Legislative Assembly which held its first session early in 1973. Shortly after these elections two political parties, the Ciskei National Independence Party (CNIP) and the Ciskei National Party (CNP), were formed and affiliation to these political parties was largely ethnic in the sense that most of the Xhosa supported the ruling CNIP and the Mfengu the opposition CNP. As such, what has come to be known as ethnicity became a major factor of concern in Ciskei politics. The present exercise is undertaken with the hope that it will not exacerbate the conflict but that more knowledge will foster understanding of the factors that are responsible for the emergence of these hostile relationships.

For some theoretical preliminaries before turning to the Ciskei case we make a few comments with regard to the nature of ethnicicity. Ethnicity, which is sometimes inappropriately referred to as 'tribalism', is a phenomenon that has attracted attention for some time. It covers a vast range of human relationships and attitudes. Ethnicity is a phenomenon that is inherently related to competition and conflict and refers primarily to problems of social organisation that are conceived in terms of politics and the allocation of scarce resources. Cohen[1] defines it as 'the strife between ethnic groups, in the course of which their members emphasize their identity and exclusiveness'. Ethnicity, also, rests not so much on the survival of conservative 'tribalistic' sentiment as on vested political and economic interests competing for hegemony in a modern national state.[2]

The resolution of these conflicting sectional interests, despite what politicians would say, is an unresolved problem in most modern states. Since World War II many peoples of Asia and Africa have discovered that the transfer of sovereignty from a colonial regime to an independent one is the easiest step. Once the colonial power goes, the larger problem of creating a viable national unity is often encountered. It may even be said of such states that their central problem, often more pressing than that of economic development, is the achievement of national unity and the integration of the different cultural units of the new state into a common political framework.[3] This is the difficulty the Ciskei is experiencing and the present divisions, though they reflect the divide and rule policies of the past, are products of the replacement of a white colonial regime by one which is rooted in the people themselves.

Instead of promoting national unity, the granting of self-government or independence has often led to the proliferation of various factions due to the fact that the citizens of the new state no longer have to close ranks against a common enemy. Divisions held in check when the foreign power controlled affairs suddenly come into the open and ethnic differences that seemed less important so long as colonial administration ruled tend to emerge after independence or self-rule. In such situations it is the very process of the formation of a sovereign state that, among other things, stimulates ethnic sentiments because it introduces into society a valuable prize over which to fight.

In Africa during the late 1950s and the 1960s decolonisation and the prospect of independence saw the rise of ethnic competition for political power. These developments even threatened national unity in many states. During this period in Nigeria, Kenya, the Gold Coast, Sierra Leone and other states, ethnic groups, some of which had never functioned as corporate entities before or during the colonial period, emerged and began to compete for power.[4] Ethnic conflict in Nigeria which involved primarily the Yoruba, Ibo, and the Hausa, delayed the independence of that state. In Uganda the Baganda fought against the 'non-Baganda'. Often there were intensive conflicts between ethnically based political parties as, for instance, in the case of Kenya where the Kikuyu and Luo who formed the Kenya African National Union (KANU) fought and managed to dominate smaller groups such as the Kamba who constituted the Kenya African Democratic Union (KADU).[5]

During these power struggles ethnicity often served political interests. Even westernised leaders, nurtured in the broader philosophy of African nationalism, found themselves in situations in which they had to use parochial ethnic group loyalties for electoral purposes. This situation even forced some of these leaders to retreat to their 'home' districts or regions where they had a political base. We have, for instance, the case of Mnandi Azikiwe of Nigeria. He was one of the founders of Pan-Africanism, studied in the United States and headed the National Council in Nigeria. As the Nigerian independence approached Azikiwe was forced to seek political support among the Ibo in eastern Nigeria.[6]

With this introduction we now consider the manner in which the ethnic division in the Ciskei occurred and how it was sustained. The Xhosa constitute a group of chiefdoms that are, with the exception of the Gqunukhwebe (who are of mixed Xhosa and Khoikhoi descent), genealogically related. In the Ciskei the Xhosa include the following related chiefdoms: Ngqika, Ndlambe, Dushane, Qhayi, Dange, Gasela, Ntinde, Hleke, Gwali, Jingqi and Ngqalase. All these chiefdoms are segments of one parent stock and chieftainship among them is held by members of the Tshawe clan to which the earliest Xhosa chiefs belonged. The Xhosa occupied the area now known as the Transkei and Ciskei at least as far back as the year 1554.[7] The Xhosa in the Transkei are the Gcaleka and those in the Ciskei are collectively known as the Rharhabe.

The Mfengu, on the other hand, are more recent immigrants to the Cape and the Ciskei and previously resided in Natal as several distinct groups. With Shaka's rise to power early in the nineteenth century a state of turmoil (the *Mfecane*) developed and forced many groups in Natal to flee. From about 1820 a stream of fugitives arrived in the Transkei and came into contact with other groups which were already in the Cape. These refugees, the majority of whom settled among the Gcaleka in the Transkei, were in an abject and forlorn condition on their arrival in the Cape and among the Gcaleka. Having left their homes in a state of turmoil they had few possessions and they suffered many hardships on their journey to the Cape, some of the leaders died en route to the Cape and during the wars in Natal. Among the people whom they met they are reported as having initiated communciation by saying *Siyamfenguze* ('We are hungry and seek shelter') and this gave rise to the name Mfengu.[8] This name has remained in general use although the Mfengu prefer the name abaMbo which refers to the region where the Mfengu resided before being scattered by the *Mfecane*. The Mfengu include diverse groups, viz. three main sections: Hlubi,

Zizi, Bhele and the smaller units known as Zotsho and Khuze. Van Warmelo[9] distinguishes the smaller Mfengu units as the Kunene, Maduna, Gubevu, Tolo, Miya, Mbuthweni and Zotsho. This classification is unsatisfactory for the following reasons:

(a) The Kunene are a segment of the Hlubi — the Hlubi of chief Msutu.
(b) The Maduna and Gubevu are also Hlubi.
(c) The Tolo and Miya belong to the Zizi section of the Mfengu while the Mbuthweni are Bhele.

This means, therefore, that the smaller Mfengu units are the Zotsho and the Khuze.

On their arrival the Mfengu were given a favourable reception by the Gcaleka as it was a Nguni custom to welcome the accession of new followers.[10] Indeed, Hintsa, the paramount chief of the Gcaleka, saw in the Mfengu a miltary and economic asset and placed them at strategic places along his borders.[11] They were given cattle on loan and those who arrived in large parties with recognised chiefs were assigned land where they could serve their own chiefs who also had an opportunity to participate in Hintsa's councils.[12] The case of the Mfengu, in fact, was unique in the sense that it was the first time that Hintsa or any other Xhosa chief before him recognised any chieftainship among immigrants. This was a gesture that clearly indicated Hintsa's intention to incorporate the Mfengu. Other Mfengu who arrived as individuals without any possessions were distributed among Hintsa's people where they performed menial tasks such as being servants or herdsmen. In return for these services they received milk and grain to support their families.[13]

Soon after their arrival the Mfengu quickly rehabilitated themselves and displayed an unusual proclivity for enriching themselves. Perhaps what accounted for this was their background of insecurity and hardship which tended to make them acquisitive and diligent. Since they were accustomed to the use of iron hoes in their homeland in Natal they became extensive cultivators especially of tobacco which they bartered for cattle. In this manner they were able to accumulate large herds of cattle. This tobacco was prepared carefully, packed in small rush baskets and hidden indoors until the opportunity to sell it arose. To sell this tobacco they formed trade parties and travelled long distances to places where tobacco was in great demand.[14]

It was the growing prosperity of the Mfengu which initiated misunderstanding between them and the Gcaleka. The unusual endeavours of the Mfengu in agriculture and trade drew the attention of some of the Gcaleka and this resulted in some cases of ill-treatment of the Mfengu. Contemporary reports reveal that some of Hintsa's subjects extracted tributes from the Mfengu who were not willing to pay them. Other Gcaleka would confiscate property which the Mfengu had acquired or would intervene in trade transactions taking possession of the articles for sale. In other instances the Gcaleka are reported to have raided the corn-pits of the Mfengu. These and other similar instances of ill-treatment provoked the Mfengu and engendered a feeling of insecurity among them. It must be pointed out that they were a 'touchy people' who had experienced many hardships before settling among the Gcaleka. After their arrival in the Cape what they needed most was an opportunity to rehabilitate themselves and it was for this reason that they developed close contact with the Rev. John Ayliff who was also extremely well-disposed towards them.

The presence of a missionary station at Butterworth at the time was undoubtedly a crucial factor in the development of enmity between the two groups. From 1826 the Rev. Shrewsbury had worked among the Gcaleka without making any headway, whereas Ayliff who took over at the Butterworth Methodist mission in 1831 became extremely sucessful because he worked closely with the Mfengu. However, by so doing he was alienating them from the Xhosa. Ayliff introduced some Mfengu to education and Christianity and his mission station became a sanctuary for those who fled from Hintsa.

It was at this time that what has come to be known as the slavery myth emerged, and it was Ayliff who did most to perpetrate this myth. Through his lack of knowledge of Xhosa society he interpreted the inferior status held by the Mfengu as proof of slavery. In championing their cause he promised them land and British protection and succeeded in winning their confidence. This was manifested by the Mfengu acceptance of education and Christianity and by their gradual drift towards Butterworth.

The so-called 'emancipation' of the Mfengu in 1835 which led to the departure of many of them to the Ciskei stemmed from the belief that they were being ill-treated in Gcalekaland and that they were in a unique situation of degradation and servitude. By 1834 the Gcaleka were already hostile to Ayliff and the Mfengu and in one instance Ayliff roused Hintsa's anger by refusing to hand over an Mfengu man whom Hintsa wanted.[15] Ayliff also encouraged the Mfengu to offer resistance to practices like *uphundlo*, an old Xhosa custom which enabled elderly men to indulge in casual sex play with young girls.

Another development which generated yet greater hostility between the Xhosa and the Mfengu was the military alliance the Mfengu made with the whites. With the outbreak of the Sixth Frontier War in 1834 they took it upon themselves to defend the mission station at Butterworth as well as other Transkeian whites. Thus, when the colonial forces entered the Transkei in April 1835, 970 Mfengu fought on the side of the colonists and played an important role in the defeat of the Xhosa.[16] It was in these circumstances that in April 1835 a number of Mfengu headmen petitioned Governor D'Urban for their removal to the Ciskei.[17] By so doing the Mfengu, who aimed primarily to serve their own interests, abandoned the Xhosa and accepted the promise of land and security offered by the colonial government. Meanwhile the Xhosa regarded this as betrayal and began to view the Mfengu as a treacherous and ungrateful people.[18] The slavery myth upon which the evacuation of the Mfengu was based is disputable as an historical fact although, as indicated earlier, there had been some cases of ill-treatment of the Mfengu by the Xhosa. However, what needs to be emphasised here is that it is not the historical facts but the beliefs concerning them that are significant in determining the relations and attitudes at the present time.

Some 17,000 Mfengu arrived in the Ciskei in May 1835 and settled originally in the district of Peddie where they pledged allegiance to the colonial government. In the Ciskei they continued to collaborate with the whites against the Xhosa and from the time of their arrival till the end of the frontier wars in 1879 they were to look to the British government for leadership, economic assistance and protection. In return, they accepted the responsibility of helping to defend the colony.[19] The Mfengu, in fact, played a significant role in the eventual defeat of the Xhosa in the frontier wars.[20] They fought zealously against the Xhosa and what the latter remember with special bitterness is the fact that during the long drawn out war of 1850-3 the Mfengu helped in the discovery of the hidden grain-pits which were of strategic importance to the Xhosa warriors during this war. The military assistance the Mfengu gave to the colonists is one of the major grievances the Xhosa have against the Mfengu.

As a reward for their collaboration the Mfengu received large tracts of land which formerly belonged to the Xhosa. In the previous century this produced great hostility between the two groups, such that in August 1837 the Mfengu at Peddie were attacked by the Ngqika, Dushane and Qhayi.[21] The Mfengu, having accepted both Christianity

Ethnic Relations in the Ciskei

and education, soon became predominantly School people.[22] Having acquired western skills they were able to take advantage of the opportunities offered by the colonial situation and they came to dominate the better paid jobs like teaching, clerical work, the clergy and trading. The Xhosa, on the other hand, rejected Christianity, education and western culture in general and remained relatively conservative. Even today there are fewer converts among the Xhosa than there are among the Mfengu. The Cattle Killing incident of 1857 (in which the Mfengu did not participate) and the dislocation the Xhosa suffered as a result of recurrent defeat in the frontier wars which continued until 1879 led finally to their loss of land and, for many, their migration to white-owned farms where they became labourers.

Consciousness of identity is relevant to our theme. The Mfengu thoughout their residence among the Xhosa did not give up their identity and instead tended to emphasise it. Particularly in the previous century their Natal origin was a live issue although it was not until the 1860s that consciousness of identity developed among them. By this time they were in more continuous contact with the missionaries. With regard to culture there are still significant differences between the two groups. Political relations have expressed themselves through these differences and have undoubtedly promoted this cultural differentiation. As a result some of the old Mfengu customs have persisted and have assumed new social and political significance.

On their arrival among the Xhosa in the 1820s the Mfengu spoke a dialect which was distinctly different from the language of the Xhosa and the Xhosa even looked down upon them for their 'outlandish' pronunciation.[23] Although the Cape Nguni as a whole speak *isiXhosa*, the various units which constitute this group speak different but related dialects of this language. Today linguistic differences between the Xhosa and the Mfengu are slight and the differences between the two dialects have been modified by the influence of the schools. It was the language of the Ngqika which was the first Cape Nguni language to be committed to writing and as a result it became the basis of *isiXhosa* used in the schools. However, even today there is *isiMfengu* which is characterised by terms of Natal Nguni ('Zulu') origin. In this regard reference can be made to the attack made by Mqhayi (Xhosa) on Jabavu (Mfengu) for the latter's use of a 'Zulu' term in a public gathering,[24] and Kawa's frequent use of 'Zulu' terms in *Ibali lamaMfengu*.

There are differences, too, with regard to dress and ornamentation. Among both groups a married woman wears a long skirt known as *umbhaco* but this garment is worn differently by the Xhosa and the Mfengu. The Mfengu place the opening of *umbhaco* at the side while the Xhosa place this in front. At the bottom edges the Xhosa decorate this skirt with black braid, the Mfengu with beads.[25] Also, the ochre used by the Mfengu is deep red in colour while the Xhosa prefer the terracotta colour.[26] Both groups practise scarification, *umvambo*, as a means of decorating the body but favour different patterns. The Xhosa pattern consists of two rows of markings that run down from the collarbone to the navel and below the breasts these vertical rows are crossed by horizontal markings. The Mfengu, on the other hand, decorate the area between the collarbone and the breasts by making elongated horizontal markings which lie parallel one beneath the other.[27] There are variations, too, in the procedure followed by Mfengu and Xhosa in initiation. This is shown, for instance, by the fact that the Mfengu perform the circumcision before sunrise and the Xhosa in the afternoon. The aim here is not to enumerate all these slight but significant cultural differences between the Mfengu and the Xhosa. What needs to be stated is that the retention of these parallel customs is undoubtedly connected with the hostile relationships between the two groups.

Consciousness of identity played a role in the choices the Xhosa and Mfengu made in affiliating to some of the independent churches which were founded at the beginning of this century. The Order of Ethiopia which was founded in 1900 by a prominent Xhosa clergyman, the Rev. James Dwane, has a predominantly Xhosa membership. Similarly, the African Presbyterian Church has a predominantly Mfengu membership. This church was founded in 1898 by a prominent Mfengu leader, the Rev. P.J. Mzimba. When he seceded from the Free Church of Scotland at Lovedale only the Mfengu (constituting two-thirds of this congregation) followed him: the Xhosa remained behind.[28]

In a more specific manner, consciousness of identity manifested itself in the 'national' celebrations observed by both groups. The annual 'Fingo Day' celebrations held on 14 May and the Ntsikana Day celebrations held in March each year are for each group occasions which symbolise a particular tradition. In 1907 the Mfengu held the first celebrations to commemorate the vows their forefathers made on their arrival in the Ciskei. In 1909 the Xhosa responded by founding the Ntsikana Day celebrations which have up to now been patronised mainly by the Xhosa. Ntsikana is held in high esteem by the Xhosa because he is regarded as the indigenous forerunner of Christianity who foresaw the future.

It is worth noting that these celebrations have been manipulated by both groups for political ends and particularly in the case of the Mfengu they have often served as platforms where political aspirations have been voiced. This is shown, for instance, by the fact that during the first 'Fingo Day' celebrations in 1907 the Mfengu made a plea to the British government to allow them to live independently of the Xhosa. The same plea was made by the 'Fingo Day' Committee in 1967 before the introduction of the reconstituted Ciskei Territorial Authority (CTA). Generally the Xhosa despise the 'Fingo' celebrations and regard them as ethnic in the sense that they serve the interests of one group. In *Ityala lamaWele*,[29] which was published in 1914, S.E.K. Mqhayi indicates that the Xhosa at that time regarded the 'Fingo' celebrations as occasions organised for the purpose of rejoicing over the death of Hintsa who is beieved to have died on 14 May 1835. During the 1976 Ciskei Legislative Assembly session a similar reference to this incident was made by a leading member of the ruling party. The member alleged that Hintsa's burial took place on 14 May 1835 the same day of the year when the Mfengu hold their celebrations.[30] As in the case of the slavery myth these assertions are not necessarily historically true although they are extremely significant in determining attitudes.

Even after 1879 when the Mfengu were no longer receiving special treatment from the colonial government, rapprochement with the Xhosa still remained difficult to achieve. When the Eastern Cape became a focal point of African political activity in the late nineteenth and early twentieth centuries, party loyalty was expressed in ethnic terms. We have, for instance, the case of Tengo Jabavu (Mfengu), an influential figure in black and white politics for more than 40 years who repeatedly clashed with Walter Rubusana (Xhosa). Jabavu and most of the Mfengu supported the Afrikaner Bond whereas Rubusana and most of the Xhosa backed the Progressive Party. Divided African politics in the region reached a climax in the Cape provincial elections in 1914 when Jabavu's candidacy drew just enough votes from Rubusana to give victory to a white man.[31] However, ethnic rivalries were temporarily subsumed under the politics of African nationalism from the 1920s until after the 1950s but polarisation between the two groups was already complete.

Separate development or the Bantustan policy was introduced in the South African 'homelands' in 1951. Before that year the policy of the white administration was to destroy chieftainship and to rule through government-appointed headmen who were placed in charge of demarcated 'locations' serving as basic administrative areas. The Bantu Authorities Act of 1951, however, changed this policy and sought to revive

the institution of chieftainship. This Act also made provision for the
establishment of Tribal Authorities which empowered officially
appointed chiefs to exercise some authority over their subjects. These
political changes roused the dormant ethnic consciousness and led
to a wave of applications for the official recognition of chieftainships.
The identity of chiefdoms which had been overlooked for decades was
thereby restored and from this time onwards politics in the Ciskei began
to centre around chieftainship and the Tribal Authorities. The establishment of these Tribal Authorities presented difficulties because
villages or administrative units in the Ciskei do not always coincide
with chiefly allegiance and in such a situation conflicting loyalties often
emerge. In the Victoria East district, for instance, some Xhosa are
under Mfengu chiefs and in the King William's Town district some
Mfengu are under Xhosa chiefs. These difficulties became more significant with the granting of self-rule to the Ciskei.

Tensions between the Mfengu and the Xhosa re-emerged in the
Ciskei during the 1960s. In 1961 the installation of the paramount
chief of the Xhosa in the Ciskei, Chief Velile Sandile, at his Great
Place in King William's Town became an occasion which drew attention
to the unresolved question of the status of the Mfengu in relation to
the Xhosa in the Ciskei. Each recognised chief in the Ciskei had to attend
this installation ceremony so as to receive a baton which signified the
authority of the new paramount over his chiefs in the territory. Among
the Mfengu chiefs who were present at this ceremony was a senior chief
of the Bhele clan, Chief Justice Mabandla, who caused a dilemma when
he refused to accept his baton from the Xhosa paramount. Chief
Mabandla's refusal to accept the baton was an indication of the tensions
which were by then developing. This was a clear indication that some
Mfengu were not prepared to pay allegiance to a Xhosa paramount as
they regarded this situation as one which could force them to forgo their
identity and 'become Xhosa'. As in the past, they were not prepared to
do this, hoping instead that they would eventually appoint their own
paramount. An attempt to nominate an Mfengu paramount, however,
failed in 1967 when the representatives of the three main Mfengu sections could not reach unanimity on the issue. When they were still in
Natal the Mfengu constituted distinct political units and these distinctions now hampered attempts to find a mutually acceptable candidate for
an Mfengu paramount.

Just before 1968, the year in which the reconstituted Ciskei Territorial Authority or New Deal was established, the growing mutual
suspicion between the two groups became clearer still. Amidst much

speculation about the implications of the New Deal meetings and caucuses were held by the Mfengu and the Xhosa separately. Xhosa leaders often met at the Great Place of their paramount in King William's Town. Mfengu leaders, on the other hand, were also active and in 1967 Mfengu representatives from various districts in the Ciskei met at Peddie. This 'closed' meeting resulted in the drafting of a document which came to be known as the 'Fingo Manifesto' in which the Mfengu petitioned the department of Bantu Administration and Development to recognise the Mfengu as a distinct ethnic unit apart from the Xhosa. This request, which the Department acceded to, meant that the Mfengu were to have separate representation in the New Deal in 1968. What is significant here is the fact that this new political structure, by its very nature, emphasised ethnic differentiation and the six members of the Executive Council were nominated on ethnic lines. It consisted of two Xhosa, two Mfengu, one Sotho and one Thembu. The chief Executive Councillor was Chief Mabandla. Members of the New Deal preferred a chief to head this Executive Council and Chief Mabandla's nomination to this position can largely be attributed to the fact that he was one of the most prominent chiefs particularly on account of his education.

Chief Mabandla's New Deal had limited powers and the political scene in the Ciskei was dominated by Mr Hans Abraham who was at the time the Commissioner-General representing the central government in the Xhosa homelands. Having piloted the formation of the New Deal Mr Abraham often evoked ethnic sentiment in the Ciskei and successfully manipulated Mfengu-Xhosa differences for political ends. For instance, at the 'Fingo Day' celebrations held in 1969 the greater portion of his speech consisted of a vehement attack on the Xhosa. He laid emphasis on what he regarded as the suffering of the Mfengu under the Xhosa and recounted atrocities the Xhosa perpetrated on the Mfengu on their arrival among the Xhosa. On other occasions Mr Abraham would identify himself with the aspirations of the Xhosa leaders.

By the end of his five-year term of office Chief Mabandla was already finding it difficult to keep the Ciskei united. Xhosa leaders, who were by this time referring to themselves and other Xhosa in the Ciskei as amaRharhabe were levelling serious accusations against Chief Mabandla and portrayed him as someone who discriminated against the Xhosa and favoured the Mfengu. For instance when Chief Mabandla addressed a meeting in Port Elizabeth towards the end of 1972 he found occasion to refer to 'certain groups of Rharhabes holding illegal meetings, digging holes for the Chief Minister (himself) and promising people land'.[32] As the 1973 election campaign gathered momentum the Rharhabe group organised extensively and even reached other Xhosa who were resident on white-owned farms. Chief Mabandla's 'failures' and the historic grievances the Xhosa have against the Mfengu in the Ciskei were common themes from public platforms and in caucuses. The Rharhabe group, for instance, often accused Chief Mabandla of ignoring the applications made by the Xhosa for chieftainship, thus, they said, perpetuating the dominance of the Mfengu in the Ciskei. The Mfengu, who were by this time feeling extremely insecure, were also uniting and their leaders were also meeting secretly.

The Rharhabe group won the election and the first political parties in the Ciskei were formed soon after the formation of the Legislative Assembly. Mr Sebe (now Chief Sebe) became the leader of the ruling CNIP which received its major support from the Xhosa just as much as most Mfengu were squarely behind Chief Mabandla's CNP. Affiliation to these political parties followed ethnic lines largely because the campaigning which preceded this election had done a great deal to rouse ethnic sentiment among the voters in the Ciskei. With the establishment of these political parties ethnicity in the Ciskei reached a climax and from this the tensions which will be illustrated in the case studies below found their source. Chief Mabandla's CNP saw itself as the party dedicated to fight *ucalucalulo lobuhlanga* (ethnicity) and called itself *Imbokotho Emnyama*, the Black Grindstone, a name that signifies the party's intention to grind out ethnicity in the Ciskei. The fight against ethnicity, in fact, became the major theme for *Imbokotho Emnyama* in political rallies of this party. On the other hand, Chief Sebe's supporters often accused Chief Mabandla of being responsible for the ethnic rift in the Ciskei particularly for the fact that he agreed to be the head of the ethnic New Deal which functioned from 1968 to 1972. Whatever personalities such as Hans Abraham or the Ciskeian politicians have done to use and abuse ethnic tensions in the course of their particular political game, we need to look more deeply into the social processes for the causal factors. This is clearly demonstrated in the following case studies.

Case Studies

Here cases relating to two villages in the Ciskei are presented. The villages are Burnshill and Nyaniso in the districts of Keiskammahoek and Peddie respectively.

1. Burnshill

Burnshill is of great interest for the purposes of our topic because it is a community which is stratified mainly on ethnic lines. Its inhabitants differ a great deal with regard to their economic standing (particularly land-ownership), educational achievement and in their association with Christianity. The village in fact includes two distinct social categories of people distinguished here as School and Semi-Red. Those who are referred to here as School are mainly the descendants of the first group of Mfengu settlers in this village and are people who have been in close contact with the missionaries and with schooling for well over a century. The majority of these School people are long-established landowners (*izimamhlaba*) who enjoy a higher status compared to other landless people in the village. This land is held predominantly in freehold and quitrent tenure both of which carry a title deed to any land bought or inherited.

The Semi-Red category, on the other hand, is closer to Xhosa tradition; it is not closely connected with Christianity or with education. This category includes the majority of Xhosa who have been landless for several generations; many of them have immigrated into Burnshill only recently. From 1936 the purchase of land under Trust enabled many landless Xhosa who previously resided on white-owned farms and other privately owned land as tenants (*amarhanuga*) to immigrate into Burnshill. Trust tenure is different from the other types and may only be used under conditions which are laid down by the Administration; many restrictions are imposed on tenants particularly with regard to stock limitation; they cannot dispose of this land at will; this type of tenure is also less secure in the sense that they can, under certain conditions, lose their land.

As a result of this large-scale immigration of Xhosa families from the farms, Burnshill now has more Xhosa than Mfengu inhabitants. The total number of the homesteads in the village is 317; 198 homesteads belong to the Xhosa and 109 to the Mfengu. A further seven are of Thembu, and another three of Mpondo origin. In spite of this demographic structure which favours the Xhosa, the Mfengu are politically dominant. The village headman is an Mfengu and, except for a brief period during the 1940s, this position has always been held by the Mfengu since their arrival in Burnshill. The headman, in turn, is subordinate to an Mfengu chief with authority over several villages in the district of Keiskammahoek. Matters affecting the inhabitants of the village are discussed by the *inkundla* which serves both the Xhosa and the Mfengu.

Distinctions between Xhosa and Mfengu in Burnshill are closely connected with the history of this village. During the early nineteenth century the Keiskammahoek district in which Burnshill is situated was occupied by the Xhosa under Chief Ngqika who had his principal homestead in what is today the village of Burnshill. After the 1850-3 war between the Xhosa and the British government Ngqika's son, Sandile, was expelled from the district which then became a 'Royal Reserve'. In accordance with the government policy of the time provision was made for the settlement of this 'Reserve' by whites and 'loyal' Africans. As a result some of the land in the Keiskammahoek district was taken up by people of German descent while the bulk of the land was granted to groups of Mfengu people who had assisted the British against the Xhosa.[33] A few Xhosa remained in Burnshill; even today there are few Xhosa who are old inhabitants of this village.

After the expulsion of the Xhosa from their territory the first group of Mfengu to settle in this village were granted what was referred to as reward land (*umhlaba webhaso*) for the services they rendered during the 1850-3 war. These were the Mfengu who were moved from the vicinity of the Fort Beaufort district and consisted originally of seven lineages with their headman, Mangqalaza. (Burnshill is also known as Mangqalaza after this settler headman.) In Burnshill these Mfengu settlers were placed under the Rev. James Laing of the United Free Church of Scotland who served the Burnshill mission from 1830-72. During this time the foundations of this School community were laid. The Rev. Laing was particularly successful in introducing the Mfengu of Burnshill to Christianity, mission education and to the use of new methods of agriculture. This missionary venture was so successful in Burnshill that towards the end of the century the inhabitants of the village were producing a large variety of crops for the markets and had orchards and an irrigation scheme. Some had training in trades like blacksmithery and building. There were other white missionaries who served this community until 1931.

As from the last century the Mfengu of Burnshill consolidated their land rights such that today they constitute a land-owning group. During the 1860s, through the insistence of the Rev. Laing, surveyed buiding sites and fields were granted to the Mfengu under quitrent tenure and a relatively large commonage was also provided for these quitrent landowners. Oral evidence also shows that soon after settling in Burnshill many Mfengu families became wealthy in land particularly through the purchase of freehold holdings. The present day situation regarding land-ownership by Xhosa and Mfengu in Burnshill illustrates the ethnic inequalities which resulted from these historical antecedents. In

Table 7.1 the 317 homesteads in Burnshill are grouped according to the type of land tenure.

Table 7.1: Ethnic Differences and Land Tenure — Burnshill

Type of tenure	Xhosa	Mfengu	Thembu	Mpondo	Total
Freehold	6	18	1	—	25
Quitrent	36	54	4	1	95
Trust	99	32	2	2	135
'Squatters' (landless)	36	5	—	—	41
Tenants (landless)	21	—	—	—	21
Total	198	109	7	3	317

From this table it can be seen that the Mfengu constitute the major land-owning group. Of the 109 Mfengu homesteads 72 (66.0 per cent) exercise the more secure land rights — freehold and quitrent tenure; 32 Mfengu families (29.4 per cent) reside on Trust land and only 5 (4.6 per cent) Mfengu are landless 'squatters'. In contrast, the Xhosa are predominantly landless. Of 198 Xhosa families only 42 (21.2 per cent) own freehold and quitrent land. Further, as many as 99 (50.0 per cent) Xhosa families reside on Trust land. The fact that the Xhosa are relatively landless is also borne out by the fact that a large proportion of them are landless 'squatters' while others are tenants. The majority of the so-called squatters are Xhosa who have been landless for several generations and have been residing on the commonage of the village. In 1940, as part of the Betterment Scheme, they were moved to the present 'squatter' section of the village where they occupy the land on a temporary basis because this commonage belongs to the land-owners of the village. Other 'squatters' are landless people who have immigrated into the village recently. In Burnshill today there are 41 'squatter' homesteads of which 36 (18.2 per cent) belong to Xhosa and 5 (4.6 per cent) to Mfengu. The tenants (*izitorhosha*) constitute yet another category of people with significant economic disabilities. Their economic position is more or less similar to that of tenants on white-owned farms and they perform services like tilling the land belonging to their landlords in return for which they receive part of the produce. The 21 families which are tenants are all Xhosa.

Also, in Burnshill there are significant differences between Mfengu and Xhosa with regard to educational achievement. In Table 7.2 information concerning 152 Xhosa and 64 Mfengu male homestead heads is presented. A village census which was undertaken at Burnshill included information on the educational standard of the homestead heads as well as their ethic affiliation. However, the sample on which Table 7.2 is based includes only living male homestead heads because information on deceased male heads was not available for all the cases. The information in the table indicates the educational differences between Xhosa and Mfengu showing the Mfengu as being on the whole better educated. There are, for instance, as many as 56 (36.8 per cent) Xhosa male homestead heads with no schooling at all as compared to only 2 (3.1 per cent) among the Mfengu. Most people with no schooling experience are those who grew up on white-owned farms where in most cases there were no schools. The table also shows that the Mfengu feature prominently among people with professional training. These professionals include teachers, clerks and ministers of religion. In this category there are 16 (25.0 per cent) Mfengu male homesteads as compared to only 5 (3.3 per cent) among the Xhosa.

Table 7.2: Education and Ethnic Differences — Burnshill

Educational standard and professional qualifications	Xhosa	Mfengu	Totals
Nil	56	2	58
Sub A & B	7	—	7
Std 1 & 2	28	11	39
Std 3 & 4	24	10	34
Std 5 & 6	29	20	49
Std 7 & 8	3	5	8
Professional (teachers, clerks, and ministers of religion)	5	16	21
Total	152	64	216

The socio-economic differences between School and Semi-Red categories, which in many instances coincide with the division between Mfengu and Xhosa, are reflected in the following cases.

Homestead A which belongs to the Mfengu of the Dlamini clan is the typical School homestead. The family is headed by a widow who inherited a 40-acre freehold plot from her husband who was the circuit steward of the Presbyterian church in Burnshill; she also played an active part in church matters. Mamswazi passed Standard six and trained as an Auxilliary Nurse in Johannesburg where the couple were married by civil rites. Of the couple's seven children three are teachers, one is a trained nurse, one son is a driver and the other is a clerk. The daughter who resided at home when the family was visited had passed Standard eight. This homestead is also comparatively wealthy in stock: it possesses 17 head of cattle and 15 goats. The maize yield for the 1975/6 season was estimated at 22 bags.

Homstead B, on the other hand, approximates the ideal type of the Semi-Red category. The homestead belongs to the Xhosa of the Qocwa clan and is headed by Mamvulane, who is a widow. With the exception of one child who passed Sub B, Mamvulane and her four surviving children have not been to school. The family immigrated into Burnshill in 1970 and today reside as tenants on freehold land owned by their landlord. Before immigrating into Burnshill they resided as tenants on a white-owned farm in Cathcart. None of the members of this family are connected with the mission churches. Mamvulane and her three married children married by *ukuthwala* (abduction).

As could be expected clashes between the Xhosa and the Mfengu in Burnshill have centred around the question of land-ownership. During the 1860s the granting of quitrent land to the Mfengu caused considerable friction. The few Xhosa who were living in the village at the time refused to accept the grants of land on the ground that the land belonged to their chief, Sandile, not to the Crown. Today the most serious conflict in this village is between the quitrent land-owners and the landless 'squatters' and this cleavage largely coincides with the Xhosa/Mfengu division. This conflict emerged during the 1950s when the quitrent land-owners prevented the 'squatters' from owning stock. With regard to the Ciskei political parties the majority of the Xhosa in Burnshill support the ruling CNIP and most Mfengu are members of the CNP. When fieldwork was undertaken in Burnshill there were occasions when Xhosa and Mfengu would hold separate meetings (*iinkundla*).

2. Nyaniso

The following case study refers to Nyaniso, a village in which political tensions emerged after the 1973 general elections. Nyaniso is inhabited almost entirely by the Hlubi who are affiliated to a major section of the Mfengu. The Hlubi of Nyaniso settled in the territory they now occupy in the middle of the last century and were brought together to form a compact settlement after the introduction of the Betterment Scheme duing the 1960s. Various factors have contributed to the unity and corporateness of the Hlubi of Nyaniso. Their exclusive occupation of their territory, the land struggles they fought against their neighbours and the long fight for the official recognition of their chieftainship are some of the factors which united them.

From the point of view of traditional authority the Hlubi of Nyaniso have always been autonomous and their chieftainship dates back to the time when the Mfengu still lived in Natal. The Hlubi of this village, too, are fully conscious of their ethnic links with other sections of the Mfengu and play an active role in the annual 'Fingo Day' celebrations which have been mentioned earlier. From about 1968 Xhosa immigrants from the farms started entering this village in search of land. In recent years many Xhosa familes have left the white-owned farms where some had settled after the Cattle Killing and the Frontier Wars. They are now resettling in various areas of the Ciskei.

The immigrants who arrived at Nyaniso were predominantly homogeneous regarding ethnic affiliation and background and had the same economic needs, especially land. Informants reported that most of these immigrants came into the village as destitute people (*abantu abaphaleleyo*) and had to accept anything the Hlubi could offer, as long as they could obtain accommodation in the village. On their arrival the majority of these immigrants were given accommodation by the Hlubi until they could build their own houses. At the beginning the immigration was slow, but it soon gathered momentum such that by 1972 over a hundred Xhosa familes had established themselves in the village and had erected their homesteads.

Up to the period of the 1973 general elections in the Ciskei the relations between these local groups were largely harmonious and informants stated that the immigrants were extremely co-operative and loyal to the chief of the Hlubi and also played an active role in the meetings of the local authority. It was also pointed out that many of them were given the opportunity to serve in the local committees in the village. The sports and welfare clubs which were introduced by the younger immigrants attracted the Hlubi youth and served to unite the two groups.

In spite of this, however, the immigrants were handicapped by the fact that they had no land rights. Due to the fact that they arrived after the allocation of land during the introduction of the Betterment Scheme they could not possess arable land and livestock. Although some were loaned land for tilling by the Hlubi and were also able to attach their stock to Hlubi friends, their need for land remained unsatisfied. Moreover, it appeared as though the immigrants would have to wait indefinitely for these rights.

It is also worth noting that the Hlubi of Nyaniso who had lived independently for over a century were now forced to interact intimately with a large body of immigrants with a different origin and background. Some form of parochialism seems to have manifested itself even at this stage. Some Hlubi referred to the immigrants as *imfiki* (newcomers) and *amarhanuga* (people from the farms) so much so that the chief had to protect the immigrants by stipulating a heavy fine for anyone who used these derogatory terms. In some measure, therefore, the behaviour of the host group towards the immigrants was broadly stereotyped and, even if unconsciously, the immigrants were viewed as cultural outsiders.

Tensions between the two groups in this village started in 1973 after the first general elections in the Ciskei and reached a climax at the beginning of 1976 when one of these groups, the Xhosa immigrants, decided to leave the village; they settled under another chief in the same district. On their departure the immigrant Xhosa destroyed their houses (at least 74 homesteads were destroyed and others were abandoned or sold) and left behind an equally dissatisfied group. When the first political parties in the Ciskei were formed in 1973 the Hlubi of Nyaniso were squarely behind the opposition party and became one of its major strongholds. It is alleged that a member of the ruling party who was defeated in the general elections in the constituency under which Nyaniso falls decided to hit back at the Hlubi who did not vote for him by appealing to the immigrants at Nyaniso to join the ruling party. After these elections this defeated candidate began to pay frequent visits to the village and initiated secret meetings which were to be held throughout the course of this struggle. The individual, however, soon withdrew from the local scene and left the struggle in the hands of local leaders.

Another factor, the religious affiliation of the immigrants, assisted them in organising themselves against the Hlubi. Since the immigrants were predominantly members of the Ethiopian Church, the local leaders began to use this church for the purposes of furthering their political interests. This Ethiopian church, which was founded in 1900 by a prominent Xhosa leader, the Rev. James Dwane, had over the years become predominantly Xhosa in its membership and as a result the immigrants were closely connected with it. After their arrival the immigrants established this religious sect in the village and built a temporary structure for their church services.

It was the involvement of the evangelist of this Ethiopian Church which led to the first clash between the immigrants and the Hlubi. The Hlubi, being ardent supporters of the opposition party, were offended by this evangelist's active promotion of the interests of the ruling party. Together with other leaders of the immigrant faction, he sold membership tickets for the ruling party. At a church meeting where he was reprimanded by other church leaders for antagonising the Hlubi by his political activities, the evangelist defended himself by saying that other Ethiopian Church leaders were also actively involved in promoting the interests of the ruling party. At the meeting where this evangelist was reprimanded, some of the members of his church committee supported his stand.

When the Hlubi noted that the evangelist was selling their opponents' tickets, they summoned him to appear before a meeting of the local authority where he was accused of causing disharmony in the village. Hlubi informants pointed out that because this evangelist was not prepared to apologise he was ordered to leave the village within two days. When this happened the evangelist went to the minister of his church in Grahamstown to seek advice, and when he returned to the village he was told to vacate the house he was occupying (the house belonged to one of the Hlubi) and he eventually found accommodation in a temporary structure belonging to one of the immigrants.

Shortly thereafter the local authority received a letter from the Superintendent of the Ethiopian Church questioning the decision made by the Hlubi who, however, ignored this letter and forced the evangelist to leave the village. On his departure arrangements had already been made by the Superintendent of this church for the evangelist to be accommodated by the leader of a group known as amaGwali in the Victoria East District.

After the departure of the evangelist the Ethiopian Church at Nyaniso became even more involved in the local struggle. Political meetings which were held in the evenings in the church building were disguised as church meetings. An informant stated that at first only 'political' announcements were made and later fully fledged political meetings were held during these church gatherings. When the Hlubi invaded one of these evening gatherings, the immigrants quickly changed over to 'church' matters and the explanation they gave for the money found on the table was that it was for church purposes. The local authority threatened to arrest the church steward if it ever found out that the gatherings were actually for 'sinister purposes'. Since the congregation was without an evangelist at the time, the church steward was summoned to appear before the local authority to give an explanation for these secret meetings.

The steward's role was even more intriguing. He said that as he lived far away from the church building and did not attend the evening services he knew nothing about the secret organisation. He further stated that the money which was found on the table was for church funds while the Hlubi believed that it was for political purposes. The local authority made further threats to arrest the church steward if it ever found out that the gatherings held by the immigrant community were actually political. It may be noted here this 'uncommitted' steward joined the exodus of the immigrants from the village.

It was alleged that after the secret 'church' meetings the immigrants began to meet regularly at night at a homestead belonging to one of the immigrants. At this time there was a recognised local leader of this group and the faction had grown in strength through the efforts of this local leader. He was in close contact with some of the leading members of the ruling party. The immigrants, too, began to refer to themselves as amaGwali.

AmaGwali, together with other newly created ethnic units in the Ciskei (for example, the Jingqi, Ngcangathelo and Khuze), are people who identify themselves with chiefdoms which existed in former times. Gwali, for instance, was the Xhosa leader who settled in the Somerset East district in the eighteenth century. After being involved in the early Frontier Wars his chiefdom was disrupted and lost its independence.[34]

Recently the present chief of the Gwali embarked on an extensive campaign of uniting the remnants of the former Gwali chiefdom and succeeded in forging them into a powerful interest group. Primarily the Gwali are landless and also aspire to social advancement and political autonomy. In the campaign for the 1973 general elections in the Ciskei the present chief of the Gwali directed his efforts to this group and received tremendous support from it. The leader of this group won in his constituency (Victoria East) with a huge majority and became a cabinet minister. In 1975 this leader was installed as the chief of the Gwali and received a grant of land for this group in the Victoria East district.

All these developments affected the community of Nyaniso. After the start of the secret meetings demands were made to the Nyaniso chief for arable land. At a meeting of the local authority the chief promised to make a few fields available to the immigrants and his intention was to give the immigrants some of the 'suspended' and abandoned fields in the village. However, the immigrants were again reminded about the fact that land in the village was not yet available and that the immigrants would have to wait till more land was made available by the government. Informants stated that the local magistrate who later visited the village reversed the decision made by the Hlubi to release the 'suspended' and abandoned fields and stated that the land at

Nyaniso was 'for the children of the Hlubi'. He further indicated that the immigrants might have to wait for up to ten yeears before getting any land.

These developments led to drastic changes in the relations between the local groups: meetings of the local authority were boycotted by the immigrants and social gatherings were held separately by the two groups. Large groups of immigrants would organise transport and attend meetings of the Gwali in other districts. Another dispute centred around the allocation of old-age pension grants. Normally applications for these grants are made through the chief but the immigrants who had severed all connections with the chief made their applications for these grants by appealing directly to the main offices of the Ciskeian government. As this created administrative problems the queries went back to the Hlubi chief; however, the Ciskei government representatives who were sent to the village to investigate these irregularities pleaded with the immigrants to recognise the authority of the Hlubi chief. Further, a local teacher was accused by the immigrants of discriminating against Xhosa pupils at the local primary school. This led to a crisis in the school and the officials of the Ciskei department of education had to investigate this 'ethnic' rift at the school. The Hlubi became all the more bitter against the immigrants when this teacher was dismissed from her teaching post.

In 1974 the Hlubi decided to eject from Nyaniso two men who had featured prominently in the anti-Hlubi faction. One of these men was the local leader of the immigrants and the other was being evicted because he used his homestead as the venue for the secret meetings which were held by the immigrants. This eviction was not effective because the two men simply refused to leave the village and instead appealed to their leaders in the ruling party for protection. During the same year these leaders (the chief minister and the chief of the Gwali) arrived at Nyaniso on the invitation of the immigrant faction. Another complaint made by the immigrants to these leaders was that the Hlubi had banned their meetings. On the day of the arrival of these leaders the two groups met at different venues — the Hlubi met outside the offices of the local authority and the immigrants gathered in their hundreds at the main gate leading into the village. Men on both sides were armed with sticks and among the immigrants women were cursing the Hlubi and their chief. When the leaders arrived they were saluted by the immigrants and traditional songs were sung to welcome them. Though these leaders pleaded for tolerance between the two groups, disharmony in the village continued. The immigrants instead negotiated

Ethnic Relations in the Ciskei

for land where they could settle independently and eventually obtained a grant at the beginning of 1976. The removal of this large group of people from the village was undertaken by the employees of the Ciskei government.

Conclusions

In the discussion above it can be seen that the current rift between the Xhosa and the Mfengu in the Ciskei stems largely from traditional grievances between the two groups. From the past century the interests of the two groups have conflicted. The Xhosa bear a substantial burden of grievance against the Mfengu because the latter assisted the colonists in their subjugation. In the process the Xhosa suffered a very great loss of land. The Mfengu, on the other hand, benefited from their white patrons. It is these ethnic inequalities which have served to maintain the divisions and antagonisms between the Xhosa and the Mfengu. As a result current developments in Ciskei politics still reflect events which occurred as early as the period of contact between the Xhosa and the Mfengu. This perhaps serves to illustrate the fact that in moments of crisis the past is reanimated and comes alive in the present, so that what one feels about the present gets emotive force from what one feels about the past as it survives not on evidence but in tradition.

At the same time, it should be said that the present ethnic conflict in the Ciskei is not based simply on old prejudices but reflects a very clear and present problem within the Ciskei today — competition for insufficient resources. With regard to the case studies presented in this chapter the particular economic disabilities of the Xhosa in Burnshill as well as the problems encountered by the immigrants at Nyaniso show that the ethnic struggle in the Ciskei is not merely a struggle for political power or political followers but relates, on the ground, to competition for scarce resources, especially land. Many Xhosa families from white-owned farms who are now resettling in various areas of the Ciskei have to contend with the problem of being landless. The Mfengu, on the other hand, are doing everything they can to safeguard the land they already possess.

We have also shown how the original ethnic differences which subsided after the 1920s — in the period of total African powerlessness — were revived by the system of Bantu Authorities which on the one hand encouraged the ideology of ethnicity and on the other hand opened new avenues for a struggle for power. In fact, the policy of separate development, based as it is on the recognition of exclusive ethnic units, has contributed a great deal to these ethnic conflicts.

Notes

1. A. Cohen, *Custom and Politics in Urban Africa* (Routledge & Kegan Paul, London, 1968) p. 4.
2. Ibid., p. 190.
3. W.H. Wriggins, 'Impediments to Unity in New Nations: the Case of Ceylon' in C.E. Welch (ed.), *Political Modernization* (Wadsworth, Belmont, 1967), pp. 188-9.
4. E.P. Skinner, 'Competition within Ethnic Systems in Africa' in L.A. Despres, *Ethnicity and Resource Competition in Plural Societies* (Mouton, The Hague, 1975), p. 143.
5. Skinner, ibid., p. 145.
6. Skinner, ibid., p.143.
7. M. Wilson, 'The Early History of the Transkei and Ciskei', *African Studies*, 18 (1959).
8. R.A. Moyer, 'Some Current Manifestations of Early Mfengu History' in *Collected Seminar Papers on the Societies of Southern Africa in the 19th and 20th Centuries* (Institute of Commonwealth Studies, University of London, London, vol. 3, 1973), p. 145.
9. H.J. Van Warmelo, 'The Classification of Cultural Groups' in W.D. Hammond-Tooke (ed.), *The Bantu Speaking Tribes of Southern Africa* (Routledge & Kegan Paul, London, 1974), p. 63.
10. W.D. Hammond-Tooke, *Command or Consensus* (D. Philip, Cape Town, 1975), p. 15.
11. R.A. Moyer, 'The Mfengu, Self-defence and the Cape Frontier Wars' in C. Saunders & R. Derricourt (eds.), *Beyond the Cape Frontier* (Longmans, London, 1974), p. 108.
12. J.B. Peires, 'A History of the Xhosa 1700-1835', unpublished dissertation, Rhodes University, Grahamstown, 1976.
13. R.A. Moyer, 'A History of the Mfengu of the Eastern Cape 1815-1865'. unpublished dissertation, University of London, 1976, p. 120
14. J. Ayliff and J. Whiteside, *History of the AbaMbo generally known as Fingos* (Struik, Cape Town, 1912, reprinted 1962), p. 19.
15. Peires, 'A History of the Xhosa', p. 200.
16. Moyer, 'The Mfengu', p. 109.
17. Moyer, 'Some Current Manifestations of Early Mfengu History', p. 145.
18. Moyer, 'The Mfengu', p. 107.
19. Moyer, 'A History of the Mfengu', p. 13.
20. Moyer, 'The Mfengu', p. 105.
21. W.D. Hammond-Tooke, *The Tribes of King William's Town District* (Department of Native Affairs, Pretoria, 1958), p. 126.
22. P. Mayer, *Townsmen or Tribesmen* (Oxford University Press, Cape Town, 1961), pp. 20-41.
23. J.D.Omer-Cooper, *The Zulu Aftermath* (Longmans, London, 1966), p. 165.
24. Moyer, 'Some Current Manifestations of Early Mfengu History', p. 148.
25. W.D. Hammond-Tooke, *The Tribes of Willowvale District* (Department of Native Affairs, Pretoria, 1957), p. 59.
26. W.D. Hammond-Tooke, 'The Present State of Cape Nguni Ethnographic Studies' in *Ethnological and Linguistic Studies in Honour of N.J. Van Warmelo* (Department of Native Affairs, Pretoria, 1969), p. 90.

27. M. de Lange, *Some Traditional Cosmetic Practices of the Xhosa*, Annals, Cape Provincial Museum (1963), p. 90.

28. B.G.M. Sundkler, *Bantu Prophets in South Africa*, 2nd edn (Oxford University Press, London, 1961), pp. 42-3.

29. S.E.K. Mqhayi, *Ityala LamaWele* (Lovedale Press, Lovedale, 1914), p. 133.

30. Ciskei Legislative Assembly Verbatim Reports, 1976, p. 589.

31. S. Trapido, 'African Divisional Politics in the Cape Colony 1884 to 1910', *Journal of African History*, 9 (1968), pp. 79-98; Moyer, 'Some Current Manifestations of Early Mfengu History', p. 147.

32. *Eastern Province Herald*, 7 October 1972.

33. M.E. Mills and M. Wilson, *Land Tenure*, Keiskammahoek Rural Survey (Shuter & Shuter, Pietermaritzburg, 1952), vol. 4, pp. 1-2.

34. C.F.J. Muller, *Five Hundred Years* (Academia, Pretoria, 1969), p. 436.

8 CISKEIAN POLITICAL PARTIES

Nancy Charton and Gordon Renton kaTywakadi

1. Early Political Activity in the Ciskei

The Eastern Cape, including the Ciskei, is the area of the earliest and most intensive contact between white settlers and the African inhabitants. White rule had been effectively extended over this area by the middle of the nineteenth century, and the long process of acculturation was set in train. The response of Africans to conquest, to administration by whites, and to the policy of acculturation and differential integration into white society was not slow to emerge. In 1884 an association of educated Africans known as *Ibumba Yama Africa* was founded in King William's Town. At the same time a black press emerged, *Isigidimi Sama Xhosa* and *Imvo Zabantusundu* which formulated and expressed the opinions of the newly emerged educated elite.

Eastern Cape personalities played leading roles in the formation of the South African National Native Convention, and the subsequent African National Congress. The existence of the Cape franchise, open to Africans who complied with the property and income qualifications, acted as a spur to political consciousness, and political activity. The local councils, perhaps rightly, were never seen as anything more than a very minor and subsidiary field of action; the aspirations of elites were firmly concentrated on the centre of white power, first in Cape Town and later in Pretoria.

During the 1950s the political campaigns of the ANC were extremely effective in the Eastern Cape; there was also a well established trade-union movement. When the African nationalist parties were banned in 1961 political activity did not cease. There emerged the Black Peoples' Congress, founded at a Convention in Bloemfontein in 1967, which was attended by many black organisations concerned with education and culture. These included the South African Students' Organisation, the Interdenominational African Ministers' Association, the Association for the Education and Cultural Advancement of the African People. In general it espoused a 'black consciousness' line. This was an attempt to interpret the experience of the black man in white-ruled South Africa at every level: social, religious, economic and political. It sought to build up the self-image of the black man, to assist him to define himself rather than to accept the definition of others. The political objective of the Black Peoples' Congress was black majority rule; their economic objective was a communal society in which wealth was more equally shared, and their immediate programme was concerned with community development and consciousness raising.

The voice of youth was particularly audible in this organisation, and the presence of Fort Hare University in the Ciskei meant that the aims and ideals of the Congress and of black consciousness were widely disseminated in the area. Their local headquarters was in King William's Town where they launched a particularly successful clinic as a community development project. In general this movement saw homeland institutions as 'phoney'. They were said to be designed to cheat people into believing they had effective communication links with Pretoria, and also to foster tribal disunity. They were seen as an example of divide and rule. They described homeland leaders as 'tools', 'quislings' and 'sell-outs'. The Black Peoples' Congress was banned during the urban emergency in 1977, together with many of its subsidiary organisations, and its community development projects. But it is important to notice that the old African nationalist movement persisted in the Ciskei throughout the period of the founding of the new Ciskeiain parties. Its socialist and unitary objectives were in competition with the more conservative regional objectives of the Ciskeian parties. And its fairly numerous community development projects were an earnest of what it wished to accomplish for the people.

2. The Emergence of Homeland Political Parties in the Ciskei

On 1 August 1972 the Ciskei was declared 'self-governing' in terms of the Bantu Homelands Constitution Act. The Legislature consisted initially of 30 chiefs and 20 elected members, representing nine constituencies. The first elections were held during February 1973.

Sixty-three candidates in all contested the nine seats, five of them multi-member constituencies. For the purpose of electioneering, candidates in Victoria East, Zwelitsha, Mdantsane, and Glen Grey grouped themselves into 'slates'; the grouping in the first three constituencies took place around Chief Justice Mabandla, who was at that time Chairman of the Executive Council of the Ciskei Legislative Assembly, and Mr Lennox Sebe who was a member of his cabinet. In Glen Grey no less than 16 candidates stood, nine belonging to three different 'slates', one led by Mr Z. Booi, one by Mr W. Jaxa, and one by Mr J. Saliwa.

There were in addition a number of independents. All candidates bar one, Mr D.R. Guzana in Zwelitsha, accepted separate development. Mr Guzana espoused a multi-racial policy, as his brother Mr Knowledge Guzana had in the Transkei. (There he led the Democratic Party, official Opposition.)

Chief Justice Mabandla is a senior chief of the Bhele, an Mfengu clan in the Tyhume Valley. He attended the school for the sons of chiefs in the Transkei, and trained as a teacher. The role which he played in heightening Mfengu consciousness during the 1960s and early 1970s has already been described. In his manifesto, he pledged himself to observe the constitution, and in particular to preserve the chieftainship and traditional authority, while at the same time observing democratic norms.[1] The constitution was to be regarded as a prelude to complete independence; but the latter could only be achieved after a clear definition of the boundaries of the Ciskei, and after a fair and just programme of consolidation. He also looked forward to amalgamation with the Transkei, if that was the wish of the leaders and citizens of the Ciskei. Mabandla rejected any form of multi-racial state, and a federal or confederal system embracing several homelands. Friendly relations with South Africa were to be maintained. Agriculture was to be improved; an attempt was to be made to improve conditions for migratory labourers; education was to be improved; industrial and commercial development was to be promoted; conditions in the townships were to be improved, and resettlement supervised and controlled. The means test for the old age pension was to be abolished.

Mabandla enjoyed the support of the majority of chiefs in the Ciskei Legislative Assembly. His group also had the support of the Mfengu, however, Chief Velile Sandile, paramount chief of the Xhosa, also supported him, seeing in him a defender of traditional institutions and, in particular, of the chieftainship. He saw Sebe, a commoner at that stage, as a threat and said that his election to the position of Chief Minister would cause the collapse of the chieftainship as an institution.[2]

Mr. Lennox Sebe (now Chief Sebe) is a Tshawe, of the royal family clan of the Rharhabe, but not of the reigning house. He too trained as a teacher at Lovedale and has, in addition, a diploma in agriculture. In 1968 he was appointed to the Ciskei Territorial Authority as a representative for the Ntinde. When the 'New Deal' was introduced, he and Mr Mtoba served on the Executive Council as representatives of the Rharhabe, under Chief Mabandla. With the transformation of the Territorial Assembly into the Legislative Assembly he became Minister of

Education until a Cabinet reshuffle gave him the new portfolio of Agriculture and Forestry. It is said that he regarded this as demotion, and that as a result enmity developed between him and Chief Mabandla. Mr Mtoba, the other Rharhabe representative, became Minister of Education in his place, so the action appears to have personal rather than tribal implications. In 1972 he visited the United States of America; many important guests were at the airport to welcome him on his return, including the Chief Minister of the Transkei. But Chief Mabandla was not present.[3] The breach between the two leaders was now obvious to all.

It was during this period that Mr Sebe emerged as the political leader of the Rharhabe, a leadership apparently endorsed by the Rharhabe Tribunal, a committee representing the various clans of the Rharhabe, which advised the paramount chief.

Mr Sebe's manifesto started significantly by stating that he stood for the aspirations and wishes of Ciskeians, within the framework of separate development.[4] He pointed out that he had sacrificed his career as an educationalist in order to give leadership. He promised equal rights for all Ciskeians, even those in the urban areas; to struggle for the recognition of all chiefs and to negotiate for additional land for new chieftaincies, to raise the salaries of chiefs and headmen; to struggle for more land and a just consolidation. He pinpointed the same development needs as did Chief Mabandla, but in each instance he promised not only increased development, but attention to the aspirations and interests of the people involved. This applies particularly to the civil servants, the teachers, medical personnel, farmers, traders and industrialists; even the workers were mentioned. This manifesto reveals a clear comprehension of the interests involved in the election, and it is framed in practical and down-to-earth terms which could be readily understood.

The group which formed around Sebe included competent businessmen from Port Elizabeth, Zwelitsha and Mdantsane, and some chiefs of the Rharhabe. It met first in Fort Beaufort in 1972, and originally called itself the *Broederbond*. This name has interesting associations. Apparently the group saw itself as having a conservatory role with regard to Xhosa culture — just as the *Broederbond* had assumed the task of protecting and promoting Afrikaaner culture. At the Fort Beaufort meeting it was decided to expand the membership of the group. They also adopted the name *Ikhonco* which means a link. This was to symbolise the unity of the Ciskei.

Members of Mabandla's group claimed that they followed the

example set by the *Ikhonco*. They acted thus in response to the electoral challenge of the other group. They took the name *Imbokotho* which can mean a grinding stone or a missile. It too was said to be symbolic of unity, of grinding out tribalism.

During the election campaign itself there was evidence of ethnic conflict. Chief Mabandla denounced the activities of the *Ikhonco* group as being conducive to a revival of the historic conflict between the two main tribal groups. They set out to create the impression that they were the true representatives of the Rharhabe, he said, and that they enjoyed the blessings of the chiefs. 'Various tribal groups . . . do not seem to take the elections as a nation, but as different entities, each working for the glorification of its racial image.'[5] The paramount chief issued a statement denying that anyone had been designed as 'the true representatives of the AmaRarabe' in the same issue of the *Daily Dispatch*.

Mr Sebe himself had little doubt about the efficacy of tribalism in electioneering. He is quoted as saying after the election:

> The reason why I now find myself in his post [i.e. Chief Mabandla's] is the fact that we belong to different tribes. Chief Mabandla is a Fingo and I am a Rharhabe. My tribe is bigger than his, therefore it was just a question of time before there was a change of premiership.[6]

These quoted statements would seem to impute blame to the Xhosa component of the electorate. The interaction between the two groups has been clearly analysed in Chapter 7. Escalating tribalism is an interactive phenomenon; both parties are responsible. Competition for local-level power between the two groups came from the historical situation, from the existence of a minority group; it was exacerbated by the political structure — the Ciskeian Territorial Authority which was organised on a tribal basis, and by the race for chieftaincies.

However, as important as the history of intergroup friction and the emphasis on ethnicity in the structures of separate development, is the nature of the electoral struggle in a political system in which there were no pre-existing political parties to organise the vote. Neither of the factions we have been describing had any available organisation to bring in the vote — except the tribal structure where it existed. Tywakadi describes very clearly how the tribal structures were used in the rural areas, and how a competitive party system puts them under very severe pressure indeed.[7] A contributory fact was of course that there was no ideological difference between the two factions at that stage.

Ciskeian Political Parties

The *Ikhonco* group won 13 out of the 20 elected seats; and two elected members joined later. From all accounts this group with competent business leaders among its members and prominent educationalists had conducted the most efficient campaign.[8] The detailed results are reflected in Table 8.1. The percentage poll was relatively high, varying from 60.6 per cent in Mdantsane to 78.4 per cent in Middledrift. The registration of voters which stood at 480,801 or 47.5 per cent of the *de jure* population of the Ciskei was also phenomenally high.

Table 8.1: General Election Results 1973

	Candidates	Votes	% Votes polled	Percentage poll
	Victoria East			
Ikhonco	Maqoma, L.M.	52,632	19.61	
	Lamani, A.Z.	52,486	19.56	
	Burns-Ncamashe	51,313	19.12	
	Ximiya, W.F.	50,327	18.75	
Imbokotho	Mabandla, M.M.	16,029	5.97	
	Matakane, R.S.	13,803	5.14	
	Mbatani, M.	13,450	5.07	
	Zantsi, W.M.	11,155	4.16	
	Zantsi, L.M.	3,143	1.17	
	Bokwe, S.T. (BNCP)	2,478	0.92	
	Spoilt papers	1,558	0.58	
	Total	268,374		74.5
	Zwelitsha			
Ikhonco	Sebe, L.L.	42,095	15.4	
	Nqezo, V.V.	38,821	14.3	
	Nkontso, D.E.	37,963	14.0	
	Sam, M.	35,878	13.2	
Imbokotho	Mtoba, S.L.	30,531	11.2	
	Guzana, P.F.	25,457	9.3	
	Sangotsha, I.L.	23,230	8.5	
	Ntshele, M.J.	22,326	8.2	
	Guzana, D.R.	8,989	3.3	
	Putu, M.M.	4.438	1.6	
	Spoilt papers	2,154	0.8	
	Total	271,882		73.6
	Mdantsane			
Ikhonco	Siyo, L.F.	25,327	18.1	
	Kewuti, Q.J.	24,164	17.3	
	Bashe	23,752	17.0	

Table 8.1 Continued

	Candidates	Votes	% Votes polled	Percentage poll
Imbokotho	Mzamo, A.N.	21,310	15.2	
	Rula, D.	20,220	14.4	
	Voyi, M.A.	20.099	14.4	
	Villie, H.K.	2,814	2.0	
	Mangala, J.K.	1,676	1.2	
	Spoilt papers	667	0.5	
	Total	140,029		60.6
	Middledrift			
	Hoyana, A.	12,159	62.7	
	Mjoji, N.W.	6,996	36.1	
	Spoilt papers	221	1.1	
	Total	19,376		78.4
	Peddie			
	Stamper, P.G.	15,449	70.7	
	Msuthwana, P.E.E.	6,125	28.0	
	Spoilt papers	264	1.2	
	Total	21,838		77.2
	Keiskammahoek			
	Peteni, R.L.	6,309	62.0	
	Ntshingwa, D.G.	1,764	17.3	
	Qalaza, H.	1,444	14.2	
	Spoilt papers	649	6.4	
	Total	10,166		77.5
	Hewu			
	Myataza, B.D.R.	6,464	46.8	
	Bandla, P.	4,657	33.7	
	Nikibathi, V.	1,118	8.0	
	Ngoma, N.T.	851	6.1	
	Sishuba, T.A.	492	3.5	
	Spoilt papers	254	1.8	
	Total	13,836		68.6
	Herschel			
	Mokhesi, S.J.	13,973	22.3	
	Mkrola, N.J.	13,284	21.2	
	Burhali, S.	12,133	19.4	
	Mei, M.	8.942	14.3	
	Kumalo, M.A.	7,209	11.5	
	Kambula, D.W.	5,187	8.3	

Table 8.1: Continued

Candidates	Votes	% Votes polled	Percentage poll
Mfaxa, M.J.	1,310	2.1	
Spoilt papers	659	1.1	
Total	62,697		62.8
Glen Grey			
Saliwa, J.H.	20,522	11.8	
Jaxa, W.T.	18,453	10.6	
Booi, Z.E.	17,846	10.3	
Gantsho, S.	17,733	10.2	
Noholoza, M.J.	17,571	10.1	
Mzazi, N.E.	16,859	9.7	
Sondlo, T.N.	16,144	9.3	
Dumezweni, M.E.	16,142	9.3	
Mhlom, W.	15,556	8.9	
Noji, W.	4,722	2.7	
Vanqa, E.T.	4,099	2.3	
Ngese, A.S.	2,762	1.5	
Mbalo, M.J.	2,256	1.3	
Joka, M.E.	774	0.4	
Zote, S.	662	0.4	
Mdyosi, G.J.	480	0.3	
Spoilt papers	601	0.3	
Total	173,182		67.1

Source: Ciskei Official Gazette no. 6; 23 March 1973.

In Mdantsane, Zwelitsha and Victoria East the *Ikhonco* slates were elected *en bloc*. Relatively few independent candidates stood in those constituencies, one in Victoria East and two each in the remaining areas. In Glen Grey the leaders of each of the three slates were successful.

Mabandla and the *Imbokotho* had been confident of winning the election. The results came as a rude awakening. But all was not lost, until the election of Chief Minister in the Legislative Assembly. The *Ikhonco* group rallied enough support from the chiefs to elect Mr Sebe Chief Minister, with a slender majority of two (*Ikhonco*: 26; *Imbokotho*: 24).

Allegations of electoral irregularities followed the announcement of the results, and electoral petitions were drawn up for Zwelitsha and Victoria East. In Zwelitsha the defeated candidates maintained that the supply of ballot papers ran out at some polling stations, with the result that voting stopped before the official closing time. During the counting and sorting of ballot papers, some were cut, resulting in some portions which contained valid votes being discarded. Intimidation was also alleged. The election was set aside on the first two counts, and white officials were found responsible. In Victoria East it was alleged that ballot papers had been replaced from another polling station, without their numbers having been recorded. Ballot boxes were not properly sealed. Secrecy was not maintained and corrupt practices were imputed to the *Ikhonco* agents. In view of the verdict in the previous case the two candidates agreed to resign. Two had recently been elevated to the chieftainship, so that their seats were vacant anyway.

Immediately after the announcement of the verdict on the Zwelitsha complaint the *Imbokotho* issued a memorandum to the Commissioner General of the Xhosa:

> On the strength of the Supreme Court proceedings and a subsequent action, we have gained the impression a deliberate effort has been made to help Mr Sebe into the Assembly in the first instance, and subsequently to keep him in a position of influence in the government of the Ciskei after he had been unseated.[9]

This refers to the appointment of Mr Sebe as Economic Advisor to the Ciskei Cabinet to tide him over until his re-election in the by-election in 1976. The memorandum continues:

> Strange that the recent visit of the Minister of Bantu Administration and Development, Mr M.C. Botha, co-incided with the meeting of the ruling party's caucus and with the hurried creation of a post for Mr Sebe, both events occurring within a few days of the Supreme Court judgment.

The implication behind the memorandum is clear: that the actions and attitudes of the white officials who were responsible for the 'chaotic state' of the Ciskei General Election in 1973, and of the white cabinet minister, meant that the Republican government favoured the success of the Sebe group.

No commission of enquiry was appointed. The electoral verdict in the by-election more than confirmed the results of the general election. However, the importance of the memorandum lies in the attitude it reveals. How fragile is the trust of participants in the homeland political system, and in the intentions of the Republican government towards the political autonomy of the homelands. Political dependency must always give rise to such problems of trust and legitimacy.

The accusations of electoral abuses and the litigation was a factor in bringing about the formation of parties. Being faced with a court case *Imbokotho* found it necessary to assume a 'legal personality' both to collect funds and to institute legal proceedings. Litigation was thus the occasion for the emergence of the parties; but their emergence was probably inevitable in view of the dynamic clearly visible during the election. Chief Mabandla stated in a memorandum announcing the formation of the Ciskei National Party that 'the formation of political parties signified the rejection of individuals as an embodiment of proper leadership. Proper leadership was expressed in principles and ideals that were embodied in constitutions.' He also mentioned the need for organisation which had been experienced during the election as reasons for the formation of his party. He felt that a Legislative Assembly necessitated the formation of parties.[10]

The announcement by Chief Mabandla of the formation of the Ciskei National Party took place at the first sitting of the Legislative Assembly in April 1973. Mr L. Sebe followed almost immediately by announcing the formation of the Ciskei National Independence Party.[11]

3. Party Structure

In the Ciskei National Independence Party the branch is the local unit of organisation, and may be formed whenever ten or more people who embrace the principles and policy of the party come together. A membership fee is payable; on payment a membership card is issued. Each branch elects an executive committee consisting of a chairman, vice-chairman, secretary, assistant secretary and treasurer. Branches may be formed in towns, on farms, in factories or compounds. Where no branches exist persons may affiliate with the central party organisation. Where branches are large they may be subdivided into *iinqila* (cells). No less than 100 branches had been established by 1976.

There are two Regional Committees in Victoria East to co-ordinate the activities of branches. They are elected by constituent branches, and were supposed to convene regional conferences; however, this has not happened so far. Instead, rallies were organised to which party leaders were invited.

Once a year a National Conference is held at which the National

Executive is elected. This conference is attended by officials and delegates from Regional Committees, and two delegates from each branch directly affiliated to the conference. The functions include policy making, election of officials and arbitration of disputes within regions and branches. In 1974 the conference was held in Zwelitsha, in 1975 in Cape Town, and in 1976 in Mdantsane, always just prior to the annual session of the Legislative Assembly.

Resolutions brought to these conferences have included the following issues: inadequate policing of Mdantsane, the abolition of the third-class pass in Std Six (the first official school leaving certificate); inadequate provision of clinics and ambulances; the abolition of migratory labour; the need for more land, more bridges and better roads.

The National Executive Committee consists of the National Leader, the National Chairman and Deputy Chairman, the General Secretary and Organising Secretary, the party Information Officer and the Treasurer. All are elected at the National Conference.

The constitution of the party gives the National Leader wide powers. He may make decisions about party policy and publicise them. The concept of collective leadership is not catered for, which may perhaps account for the considerable turnover of cabinet ministers in 1976 and for the numerous fissures which opened up in party leadership particularly in 1977.

The party uses the rally as a means of political recruitment and mobilisation. It is a cross between a prayer meeting and a conventional party meeting. During a rally prayers are said, hymns are sung and speeches made. These are interrupted by shouts of the party salute 'Bopha!' Hands are raised with fingers linked, indicating a chain. Usually the words of a hymn are changed and names of present leaders of the party and current events are substituted. This was reminiscent of the fifties when the Defiance Campaign of the African National Congress was at its height. The message of the songs then was directed at the white ruling regime, but the songs in the homeland elections conveyed messages that were directed at the other Africans. For instance during the fifties, people would sing a song with the following message: 'Verwoerd (or Malan or Strydom), set Africa free'.

The Congress had a salute: 'Mayibuy' iAfrika' (Africa must return); at the same time the right-hand fist with the thumb pointing backwards would be raised. Homeland parties tended to copy these procedures. Rallies are usually preceded by a motorcade; women are expected to appear in traditional dress. In the speeches by party leaders party policy is explained and new members are recruited. Rallies are usually accompanied by much pomp and grandeur, feasting and singing.

Membership is open to all Ciskeians from the age of 18 years. The party did not have a functioning youth wing, although efforts had been made to organise one. The presence of the Black Peoples' Congress, and the strength of the South African Students Organisation in the Eastern Cape may well have some relevance to this situation. Youth remains attracted to the old African nationalist politics directed at the central organs of white power. It refuses to be deflected into regional channels which it sees as powerless, and inadequate to realise the freedom and equality to which they aspire.

The party colours are blue and white, which coincide with the official colours of the Ciskei government. This is interesting, and may betoken a tendency to equate the ruling party with the government, a tendency by no means unknown in the rest of Africa.

In the Ciskei National Party, at one time the official opposition, the branch was also the basic unit and might be established where there were 20 or more members. In rural areas it might be established in a chieftaincy, or a village. Where no branches existed members might affiliate directly to the central body. There were only eleven branches in 1976, in Zwelitsha, Alice, Mdantsane, Glen Grey and in the Western Cape. Each branch elected its own officials. Where two branches existed in close proximity a Regional Committee might be formed to coordinate their work. Constitutionally they appeared to be distinct, yet they seemed to perform the same functions as branches.

The National Conference consisted of the National Executive, the chairman, secretary, and two representatives from each region, and members of the Legislative Assembly who were not party officers. It was the main policy-making body. Since the inception of the party only two Conferences have been held. In 1974 they affirmed the new policy of non-racialism — a complete *volte face* on Mabandla's previously enunciated policy; amalgamation with the Transkei was looked upon favourably, as were African trade unions. There were also resolutions on sport.

The National Executive was elected at the National Conference, and was entrusted with decision making when the Conference was not in session. It consisted of a National Leader, Deputy Leader, National Secretary, Assistant Secretary, Treasurer, and members of the Ciskei Legislative Assembly.

It too used rallies to mobilise and recruit members. Membership was open to all Ciskeians over 18 years; a membership fee was payable, and a card was issued. Members had to swear an oath of loyalty. The party had no functioning youth wing either; there was apparently one at Glen Grey which petered out. The emblem was a black woman kneeling by a grindstone; the salute was a raised fist accompanied by the cry 'Khulula' (Make free).

Organisationally speaking both parties were very similar. The CNIP had a wider network of branches. But both apparently failed to achieve mass mobilisation at grass-roots level. In the survey of workers in certain factories in the East London area in 1974 52 per cent of the workers claimed to be members of a party, 88 per cent belonging to the CNIP and 12 per cent to the CNP. A significantly larger proportion of workers not born in East London claim membership of a political party than do workers born in East London (70 per cent as against 62 per cent).[12]

In the Mdantsane survey (1976) only 32 per cent claimed to be party members — 84 per cent of the CNIP and 16 per cent of the CNP. Considering the length of time which had elapsed since the creation of parties — barely one year during the factory survey and three years during the Mdantsane survey, it is apparent that party organisations had made a significant impact, even though they had not achieved mass mobilisation. However, failure to organise youth wings points to a serious failure to win the youth for their cause.

The opposition complained of apathy in the rural areas: 'Nobody ever cared to renew membership.'[13] In all areas party structure tended to shrink between elections as a result of apathy. However, percentage polls were relatively high, especially in the rural areas. Although the Mdantsane poll was the lowest in the Ciskei, it was not extraordinarily low. No separate figures are available for the urban area itself. But the hypothesis would be that registration of voters might be lowest there, in view of the alienation of the urban voter from the homeland system as a whole. The alienation of a certain group of Ciskeians in Mdantsane was clearly reflected in the results of the survey (see Chapter 9).

Constitutionally the governing party delegates a great deal of power to Chief Sebe, the National Leader. The nomination controversy in Mdantsane confirms that this power is utilised. The opposition leader on the other hand would appear to have deferred to the opinions of his party colleagues. Chief Burns-Ncamashe maintained that Mabandla had the new policy of multi-racialism 'forced down his throat'.[14] He maintained that statements from the party were sometimes released with only the signature of the General Secretary and one other member of the Executive, not necessarily that of the Leader.

4. The Party in the Rural Areas

A study of the political process in the village of Gobozana revealed several interestings facts.[15] Parties have failed to establish permanent branches which could serve as communicating links with the legislature. Instead they used the tribal structure initially, and have continued to rely on it. In a two-party system this must create immediate problems for the tribal structure.

For instance in ImiDushane the chief has an inner circle of advisers called *amaphakathi*.[16] Included among the members of this inner council were two men who were prominent in party affairs, on opposing sides, namely Mr Sangotsha and Mr Nkontso. The Chief joined the CNIP; the effect of the party split on the inner council was to refract and 'kill' it.

The headman moved in a field of forces which included the chief, the bureaucracy, and the antagonistic political parties. The key role of the headman in the political process in a village makes his post a target for manipulation by the party in power. In other words, all things being equal, the ruling party will aways prefer to appoint a headman whose loyalty to them is known.

Where a headman is installed against the wishes of the community the people may well accept him on the assumption that the government's will may not be opposed. However, if this happens he will lose his legitimacy among his people. His role as a catalyst in the achievement of consensus will be well nigh impossible.

Ironically then even the weakly articulated party system in the Ciskei was contributing to the undermining of traditional institutions, and traditional political culture.

Traditional structures were accepted as the pivot on which constitutional development in the homelands was to be based. This is the principle which underlies the Bantu Authorities Act of 1951. This Act encouraged the resuscitation of defunct chiefdoms and promoted headmen to vacant chieftaincies. It is these actions which gave Gobozana aspirations towards becoming a separate chiefdom, and Gobozana is not alone in cherishing such ambitions. In 1975 in the Legislative Assembly Chief Justice Mabandla accused the government of neglecting the claims of six areas for separate chieftaincies: Khawulela, Ngcelwane and Ndlazi, Zibi, Mrwebo and Zali.[17] It should be noted that Gobozana is not mentioned.

Communication between the village and the authorities did not seem to be at all good. Villagers misunderstood the reasons for official actions, as for instance when a high school was built in a neighbouring village and not at Gobozana. They maintained that this was clearly ethnic discrimination against a Fingo minority by a Xhosa government. They have been unable to push the case for a clinic further than the Tribal Authority. When questioned the Minister of Health stated that he had never heard of the need there, nor of the action which the local community had taken in building a clinic. One may infer that the troubled relationship between village and Tribal Authority has reflected adversely on its ability to communicate felt needs up the traditional hierarchy, and the modern channels. The latter consists of headman, bureaucracy, that is, Bantu Affairs Commissioner, officials of functional departments, members of the Legislative Assembly for that constituency and finally the members of the Cabinet (one of whom actually represented the constituency — another is their chief).

Perhaps most interesting has been the exploration of the perceptions of the headman and of his people with regard to ethnicity and its significance. As amaMfengu they were conscious of being a minority in their particular tribal authority. All their frustrations were consequently attributed to this cause, which in turn heightened their feelings of alienation and rejection. Equally interesting were their perceptions of the party game as a zero sum game; they felt the need to identify with the winning side, in order to be able to share in the spoils of office. It may be conceded that these perceptions were mistaken. The school was not awarded to a CNIP village, but to a village whose centrality commended it. Many CNP areas with able members of the Legislative Assembly have obtained benefits, in spite of their known political allegiance. However, perceptions are important for they determine political actions. In Gobozana the headman and his councillors bought CNIP membership cards, though their real inclinations were said to be otherwise. They did so 'in the interests of the village', and on the assumption that they were playing a zero sum game in which their interests must always lie with the winning side. Such perceptions must contribute powerfully to the emergence of a one-party political system.

5. The Party at Local Level in Mdantsane and Zwelitsha

A study of local government elections in 1974 in Mdantsane and

Zwelitsha revealed that they were fought on a party basis.[18] CNIP nominations were made by the cabinet. In Mdantsane the CNIP won a resounding victory in the five contested zones and then packed the council with nominated members from its own ranks. By February 1975 the party had ousted all CNP members. The elections at Zwelitsha followed the same pattern. The ruling party had set itself a political objective — the control of township councils. It had shown itself to be efficient and well organised, and intolerant of opposition, for opposing candidates were harassed in many ways.

Government involvement at local level does not always redound to the credit of the government, or promote its legitimacy. Neither does it always facilitate communication of needs. However, the opportunity to build up a political machine after the model of Tamany Hall is obviously present in the township situation. The pay-off is in terms of commodities, which are very scarce and therefore highly prized: housing, jobs and trading licences.[19] Mdantsane comprises 98,289 people or 16 per cent of the *de jure* population of the Ciskei. It elected four members of the legislature, or 20 per cent of elected members. It was thus a political prize worth wooing, and impounding. The temptation to do so must be great, and it may bring short-term political advantage. But in the long term it could be disastrous to legitimacy, especially if the 'machine' is both inefficient and corrupt, and is seen by the people to be so. One of the grave disadvantages of political centralisation of any kind is that the central government is called upon to answer for all the sins of its agencies in the hierarchy; the resentment of the people can then be directed only at the apex, at the central government itself. In a pluralistic structure resentments can be directed at many different agencies at different levels. It is thus dispersed, to an extent, making greater stability possible for the central government.

6. Party Policy

A close examination of the Sebe manifesto reveals CNIP consistency throughout the period under review. The party has not deviated from the framework of the policy of separate development. Strides have been made in the recognition of new chieftaincies; some land has even been found for them, often at the expense of existing chieftaincies which support the opposition. Salaries and conditions of service have been improved for chiefs and headmen, civil servants, teachers, medical personnel, and pensions have been increased. Attention has been given to the needs of farmers, especially by providing for irrigation schemes. New townships have been built and existing ones improved; educational and health services have been greatly expanded. Industry and commerce have been encouraged, and the commercial sector, like the bureaucracy, has been Africanised.

However there have been frustrations, especially at the level of financial resources. Land consolidation has been achieved, but at a price which not all would agree was just. This issue is explored in Chapter 9. Chief Sebe has, together with other homeland leaders taken up the cudgels on behalf of the urban blacks, with minimal results. He is sympathetic to the interests of the urban worker, in theory; in practice he has played a mediating role between employers and employees, torn between the need for low wages and more job opportunities and the need for a reasonable standard of living for all his people. He does not see trade unions as necessary. His manifesto does not mention amalgamation with the Transkei. He remains opposed to it on economic grounds. His manifesto does not raise the topic of independence; he saw it as a possibility only after the land and the economic issues have been solved.[20] Chief Maqoma defines the party position clearly: 'We cannot therefore separate ourselves from the Republic of South Africa before we have made use of our wealth there, namely in developing the Homelands we reside in first.'[21]

However, a Commission of Inquiry which includes among its members foreign experts, has now (1979) been appointed to go into the desirability of independence. The Ciskei government would appear to be considering the matter seriously.

The CNIP has followed a consistent policy ever since it was formed. The CNP on the other hand, finding itself out of power, had to seek issues on which to oppose the governing party, or die as an opposition. The Minister of Justice put the position clearly in the 1973 sitting: 'They cannot be opposed to our policy of separate development. We better ask the members of the opposite side to come over to our side'.[22] Mr Siyo commented at the same sitting: 'The only opposition we have is that we are opposing each other on the question of leadership'.[23] They were not slow to remedy this defect. At their 1974 Grahamstown Conference they approved a policy of multi-racialism which runs completely counter to the 1973 Mabandla Manifesto. The adoption of this policy enabled the CNP to offer an ideological alternative to separate development. They were no longer merely opposed on the question of leadership. It thus came to resemble the opposition party in the Transkei, in a very real way. Tywakadi points out that the CNP owed its existence to the policy of separate development; as official opposition it was actively co-operating in legitimising the institutions created by this policy. There was thus a contradiction between its situation within the system, and its policy. Discussion with members of the party established that they had considered the possibility of rendering the homeland machinery unworkable, if and when they came to power as the Labour Party had done in the Coloured Persons' Representative Council.[24]

At the Grahamstown Conference Mr P.G. Stamper, MLA for Peddie, pleaded for dialogue with the Transkei with a view to amalgamation.[25] This issue is raised at almost every sitting of Assembly. The Mdantsane survey revealed that there was a considerable degree of public support for such a policy, at least in that area (57 per cent were in favour of amalgamation, 17 per cent against and 26 per cent were uncommitted: see Table 8.2(e)).

On the land issue the CNP took a stronger line than most members of the governing party. The party claimed all the land between the Great Kei and the Fish rivers, and they attacked the consolidation plans and the excision of the two northern districts with fervour.

At the 1974 Conference they also raised the issue of resettlement; they were against the removal of people from their established areas. The governing party too has opposed the policy on specific occasions, for instance, the plan to resettle Grahamstown's 40,000 Africans at Committees Drift in the Ciskei. But for the most part it has been powerless to resist the Republican government on this issue.

Complaints from the government benches in 1973 about the lack of an effective opposition were perhaps premature. The opposition took up a new position, and was not afraid to attack the government on basic policy issues as well as on administrative details.

7. Party Interaction 1973-8

The ruling party consolidated its position between 1973 and 1975 by electoral victories in local government, and in the by-elections which came about, for various reasons. In his analysis of some of these elections, and of party activity in a typical rural area Tywakadi maintains that several factors contributed to their success. He feels that the governing party had an automatic advantage. The electorate 'cannot see the difference between the ruling party and the government'. People

	%
Table 8.2(a): Significance of Tribalism in Mdantsane: Mdantsane Survey 1976	
It is becoming less important	53
It is not becoming less important	28
No response	19
Table 8.2 (b): Identific Group	**%**
Tribal	6
Ciskei	37
South Africa	44
No response	13
Table 8.2 (c): Reasons for Identifying with South Africa	**%**
It would enable me to work, or settle without restriction	86
It would give me more rights/money	6
I belong to South Africa/South African belongs to me	5
Other	3
Table 8.2 (d): Political Preference for United South Africa or Homeland System	**%**
A united South Africa with black majority rule	45
The homeland system	28
Other	2
No response	25
Table 8.2 (e): Desirability of Amalgamation with Transkei	**%**
In favour of amalgamation	57
Not in favour of amalgamation	17
No response	26

were being asked to vote for 'government approved' candidates. This wold ensure that pensions, houses, sports facilities and schools would be made available to the community concerned.[26]

The Mdantsane survey lends support to this view. Table 8.3 reflects the fact that informants voted for a party primarily because they admired the leader of the party or the candidate (27 per cent) or because they did what the majority did (10 per cent). Similarly those who joined a party did so because they approved of its policy (9 per cent), admired the leader (8 per cent), or did what the majority did (6 per cent). There are two clear tendencies in these responses to open questions, one to follow approved leaders, and the other to take the side of the majority. Similarly in the rural areas Tywakadi found that the villagers saw party politics as a zero sum game in which their real interests had always to lie with the winning side, whatever their inclinations. Chief Mabandla formulated this attitude very clearly in the legis-

Table 8.3: Party Choice: Mdantsane 1976

	Percentage Total Respondents	
	Why did you vote?	Why did you join?
Did what leaders told me	4	2
Feared intimidation	2	2
Did what the majority were doing	10	6
My clan or tribe involved in party	—	8
Admired leader or candidate	27	1
Admired party achievements	—	5
Admired policy of party	—	9
Do not know why	1	—
Did not vote/join	54	64

lature: 'The ruling party is only acting in the interests of a section of the community which excludes the members of the Opposition.'[27] In Ciskeian politics in the short run, nothing succeeds like success apparently. Such attitudes are a powerful factor in producing the so called 'bandwagon syndrome' in electoral behaviour.

The initial rise in the fortunes of the governing party and the decline in those of the opposition was not the only indication of a tendency towards a one-party dominant system. Attitudes towards the opposition among legislators, and among the people of Mdantsane tend to be ambivalent. In 1972 Chief Mabandla said there was no institutionalised opposition in traditional courts.[28] The following year he said he could not find an appropriate word in Xhosa to express its meaning: It is now called *abaxhoxhonxi* from the verb 'to provoke'. However, the chief has a clear understanding of the opposition's role:

> Our main object is to apply our brakes if the cabinet is dangerously running downhill or if the cabinet is asleep. Our whole job is to prick it into action. The government is our government.[29]

Initially opposition criticism in the Assembly provoked government members into ridiculing its lack of a different platform from that of the government. Thus in 1973 Siyo said: 'Both sides are agreed in toto with the policy of separate development'.[30] When the opposition remedied this defect at its 1974 Conference the response of the government was swift and ominous. During the 1974 session the chiefs in the opposition were told that they were endangering their position as civil servants by associating with a 'subversive' party such as the CNP. These threats had no effect whatever, but they were made. 'I descry a tendency towards Communism!' said the Chief Whip of the governing party about the opposition.[31] This could be said to be the ultimate in political invective in South Africa! The Chief Minister moved from threats in 1974 to blandishments in 1975. He invited the Leader of the Opposition to confer with him 'on national matters ... for the good of Ciskeians'. He implied that they had no experts and that the debate would consequently be 'drowned' or take the form of character assassination.[32] Cabinet Ministers are obviously irritated by minor complaints which come up in the budget debates and during the votes of no confidence, as if purely administrative matters should not be mentioned in the Assembly. Sebe says: 'The duty of the Opposition is to join forces with the government and attack poverty and hunger.'[33] Obviously the ruling party desired the support of the opposition in areas where they were involved in fighting the Republican Government. They did not see that support as forthcoming. There is much evidence in Ciskei debates to support Apter's conclusion that political leaders in Africa 'easily accept the view that a political opposition is troublesome'.[34]

In a survey of Legislative Assembly members undertaken in 1975, members were asked to name two important functions of the opposition. Table 8.4 reflects a clear consensus that it has a 'watchdog' function. Tywakadi remarks that the association with the dog image is itself derogatory.[35] There may well be something in this. Mystification was by no means confined to the traditional groups. Those who did not know what the functions of the opposition were or who thought it had no function, were very few, but they included both chiefs and business men. The troublesome images are clearly reflected in some of the free responses: 'The opposition counters whatever the government proposes.' '[It] opposes even a good thing.'

Table 8.4: How Legislators See Function of Opposition: Ciskei Legislative Assembly Survey 1975

Function	Number Attributing Function	
	CNIP	CNP
Watchdog	22	14
To overthrow the government	2	—
To help the government	2	2
Do not know	3	1
Nothing	2	—

Ciskeian Political Parties

In the Mdantsane survey in 1976, questions were asked which indirectly probed people's attitudes towards political conflict and opposition. Table 8.5 shows that between 37 per cent and 40 per cent of respondents would not attend certain meetings, or join certain organisations, or talk to people about politics; 40 per cent would disapprove of friends or relatives joining a party other than the one they supported. Those reluctant to attend certain meetings said they would be deterred by meetings where violence might erupt, which were secret, or illegal, political, or Bantustan, or 'opposition'; 16 per cent of all respondents would not go to political-type meetings of one sort or another.

Table 8.5: Attitudes Towards Political Strife: Mdantsane Survey 1976

	Percentage of Respondents
Would not attend certain meetings	38
Felt free to attend any meetings	53
No response	8
Would not join certain organisations	40
Felt free to join any organisation	48
No response	11
Would not discuss politics with some people	37
Felt free to discuss politics with anyone	37
No response	25
Would not approve of friends joining a party other than own	40
Would approve of them joining any party	55
No response	6

Many respondents saw political parties as divisive. In response to the question 'Is there unity in the Ciskei?' 48 per cent responded that there was not, and 13 per cent attributed this lack of unity, on an open-ended response, to the existence of political parties (Table 8.6).

Table 8.6: Unity in the Ciskei: Mdantsane Survey 1976

	Percentage of Respondents
There is unity	32
There is no unity	48
No response	20

The survey of Legislative Assembly members gave evidence of sensitivity to criticism in another way. When asked which of the news media had the interests of the Ciskei at heart, only five members felt that the media identified as being critical of the Ciskei government were making a contribution to development. The majority felt that the 'reasonable' or the 'not critical' press was more interested in the Ciskei and more constructive. Most emphasised that criticism had to be constructive. D.W. Wilcox points out that there is tremendous pressure for 'constructive' or 'responsible' criticism. He maintains that this concept of constructive criticism is not just a political expedient:

> It has a basis in traditional African values. Although the Western world places high value on criticism of government officials as a criterion of press independence, the African framework is different. Most traditional African cultures have a high respect for authority, and it is considered disrespectful to challenge or gossip about ethnic, and now about national, leadership.[36]

It is possible then that the ephemeral nature of most opposition parties in African politics is due to cultural norms which are inimical to their existence, as well as to the fragility of national unity.

The move against the opposition did not remain merely at the level of threats. In the wake of the Mdantsane local elections in 1974 Mr Mtshizana, a lawyer, was banished from his home and practice to Herschel.[37] The position was exacerbated by the imposition of a ban on open-air gatherings imposed in September 1977. By the same Proclamation R252 it became an offence to organise a boycott of meetings called by chiefs, or to embarrass any officer of the Ciskei government.[38] This came in the wake of countrywide disturbances in urban areas.

It can thus be seen that there are a number of features in the Ciskei which are promoting the development of a one party dominant system:

> the strangeness of the concept of 'opposition', which is not institutionalised in traditional political structures;
> the importance of solidarity in African eyes at the level of family, clan and tribe;
> a natural sensitivity to criticism due to the insecurity of new rulers, working new institutions;
> the security legislation of the Republican government which has twice been used, once against the CNP when Mtshizana was

banished, and subsequently against the Black Peoples' Congress and the South African Students' Organisation when Steve Biko and many others were arrested, and the organisations themselves banned;

the marginal position of chiefs who shifted support to the ruling party, and the creation of new Xhosa chieftainships to swell support for the CNIP government (Table 8.7).

Tywakadi in his analysis points out that the opposition was not always knowledgeable about the rules of procedure in the Assembly. Furthermore it tended to be suspicious of the government's intentions, and to be driven to actions which could then be seen as 'troublesome', for instance in issuing press material on the No Confidence debate which had never in fact been used.[39]

However, in spite of all these quite formidable problems, and in spite of their tribal and traditional image, the opposition was alive and well in 1977, and reputedly gaining membership at the expense of the ruling party, where in-party conflict and fission had been endemic since the end of 1975.

8. L'Envoi

In June 1978 the second general election took place. It was presaged by a wave of detentions and arrests, both by the Republican Security police and the Ciskeian police. An opposition candidate and former chief whip of the CNIP, Mr A.Z. Lamani, was detained in Port Elizabeth.[40] The following day Mr L.F. Siyo went into hiding. He was an ex-Cabinet Minister and is still living in exile in the Transkei. Chief Burns Ncamashe, an opposition leader, stated that there was evidence of threats and intimidation aimed at opposition leaders. He called in vain for the postponement of the election.

Given the proclivity of people to support the existing government, and the climate of harassment and intimidation, the results of the election are not surprising. Chief Sebe's CNIP won every seat, with 13 opposition candidates losing their deposits. Twenty-one of the 22 seats had been contested. There was however, a low percentage poll, only 53 per cent. After the election Chief Sebe stated that his people had spoken clearly. 'They have effectively made the Ciskei into a one-party state.'[41]

Pre-election tactics had robbed the opposition of the support of all

Table 8.7: Party Representation: Ciskei Legislative Assembly 1973-1976

Party	1973		1974		1975		1976	
	Chiefs	Elected	Chiefs	Elected	Chiefs	Elected	Chiefs	Elected
CNIP	11	15	16	16	18	16	15	14
CNP	19	5	17	4	18	4	12	1

Source: Ciskei Legislative Assembly Debates. Representation during main session of the year.

but six of the Chiefs. When the Legislative Assembly reconvened there were only three left supporting the opposition, and they were denied the status of official opposition because they were not elected! Chief Ncamashe was thus unable to move the customary No Confidence motion.

The Ciskei is now a *de facto* one-party 'state'. And in the 1979 session there were resolutions tabled which presaged the initiation of a more formalised situation in which any opposition party would need to be licensed.[42] Bannings and detentions have continued well into 1979. By March this year there were said to be at least ten political detainees; 65 persons who had been involved in a bus boycott in Mdantsane in January were also held in detention.[43] It is a one-party 'state' with an authoritarian rather than a participatory emphasis, for as we have seen the party hardly exists as a channel of communication from people to rulers.

Notes

1. N. Charton, 'A Socio-Economic Survey of the Border and Ciskei Regions', unpublished report, Institute of Social and Economic Research, Rhodes University, Grahamstown, 1978.
2. D. Kotze, *African Politics in South Africa 1964-1974* (Hurst, London, 1975), pp. 136 and 138.
3. *Daily Dispatch*, October 1972.
4. Charton, 'A Socio-Economic Survey', p. 241.
5. *Daily Dispatch*, 17 October 1972.
6. W.J. Breytenbach, *Bantoetuislande: Verkiesings en Politieke Partye*, Mededelinge van die Afrika Instituut, no 23 (Africa Institute, Pretoria, 1974), p. 46. Translated from the Afrikaans.
7. G.R. kaTywakadi, 'The Development of the Political Party System in the Ciskei', unpublished dissertation, Rhodes University, Grahamstown, 1977, pp. 160ff.
8. Kotze, *African Politics*, B. Streek, 'All you Need to Know About Ciskei's Election' in *Daily Dispatch*, 19 August 1977.
9. *World*, 25 June 1975.
10. J. Mabandla, mimeographed statement, 24 April 1973.
11. Ciskei Legislative Assembly, Verbatim Debates, 1973.
12. R.W. Waxmonsky, 'Selected Characteristics of Bantus Employed by East London Industrial Firms', unpublished paper, Institute of Social and Economic Research, Rhodes University, Grahamstown, 1975, p. 35.
13. Tywakadi, 'The Development of the Political Party System', p. 144.
14. Ciskei Legislative Assembly, Verbatim Debates, 1975, p. 216.
15. N. Charton and G.R. kaTywakadi in Charton, 'A Socio-Economic Survey', pp. 264ff.
16. W.D. Hammond-Tooke, *The Tribes of King William's Town District*, Department of Native Affairs, Pretoria, 1958, p. 57.
17. Ciskei Legislative Assembly, Verbatim Debates, p. 18.

18. Charton and Twyakadi in Charton, 'A Socio-Economic Survey', p. 253.
19. T.J. Gordon, 'Mdantsane: City Satellite or Suburb', unpublished dissertation, Rhodes University, Grahamstown, 1977.
20. Streek, 'All you Need to Know About Ciskei's Election'
21. Ciskei Legislative Assembly, Verbatim Debates, 1976, p. 151.
22. Ciskei Legislative Assembly, Verbatim Debates, 1973, p. 40.
23. Ciskei Legislative Assembly, Verbatim Debates, 1973, p. 113.
24. Tywakadi, 'The Development of the Political Party System', p. 141.
25. *Daily Dispatch*, 7 June 1974.
26. Tywakadi, 'The Development of the Political Party System'.
27. Ciskei Legislative Assembly, Verbatim Debates, 1975, p. 45.
28. Ciskei Legislative Assembly, Verbatim Debates, 1972, p. 327.
29. Ciskei Legislative Assembly, Verbatim Debates, 1973, p. 20.
30. Ibid. p. 113.
31. Ciskei Legislative Assembly, Verbatim Debates, 1974, p. 473.
32. Ciskei Legislative Assembly, Verbatim Debates, 1975, p. 66.
33. Ibid.
34. D.E. Apter, 'Some Reflections on the Role of a Political Opposition in New Nations' in I. Markowitz, *African Politics and Society* (Free Press, New York, 1970).
35 Tywakadi, 'The Development of the Political Party System', p. 234.
36. D.W. Wilcox, *Mass Media in Black Africa: Philosophy and Control* (Praeger, New York, 1975), pp. 33-6.
37. *Daily Dispatch*, 31 December 1974.
38. *Guardian*, 1 October 1977.
39. Twyakadi, 'The Development of the Political Party System', p. 236.
40. *Sunday Tribune*, 11 June 1978.
41. *Evening Post*, 7 July 1978.
42. *To the Point*, 14 August 1978.
43. *Daily Dispatch*, 20 March 1979.

9 THE LEGISLATURE

Nancy Charton

1. The Functions of Legislatures

Traditionally the legislature has been seen as the law-making body. This overstates the matter in most modern polities, democratic or authoritarian. No legislature wholly dominates the law-making process: however, all are in some measure channels of communication between the rulers and the ruled.

Of course, legislatures were invented not merely to furnish chambers of debate and dialogue but, perhaps even more importantly, they were invented in order to control the actions and exactions of executives. 'When an American thinks about the problem of government-building, he directs himself not to the creation of authority and accumulation of power, but rather to the limitation of authority and the division of power'.[1] John Stuart Mill stresses that the proper function of the legislature is not that of governing,

> for which it is radically unfit, the proper office of a representative assembly is to watch and control the government; to throw the light of publicity on its acts; to compel a full exposition and justification of all of them which anyone considers questionable; to censure them if found condemnable; and, if the men who compose the government abuse their trust, or fulfil it in a manner which conflicts with the deliberate sense of the nation, to expel them from office, and either expressly or virtually appoint their successors.[2]

Debates are significant not only in respect of their policy outcomes; in a society where the radio and press exist, debates in the legislature, and issues highlighted there, are disseminated among the population; they make people politically aware. Many political scientists working in Africa have pointed to the important tutelary role of the legislature. R.F. Hopkins writes of the Bunge in Tanzania 'the M.P. who is not a member of government is above all else a communication link, a popularizer and legitimizer for the party and the government. He is not a law maker.'[3]

These legislative, controlling and tutelary functions will be examined

150 *The Legislature*

in the Ciskei Legislative Assembly in the pages which follow.

As a Law-Making Body

When examining the legislative record of the Ciskei Legislative Assembly it is obvious that law making is really a function of the executive. Bills are prepared by the public service, approved by the Cabinet and are not often heavily debated. Table 9.1 reveals that 15 bills out of 30 between 1973 and 1976 were contested in some respect. Table 9.2 shows most legislation was very rapidly dealt with. Two minor amendments were achieved, one at the instance of the opposition, and the other at the instance of the minister concerned. Not included in the record are several resolutions to amend the constitution. These resolutions go forward to the Republican government for the necessary amendment of the instrument. All such resolutions have been presented at special sessions of the legislature. They included such important matters as the creation of new chieftaincies, the amendment of the boundaries of the Ciskei owing to consolidation and excision, the appointment of cabinet ministers and their dismissal by the Chief Minister, the dissolution of the Assembly on request, the extension the period of absence allowable to the Chief Minister and the designation of electoral districts. Many of these resolutions were passionately contested by the opposition, to no avail. There was really no question of trying to achieve consensus on such important matters.

The appropriation bills have also been heavily debated. In the years under review no amendments have been achieved, but many informal questions have been raised, and grievances ventilated from the floor. The issues were both local and general, comment was both complimentary and critical. The Agricultural Development Bill, 1973 sparked off a long debate on consultation and Brown Swiss bulls, anathema to farmers largely because the previous administration had prescribed their use in stock improvement schemes. The Liquor Bill of the same year was challenged because it was said to create a monopoly, and one opposition amendment was carried. The Education Bill, 1974 was also heavily debated, the opposition challenging 14 clauses out of 38; however no challenges were pressed to a division. One minor amendment was proposed by the minister.

In 1975 the opposition challenged the Bill to amend the payment and privileges of members of the legislature. They were under a misapprehension about the loss of salary incurred for unauthorised absence from the sittings. When later in the same session they attempted to increase the rates of remuneration they were foiled by

The Legislature

Table 9.1: Legislation

Year	Act	Amendments	Comments
1973	Appropriation	Nil	Many issues raised in committee stage.
	Payment and privileges of Members of Legislative Assembly	"	Objections to proposed allowances as too low
	Recision of certain rates	"	No debate
	Agricultural development	"	Debate on Brown Swiss bulls and right to expropriate land
	Apprenticeship	"	No debate
	Ciskeian Liquor	1 clause Proposed by Opposition	Monopoly position of XDC attacked

There was debate on four out of six bills, and one was amended in deference to the wishes of the Opposition.

Year	Act	Amendments	Comments
1974	Education	1 clause Proposed by Minister	Fourteen out of 38 clauses were disputed, but divisions were not called
	Tribal Tax	Nil	No debate
	Public Service Amendment	"	" "
	Liquor Amendment	"	" "
	Additional Appropriation	"	" "
	Appropriation	"	Many issues raised in committee stage

There was debate on two out of six bills, and one minor amendment was proposed by a Minister.

Year	Act	Amendments	Comments
1975	Payment and Privileges of Members of Legislative Assembly: Amendment	Nil	Opposed because of a misapprehension which was clarified.
	Ciskei General Loans	"	Questions raised
	Liquor Amendment	"	Some debate on employment of experts to test beer and on opening times
	Appropriation	"	Many issues raised in committee stage
	Additional Appropriation	"	No debate
	Payment and Privileges of Members of Legislative Assembly: Amendment	"	Opposition attempted to increase scales

There was debate on four out of six bills, but no amendments were successful.

Table 9.1 Continued

Year	Act	Amendments	Comments
1976	Additional Appropriation	Nil	No debate
	Payment and Privilege of Members of Legislative Assembly	''	'' ''
	Appropriation	''	Many issues raised in committee stage
	Archives	''	CNUP failed to raise principle during second reading
	Public Service Amendment	''	No debate
	Forestry	''	Debate on expropriation and permits for hunting and fishing, naming of forests, immunity of Forester for injury caused. No point pressed to division.
	Nature Conservation Bill	Nil	Opposition wished to reduce obligatory penalty. Failed: procedural ineptitude.
	Marketing Board	''	Heavy debate on dangers of control
	Social Pensions	''	No debate
	Liquor Amendments	''	No debate
	Unauthorised Expenditure	''	No debate

There was debate on five out of eleven bills. None were amended.

Source: Office of the Chief Minister and CLA Debates: 1973 to 1976.

the fact that the budget had already been approved. In the same year they challenged the Liquor Amendment Bill with regard to employing white experts to assay Bantu beer, and the provision for opening times.

In 1976 Chief Ncamashe challenged the Archives Bill, but failed to do it at the right time. The opposition challenged the Forestry Bill with regard to procedures for expropriation, permits for fishing and hunting, and the immunity of government employees for damage to property; they also challenged on the issue of naming forests; but no points were pressed to a division. On the Nature Conservation Bill their amendment failed through procedural ineptitude. In the Marketing Bill

Table 9.2: Structure of Debates

Dates of Main Session	Nature of Legislative Activity	Days Utilised	Total
1975	Appropriation Bill	3	
19-27 May	Legislation (3 Bills)	1	
	Motions (10)	2	
	Questions and General, including election of and reports of sessional committees	1	7
1976	Appropriation Bill	9	
27 April-25 May	No Confidence debate	5	
	Legislation (8 bills)	2	
	Motions (13)	2	
	General Business, including formal questions, election of and reports from sessional committees	2	20

Source: CLA Debates: 1975 and 1976.

they clearly saw the dangers of control, but points were not pressed home.

Facility in debate, and ability to use and exploit the parliamentary procedure are clearly problems. Such facility can only come with experience, and competence has certainly grown between 1973 and 1976. However there was a more serious problem for the opposition in that when challenging technical legislation they did not have the necessary knowledge to challenge in detail. One member said in the budget debate on the Department of Health: 'In fact the department we are now dealing with is highly scientific and technical. That alone makes it too high to grasp for some of us.' The Ciskeian legislature is not the only one where the technical nature of modern law making puts the opposition at a disadvantage; the cabinet on the other hand can call upon the expertise of their officials. Language too may be a problem. Thus in 1972 a member requested a translation of the draft constitution into Xhosa.[4]

It is even more interesting, when examining the law-making function, to look at the nature of the issues raised in formal questions, motions, the No Confidence debate, and in legislation. It is possible from such an examination to diagnose non-issues, and to see which issues put into the parliamentary mill come out at the other end in the form of legislation, or appropriation of resources. Table 9.3 indicates that there are areas of heavy pressure: namely the chieftainship, the bureaucracy, agriculture, education and the legislature itself. In all these areas favourable results were achieved. New chieftaincies have been created, Africanisation of the bureaucracy has been rapid, salaries have been increased across the board for traditional elites, public servants, teachers and the members of the legislature; four acts passed have been concerned with agriculture, marketing, forestry and nature conservation. There has also been a comprehensive Education Act.

Table 9.3 (a): Issues Raised and Debated in Formal Questions

Issues	Year				
	1973	1974	1975	1976	Total
Local development plans	3	1	—	1	5
Tribal Authorities, chiefs and headmen	5	1	3	1	10
Roads and bridges	8	3	2	2	15
Agriculture, dams, boreholes	17	2	3	—	22
Nature Preservation	—	1	—	—	1
Land	8	—	—	1	9
Resettlement	3	2	1	—	6
Labour	1	1	—	1	3
Housing	5	1	—	3	9
Postal communications	—	—	—	1	1
Education	20	3 (2 local)	—	4	27
Taxation	1	—	—	1	2
Bureaucracy	6	2	6	1	15
Use of Government cars	—	—	1	—	1
Health	3	—	—	—	3
Commerce	2	—	—	—	2
Law	1	—	—	—	1
Withdrawn/Private answers/ unaccounted for (2)	11	—	—	—	11
Total	94	17	16	16	143

One area of heavy pressure has been land and resettlement. Results in this area have been frustrating and indifferent. Consolidation has been achieved at a price. Those opposed to resettlement have been asking for amelioration of conditions in such areas, or objecting to resettlement in principle. Table 9.4 shows how this type of expenditure, laid upon the Ciskei by Republican policies of influx control to the cities has increased by 571 per cent in the three years under review.

Table 9.3 (b): Issues raised in Motions before the House

Issues	Year				
	1973	1974	1975	1976	Total
Tribal Authority Affairs	–	1	–	2	3
Agriculture	–	1	–	–	1
Land	–	2	–	2	4
Resettlement	–	–	–	1	1
Labour and wages	–	2	–	–	2
Education	–	2	1	1	4
Taxation	–	–	–	1	1
Bureaucracy	–	1	1	1	3
Law	–	2	4	–	6
Planning and economic development	–	2	–	–	2
Housing and townships	–	1	1	–	2
Citizenship	–	–	–	1	1
CLA, composition, accommodation	–	2	2	2	6
Dangerous weapons	–	–	–	1	1
Capital site	–	–	–	1	1
Recreation rural areas	–	–	–	1	1
Total	0	16	10	13	39

Source: CLA Debates: 1973 to 1976.

Ciskeian income increased by R18,520,000 between 1973 and 1976; expenditure on resettlement increased by R4,500,000. More than a quarter of all its additional funds then went to an area of which most members of the Legislative Assembly, both government and opposition, gravely disapproved.

Some areas of heavy pressure, notably housing and roads and bridges, did not achieve any obvious legislative results, although allocations which cover these two areas did increase by 226 per cent. Only one act touched the problem of labour, the Apprenticeship Act; issues in regard to migrant labour, wages, job reservation and urban poverty come up moderately frequently.

It may be concluded that in spite of the representational deficiencies of the legislature, issues are being raised on behalf of urban workers and landless peasants. But the lack of competence of the legislature to achieve results for either is reflected in the limited or negative output either in terms of legislation or of financial resources.

Being a rubber stamp for the executive arm of government in the field of legislation has not inhibited debate and dialogue. The legislature did constitute a channel of communication between the people and the

Table 9.3 (c): Issues Raised During No Confidence Debate

1974 CLA Debates, vol. 2, 55 pages	1975 CLA Debates, vol 5, 66 pages	1976 CLA Debates, vol. 7, 156 pages
Issues		
Land	Land	Land
Chieftainship	Chieftainship Headmanship	Chieftainship
Corruption	Use of government vehicles	Use of government vehicles
Jobs for pals	Jobs for pals	Jobs for pals
Economic development	—	Border industries
Amalgamation with Transkei	—	Amalgamation with Transkei
	Tribalism	
	Wage gap	Job reservation
	Broken promises re provision of roads and water	
		Interference with local government, urban and rural
		Pay off to Government supporters
		Capital site
		Resettlement
		Education
		Zwelitsha

Source: CLA Debates: 1974 to 1976.

executive. This was particularly noticeable in matters of administrative detail, and in local issues. In both areas where we had observers, certain major local issues arose. In both cases these issues were discussed in the legislature, though they were not necessarily resolved.

As an Instrument of Control

The opposition has attempted to bring administrative and other abuses to the notice of the exectuive. There has been a gradual growth in the length and depth of the No Confidence debate; Table 9.5 reflects the improvement in the participation of opposition members, particularly in 1976. After initial struggles with parliamentary procedure, the members of the legislature showed greater ease and ability in using the system to their advantage although they still had much to learn in the actual legislative process. All members had a clear concept of their role. Appointed members had to speak always as delegates, rather than as representatives which could account for their greater freedom in formu-

The Legislature

Table 9.4: Public Expenditure

	1973/4	1974/5	1975/6	% Increase
		R1,000		
Land planning and conservation	356	838	1,266	151
Population settlement	955	2,583	5,455	571
Employment and income creation	1,265	1,765	2,077	61
Development of human potential	6,960	7,742	12,757	183
Provision of social services	2,758	3,535	5,309	192
Government planning and administration	1,477	1,773	2,662	180
Infrastructure creation	2,186	2,036	4,951	226
Total	15,957	20,272	34,477	216

Source: Benbo: *Black Development in South Africa*.

Table 9.5: Intervention in Debates

Year	Members' Status	0	1-5	6-10	11-15	16-20	21-25	26-30	31	Total
1973	Chiefs	12	8	6	1	—	—	—	2	29
	Commoners	—	1	2	1	3	2	1	4	14
1974	Chiefs	18	8	4	1	—	—	—	2	33
	Commoners	—	—	7	1	2	1	1	2	14
1975	Chiefs	24	5	2	—	1	—	—	2	34
	Commoners	2	4	1	3	1	—	—	3	14
1976	Chiefs	9	9	1	—	—	—	—	3	22
	Commoners	—	2	—	2	3	—	—	3	10

Note: Every intervention has been counted. The paramount chief was not counted for the years 1973 to 1975, but his personal representative was counted as a chief in his place. The chairman and cabinet members were excluded from the count.

Source: CLA Debates 1973 to 1976.

lating formal questions, or proposing motions; in general debate they tend to constitute the silent majority (Table 9.5). Elected members look 'in particular to the needs of the people' who elected them.[5] They are 'the servants of the people'.[6] 'The voters listen. They are judge; they are the people who sent the members to this House.'[7] They have a clear concept of their responsibility to those who elected them; they also see their role in an educational light: 'It is imperative that we go around and educate the people.'[8] When asked to name two important functions of government the cabinet members emphasised development, elected members emphasised development, welfare and satisfaction; appointed members emphasised peace, order and welfare, with development secondary.

In their challenges to proposed legislation the opposition showed itself to be very aware of the dangers of granting ministers and public servants too much power. But their ability to keep delegated power in check was minimal in the face of government insistence on the clauses in question.

The great weakness of the Legislative Assembly lay in its poorly developed committee system. In the four years under review the Sessional Committee on Accounts, on which both government and opposition have representatives, never reported anything of substance to the House. A complaint was made in 1976 that members of the opposition did not attend the meetings of this Committee satisfactorily. The opposition response indicated that notices always went out late.[9] Modern governments cannot be adequately watched and controlled in a desultory fashion from the floor of the House. Members need training and knowledge, and a committee structure which will allow them to acquire that knowledge, and to come face to face with executive members, both ministers and public servants. The control of delegated legislation and of the executive is not one of the strong points of the South African parliamentary system. Maybe the Ciskei needs to look further afield for more effective ways of institutionalising control of the bureaucracy and the executive.

As an Agent of Political Socialisation

Members of the legislature are aware of their role in this respect. Most elected members had addressed public meetings during the session in which they were interviewed (1975); most had received resolutions passed at public meetings. Almost half the elected members had addressed voluntary associations of some kind. All said they were easily accessible for interview by the public, and more than half of both elected and nominated members had conducted such interviews within the month of being interviewed. All cabinet members had been involved in this way; they had also all received deputations from farmers', teachers', traders', sports and other organisations, as had many of the ordinary members of the Assembly.

On the evaluation of the members of the Assembly, informal communications between them and their voters is good. However the Mdantsane survey attempted to test the relationship of people to their political institutions at a behavioural level by asking whether they had had a problem with the authorities in the past year; 50 said they had, 20 in connection with unemployment, 18 in connection with housing, others in connection with pensions (3), business licences (2), Post Office (2), citizenship and other sundry legal matters (5). They were then asked whom they had approached for help. The nature of the problems probably conditioned the response: 45 approached bureaucrats or state functionaries; one went to a lawyer; one did not go to anyone, and three only approached politicians, two saw town councillors, and one went to a member of the opposition. This would seem to indicate that the people of Mdantsane, conditioned by nearly a century of bureaucratic control, have not seen members of the Legislative Assembly as possible recourses in time of trouble; we also remarked in Chapter 8 on the ignorance of the village of Gobozana of the existence of such channels. One may reasonably conclude that much remains to be done to teach people about the new channels which have been created.

In fulfilling its tutelary role the Assembly is very dependant on the mass media. And the position in that regard is not altogether satisfactory, as is demonstrated in Chapter 10.

2. The Problems of New Legislatures

Men obey the commands of the state for various reasons: either they accept that it has an authority to command them or that it is acting in their interests, and they obey voluntarily; or they obey because they fear the sanction of force which it may bring to bear on dissenters. Institutions are said to be legitimate insofar as they command the consent of men. How do institutions become legitimate? Max Weber is one of the early sociologists who attempted to tease out the stuff on which consent is built. Modern writing on the subject has not progressed much, if at all, beyond the three ideal types which he built to explain why men obeyed the law. In the first instance, he identified traditional legitimacy. Tradition and history sanctify law and government. This type of legitimacy, he maintained, predominates in static, ascriptive societies, and it is often associated with the sanctity endowed by religious and mystical forces. In times of change and danger, charismatic authority is often encountered. This is exercised by a leader with personal courage and magnetism, who is recognised by the people as having a message of salvation relevant to their particular situation. There is a strong religious or other worldly element present both in the convictions held by the leader about the one and only true path to salvation, and in the commitment of his followers to the way he indicates. Finally Weber identified a rational legal form where legitimacy is based on law, experience, merit and achievement. In this type the element of rationality is predominant.[10]

These types of legitimacy are never found in isolation; all may be discerned in varying proportion in any polity. All are necessary in some measure; none is in itself sufficient. Emperor Haile Selassie of Ethiopia, King of Kings, Lion of Judah, was deposed at the very end of his long and eventful reign. All his traditional and religious legitimacy and considerable achievements could not save him from the wrath of certain disadvantaged groups in Ethiopian society. In many African states charismatic leadership has emerged, and endured, as in the case of Felix Houphouet Boigny and Julius Nyerere, to name only two. However, there are also many charismatic leaders who have met their political demise in coup or assassination. Kwameh Nkrumah, Osagyefo (Saviour), is perhaps the best known example in Africa. Identification with legal and rational norms has been equally fragile. In a reaction to racist and authoritarian colonial regimes, many new African states drew up constitutions incorporating bills of rights; yet these bills of rights have never commanded the commitment which the American one elicited. As at this moment none is operative. And the constitutions have evaporated like the morning dew when exposed to the heat of conflict over scarce resources.

Beside these important variables identified by Weber we may place one identified by the systems theorists, namely 'capability'. Thus Potholm maintains that political leaders use 'their regulative, extractive and distributive powers' to enhance identification with the political system, and to build support for it.[11] Marxists would argue that these powers are used only in the interests of the property-owning or controlling class.

Political institutions in new states normally lack the sanctity of history and tradition. In Africa particularly, these institutions have been grafted on, as it were, from the top down. There is a diversity of tradition, and little if any consensus with regard to religion, or norms and values in general. And new political systems are often notoriously short of capability. They have the capacity to raise expectations, both material and political, without the capacity to fulfil those expectations. It is no wonder that political institutions in new states have proved to be fragile.

What has the new legislature to do in order to acquire legitimacy? Time is all important. Legislatures need a long gestation period. Legis-

The Legislature

lators need to learn their trade; constituents need to learn how to manipulate and control the legislators; the institution must develop its own ethos in the crises and experiences to which it is subjected and ultimately legislators will conform to its ethos. New legislatures need time then to develop autonomy, power and influence. When the norms of representative government are sanctified by religious and moral values within the community, the legislature will be strengthened. When a political leader emerges who enhances the image of the legislature, the legitimacy of the leader will impart itself to the legislature. 'He legitimizes the state by ordaining obedience to its norms out of loyalty to his person.'[12] But such leaders must be seen to operate within the legislature itself, if it is to be legitimised.

Perhaps most important of all, a legislature needs to prove of practical value to significant groups in society. Men only invest themselves in an institution which gives them a return on their investment in cultural or material terms. In politics nothing succeeds like success. A legislature must prove to be an effective channel for the exercise of influence and power, at least for some dominant groups in society. If that is so, it will have drawing power. As other groups arise in society to contest the hegemony of the dominant groups, the legislature will become the focus of their endeavours. If it is sufficiently open, it will become the arena for the power struggle, and dominant group will succeed to dominant group. In western parliaments, the aristocrats yielded to the middle class. Finally, the working class entered the arena, making their demands effective in their turn. In this model of institutional development, there was adaptation and change and persistence. The combatants in the arena tended to change; the issues changed; but the institution remained, permitting change, yet moderating it. It was made possible by the openness of the legislature to newly emerging groups.

Surely this is the secret of institutionalisation which Huntington defines as 'the process by which organizations and procedures acquire value and stability'.[13] The following section explores the prospects for the institutionalisation of the Ciskei Legislative Assembly in these terms.

3. Factors which may limit the Institutionalisation of the Ciskeian Legislative Assembly

The Identity Crisis

All new nation states suffer from an identity crisis. 'The development of a clear and unambiguous sense of identity is more than a facilitating factor in the creation of a nation; it may be in some sense the major constituting factor.'[14] Most African nations are merely geographical expressions at their birth, whose people relate primarily to village, clan, tribe or region. To diversity of language, culture, and kinship group may be added the complications of socio-economic and educational stratification. While some relate to the village, the clan or the tribe, those who have enjoyed a western style education are seeking a 'national' identification. It is this group which normally spearheads the nationalist movement in a colonial state.

Ciskeian Africans have these problems in ample measure. There are many whose primary loyalty is to the tribe or clan, especially in the rural areas. In the socio-political survey of Mdantsane undertaken in 1976, 28 per cent of the 297 respondents said that tribalism was still important in Mdantsane (see Table 8.2a). When asked whether unity prevailed in the Ciskei nearly half (48 per cent) responded that it did not; and 22 per cent identified tribalism as the major disruptive factor (see Table 8.6). Even in the urban situation then tribalism is seen as being pervasive, and as being a factor in the political process. However, when asked to identify the most important group to which they belonged only 6 per cent opted for the tribe, as distinct from the Ciskei (37 per cent) and South Africa (44 per cent) (Table 8.2b). An open-ended question explored the reasons for their identification. Of the 140 respondents relating to South Africa no less than 113 (or 86 per cent) did so for essentially pragmatic reasons: because this would enable them to work anywhere in South Africa, or to settle anywhere; it would cause restrictions and the need for different citizenship certificates to be eliminated. A further nine (6 per cent of that particular group) felt that to be a South African would give them more rights, more money, more land or 'all I need'. Only nine identified for ideological reasons, namely: because 'I belong to South Africa', or 'South Africa belongs to all of us', or because 'all blacks desire this' (Table 8.2c).

A subsequent question asked whether respondents would prefer a united South Africa with black majority rule or the homeland system. Here again 45 per cent opted for a united South Africa, and only 28 per cent for the homeland system; 25 per cent refused to commit themselves (Table 8.2d). In this question reasons given for the identification with South Africa were ideological: 52 per cent of that group felt it would be more democratic, fairer, and that it would eliminate racialism and tribalism; a further 26 per cent felt that whites and blacks should share power and that ethnic groups should not be separated; 12 per cent said separate development was a failure.

Over 40 per cent of the Mdantsane respondents in 1976 then identified primarily with a united South Africa. To an extent, this confirms research done in 1971 in towns and cities of the Eastern Cape which found that:

> When people referred to their ideal model of society as they felt it ought to be, they generally did not speak of independent Bantustans, but of single South Africa, whole and undivided, with equal opportunities, where race and colour would not matter.[15]

This was the goal increasingly embraced by the opposition Ciskei National Party. Thus Chief J. Mabandla says of separate development, during the No Confidence debate in 1975:

> The horse they [the Ciskei National Independence Party] are riding, is a borrowed one from their fathers, the Nationalist Party. We have ours which has not been borrowed from any Baas. Your Policy is that of Separate Development and ours is non-racialism.[16]

This was the goal of the old African Nationalist movement during the first half of the century, a movement which, in many ways, was cradled in the Eastern Cape. The existence during the early part of this period of the non-racial Cape franchise, underscored the goal. One might say that the weight of tradition and history lie behind it to a far greater extent than behind a Ciskeian identity as such. The unitary, non-racial goal was also espoused by the Black Peoples' Convention and the South African Students' Organisation, the successors of the old liberation movements. Both were active in the Ciskei, especially among the young until banned in 1977. These movements also tended to emphasise the unity of Africans, Coloureds and Asians, the common denominator being the yoke of oppression which afflicts all alike.

The Ciskei then has an identity crisis which at the present time is much more difficult to resolve than in most other African territories. Not only is there a difference between rural and urban attitudes, but the urban people and the intelligentsia who normally head up the nationalist movement are divided in their loyalties, one group relating to the Ciskei and the homeland concept, and another, apparently larger, group relating to a united South Africa.

However, that is not the end of the story. Because the Ciskei and the Transkei share a common language and culture, there have been thoughts about amalgamation since the early years of this decade. This is obvious from Mabandla's election manifesto, which rejected it by implication.[17] However, these thoughts persisted particularly among the members of the opposition parties. 'You will notice that the people over the Kei, and those on this side, are one and the same people. The tribes here, and those on the other side are related to each other.'[18] Chief Burns-Ncamashe of the Ciskei National Unionist Party was also keen to see a linkage between the two territories. In 1976 Chief Mabandla proposed a motion in the Legislative Assembly supporting amalgamation, and he was enthusiastically seconded by Chief Ncamashe. Both however stressed that this issue must be decided by the people.[19]

However, Chief L Sebe stated his objections to amalgamation during the same session.

> I have often said that our people cannot eat flags or constitutions ... Now, I would ask you this, of what benefit would it be to the Ciskei to become part of an independent Transkei which even at this very time has completely inadequate financial resources to provide for the development of the area it presently administers? Is any benefit to be found in one destitute family joining another to sit down to an empty table?[20]

The governing party clearly had their eyes fixed on the Southern cornucopia — the Republican government, and on the material development of the Ciskei. Their reasoning is very much in line with that of the supporters of a united South Africa in the Mdantsane survey.

What do the people themselves think of this issue? In the Mdantsane survey respondents were asked whether they would approve or disapprove of the amalgamation between Ciskei and Transkei. More than half (57 per cent) said they would approve; 17 per cent disapproved, and 26 per cent were uncommitted (Table 8.2c). In probing for reasons 66 per cent of those in favour of amalgamation were thinking in terms of cultural identification: 'we are all Xhosa', or 'we speak the same language'. Only 30, or 18 per cent advanced reasons of material or political benefit. A further 10 per cent advanced ideological reasons: 'because we are all human beings', or 'we all belong to one South Africa', or 'blacks must unite', or 'this would end friction'. About half the dissenting group feared Transkeian dominance and resulting disunity: 'You can't have two bulls in one kraal'.

It is interesting in this regard to review the events which led to the handover of the Glen Grey and Herschel districts to the Transkei in

1976. In 1971 Glen Grey had voted by an overwhelming majority, 37,842 to 6,634, to stay with the Ciskei.[21] Despite this decision the area was ceded to the Transkei in 1976. Residents had the option of choosing to stay where they were, becoming Transkeians, or remaining Ciskeians by being resettled on newly appropriated compensatory land, at the expense of the Republican government, who paid compensation for the improvements they left behind. During the course of 1976 many thousands of Ciskeians availed themselves of the offer of alternative land in the Queenstown district, and the Ciskeian government was faced with a massive resettlement problem. This could be seen as voting with their feet. However, figures furnished by the Ciskeian Secretary for the Interior on 14 June 1977 reveal that a minority of registered voters had in fact left the two districts:

Table 9.6

Ciskeian Registered Voters Herschel and Glen Grey prior to 1976		Reregistered in Ciskei after resettlement up to 14 June 1977	
			%
Herschel	49.019	12,067	25
Glen Grey	86,188	15,432	18

Debate in the Legislative Assembly was prolonged and bitter, but it is apparent that only a minority of the people felt sufficiently threatened by the Transkeian take-over to actually walk out.

Both Chief Kaiser Matanzima and his brother Chief George have expressed themselves in favour of amalgamation and the press has often accused them of intervening in Ciskeian politics in order to bring it about.[22]

The acceptance of the Ciskei Legislative Assembly as a legitimate organ of government will obviously hinge to a considerable extent on how people define their boundaries. For those relating to the tribe, and to the homeland, it will more easily achieve legitimacy than for those relating to a united South Africa. The whole problem is further complicated by the legal issue of citizenship explored in Chapter 5.

The Issue of Power and Autonomy

It is important that the Ciskei Legislative Assembly is seen to have the power necessary to accomplish goals. At present it is a subordinate legislature, and many dissenters are inclined to total scepticism. 'It is fake story.' 'The whole thing is not genuine.' This view seemed common among people of all degrees of education, and of both rural and urban background.[23] This research was done prior to the Ciskei moving to self-government in 1972. However, it is an opinion sometimes shared by members of the Legislature when the Republican government forces through an unpopular policy, such as the excision of Glen Grey and Herschel. The Chief Minister, speaking in response to criticisms of the process of resettlement as a result of the exodus from the two districts, cried out: 'The problem in Herschel cannot be blamed on the governing party ... Black men should say evil is evil and not put this at the doorsteps of my government.' He maintained that the Republican government had failed to carry out their promise to move people, relocate them and maintain them in the interim period. He saw clearly the political implication which such actions could hold for his government, and talked darkly about sowing seeds of distrust in the leaders of the people and 'trying to get rid of a government that works for the needs of the people'.[24]

In theory the homeland political institutions have been designed to articulate the interest of both those resident in the homelands and in the so-called white areas of South Africa. In 1970 there were 411,300 Ciskeian Xhosas in the 'white' areas compared with 525,200 in the homeland itself. Thus 44 per cent of the *de jure* population reside outside the homeland.[25] Urban dwellers have the right to elect members of the Legislative Assembly, but their influence is dissipated by blending them into their constituencies of origin. Thus the citizens of Soweto cannot really get together and demand action on their behalf from any particular candidate or slate of candidates. They will in all probability be voting for candidates across the board in all the constituencies of the Ciskei. Members of the Legislative Assembly complain about the difficulties of even contacting such voters.

> I could even say my area is as big as the whole Republic of South Africa. Hundreds of my voters reside in the Western Cape. If I have to perform these duties well I must visit these people in Cape Town twice a year, at my own expense. I must also visit Johannesburg ... I have to finance all this personally.[26]

During 1975 the chief minister reported to the Assembly on an interview with the Prime Minister of the Republic, attended by all the homeland leaders. Issues raised were the need for home ownership schemes in 'white' areas, trading rights, the medium of instruction in schools, and ethnic grouping.[27] From this meeting flowed the acceptance by the Republican government of the right to home ownership in certain urban areas. But the white government often reacts tardily and with an ill-grace to such representations. It is interesting to note that the thorny problem of medium of instruction in schools was raised at this meeting, and ignored. It later became one of the contributory causes of the explosion among school children in 1976 in Soweto. Since the early years of this decade the Ciskei government has been resisting the plan to move 40,000 Africans from Grahamstown. The plan for resettlement in the Ciskei was stalled, in deference to their wishes; but the Department of Bantu Administration and Development promptly bought additional land in the close vicinity, and plans to go ahead with a resettlement scheme of its own.

Clearly the Ciskei government does not have the political muscle to move the Republican government on behalf of its absentee urban citizens. It is not surprising that urban blacks have little confidence in homeland governments. When the Mdantsane sample was asked whether the Ciskei government coud improve the situation of urban blacks in the white areas, only 15 per cent responded in the affirmative; 25 per cent felt they could do nothing, and 57 per cent did not know or did not respond (Table 9.7). As reasons for the lack of confidence they

Table 9.7: Can the Ciskei Government Improve the Situation of the Urban Blacks?

	%
Yes	15
No	28
No Response	57

Source: Mdantsane Survey 1976.

stated that the Ciskei government had no power, was not interested in the urban black, or did not understand his problems. When a government lacks any real 'capability' with regard to 44 per cent of its citizens it will obviously be faced with difficulty in making itself legitimate to them, and perhaps to others resident in the homeland itself, who commute back and forth as migrant labourers, and are conversant with the problems of those living in 'white' areas.

The Issue of Economic Dependence

Ciskeians are men of several political worlds, the world of tribe and clan, of language group and region, of South Africa, of white cities and black rural areas; there is also the world of the black oppressed. They are in addition men of two worlds in an economic sense. All African countries, consequent on their colonial contact with the West, have suffered a revolution of rising expectations. South Africa has been no exception to this rule. Where black and white have lived in close contact for nearly two centuries, this revolution has been fuelled to an even greater extent than in the rest of Africa. In 1975 it was estimated that approximately 137,000 Africans lived in the towns of the Ciskei encircling East London and King William's Town, namely Mdantsane, Zwelitsha and Dimbaza.[28] The affluent white society is the shop window and the standard setter in such a situation. As consumers, Ciskeians have been incorporated into an affluent cash economy.

> We are black people and we are Ciskeians who also want to possess things which are owned by the white community. We would like to own furniture shops, general dealers, and proper supermarkets. We want garages, hotels and many other properties which are agencies of development.[29]

The Mdantsane survey revealed that the essentially middle-class aspirations of all economic groups are rising. Thus 45 per cent felt that their family would be economically better off in five years' time, 41 per cent expected to remain the same, and only 13 per cent thought they would be worse off (Table 9.8a). These rising expectations are reflected in answers to other more concrete questions. When asked what their highest ambition had been 78 per cent stated they had had aspirations to middle-class occupations, 53 per cent opting for nursing or teaching and only 11 per cent for the higher professions such as law and medicine (Table 9.8b). Educational ambitions matched the professional ones; 62 per cent had aimed at a Junior Certificate or a Senior Certificate, and 22 per cent at a degree. Only 3 per cent had achieved their ambition, and the vast majority felt they had been prevented from achieving it by poverty. Asked to state what kind of a job they would like their children to have only 3 per cent mentioned skilled trades, and 1 per cent factory or semi-skilled work; 5 per cent said it would depend on the child, or did not respond; 90 per cent now aspired to middle-class occupations for their children, and no less than 28 per cent to the higher professions. Educational aspirations have also risen; 90 per cent now aimed at the Junior Certificate or higher, and no less than 41 per cent wanted their children to obtain a degree.

When asked whether they thought there were other people who lived

Table 9.8 (a): Economic Expectations

	Position of family today, compared to 5 years ago	5 years hence
	%	%
Better off	30	45
The same	32	41
Worse off	37	13
No response	2	2

Table 9.8 (b): Highest Ambitions

Occupational	For self	For children
	%	%
Teacher/nurse	53	51
Law/engineering/architecture	11	28
Clerical/civil servant	8	7
Minister of religion/social worker	4	3
Business man	2	1
Farmer	1	1
Skilled/semi-skilled artisan	9	3
Domestic servant	1	
Nothing/depends on child	10	5
Factory worker		1
Educational		
	%	%
Post-matriculation	22	43
Matriculation	24	37
Form 4	1	1
Junior certificate	37	9
Form 2	1	
Form 1/Std 6	2	1
None/highest possible/do not know/ No response	12	9

noticeably better than they did themselves, 90 per cent agreed that this was so, and 66 per cent disapproved of the situation (Table 9.8d). When asked what sort of people lived better than they did, they mentioned business people, educated people, professionals, property owners, important or rich people (76 per cent). Only 9 per cent responded racially, indicating white people (Table 9.8c).

The concern of the residents of Mdantsane with their low socio-economic status is revealed in many questions. Thus 40 per cent saw poverty as the most important obstacle to their advancement (Table

Table 9.8 (c): Relative Deprivation

Do you think there are other people who live better than you?

	%
Yes	90
No	4
No response	5

What sort of people are they?

	%
Business men, educated people, professional people, property owners, important people, rich people	76
Political leaders	1
Whole families, small families, healthy people, those employed, those with houses	7
Whites	9
No response	5

Table 9.8 (d): Relative Deprivation (continued)

Do you approve or disapprove of people living better than you?

	%
Approve	26
Disapprove	66
No response	8

Table 9.8 (e): Blocked Aspirations

Why did you not achieve your highest ambition?

	%
Poverty	83
Domestic problems	4
Lack of educational opportunities	4
Lack of motivation	6
Ill health	2
Bad company	1

9.8e). Only 3 per cent felt there were no obstacles in their way. When asked what made people happy and content with life 84 per cent of the replies focused on socio-economic factors, mainly money (30 per cent), occupation (7 per cent), land (5 per cent) and house and furniture (22 per cent); only 5 per cent of the replies concerned political factors, and 6 per cent personal factors such as family, religion and personality (Table 9.9a). The most important problem in the family was identified as lack of money by 72 per cent. Asked to identify the biggest problem of the black people, 73 per cent mentioned lack of money, employ-

The Legislature

Table 9.9 (a): What Makes People Happy and Content?

	%	
Money, good wages	30	
A good job	7	
House and/or furniture	22	
Education	9	
To own land	5	
To have a car	5	
To own stock	3	
To be healthy	2	
To have good food	1	Socio-economic factors 84%
Good relations with community	1	Social factors
Freedom, rights, good government, security	5	Political factors
Family	5	Personal/psychological factors
Religion	1	
No response	3	

Table 9.9 (b): What is the Most Important Problem in Your Family?

	%
Lack of money	72
Lack of housing	8
Lack of employment	2
Separation of family	2
Ill health, family disunity	2
Family too large	2
Lack of pension	1
No response	10
No problem	1

Table 9.9 (c): What is the Biggest Problem of the Black People?

	%
Lack of money, employment, stock, land	73
Too many restrictions, lack of rights, work too hard, are ill treated	12
Lack of housing, transport, education	3
Lack of unity, self-control, compassion, initiative and leadership	7
No problems	4
No response	0

Table 9.9 (d): How Would You Spend R10,000?

	%
Invest in: land/house/farm	29
education	16
bank/stocks/shares/insurance	20
business	9
agricultural implements/stock	4
Buy household goods	4
Buy durable consumer goods	13
Give to others	2
No response	3

ment, stock or land; 12 per cent concerned the lack of civil rights, restrictions, ill treatment and hard work. Only 3 per cent mentioned lack of amenities (Table 9.9c).

The desire for economic security came out clearly too in replies to the question: 'How would you spend R10,000?' Respondents indicated that they would invest it in land or a house (29 per cent), in education (16 per cent), in the bank or stocks and shares (20 per cent), in a business (9 per cent), in agricultural implements or stock (4 per cent). Only 4 per cent wanted to buy consumer goods, and 13 per cent indicated that they would buy durable consumer goods (Table 9.9d).

The Mdantsane survey demonstrated that people are concerned about and frustrated by low economic status, that they take note of inequalities in the economic system and do not approve of them. Most interesting finding in this respect was that the sense of relative deprivation had a class rather than a racial connotation. Finally the replies demonstrated the middle-class aspirations of the vast majority, and showed that they appeared to be rising. Mr E.D. Nkontso spoke for all Ciskeians when he said: 'All it is is grief and nothing else. It is South African grief. It is grief for all Ciskeians to have no money.'[30] Unfortunately the Ciskeian government has no control over the economic system which has to fulfil such expectations. 'Like the weather, it is there, to be suffered or enjoyed as the wind blows hot or cold.'[31]

In many ways the Republican government has been helpful. The gross fixed investment in the Ciskei by the public sector has risen from R559,000 in 1960/1 to R10,503,000 in 1973/4.[32] The Republican subsidy has risen from R7,709,000 in 1970/1 to R27,352,000 in 1975/6, constituting 79.3 per cent of Ciskeian revenue,[33] which was severely pruned by the Republican government, causing much bitterness. 'Eleven million rand is all that the Ciskei needs this year to make the difference between marking time and advancing. Eleven million rand is less than one-thirtieth of the increase in the South African defence spending'.[34] It was reported that ministers had flown to Pretoria to put their case. 'However, the whites there took very little notice of what we said to them.'[35]

In 1973 the Chief Minister had promised to improve the situation of various interest groups, for instance of chiefs and headmen, public servants, medical personnel, farmers and workers. Wherever it has been possible for them to take the initiative the Ciskeian government has honoured those promises. Africanisation has proceeded apace in the bureaucracy; salaries and pensions have been improved across the board; agricultural development has been offered to farmers in various ways. Loans and training have been provided for business men. The claims of all these groups, to at least a limited extent, have been met; to use Potholm's phrase, the government has utilised 'their regulative, extractive and distributive powers' to enhance identification with the political system and to build support for it.

Unhappily for the Ciskei government, their domain does not extend to the private sector of the South African economy, which is responsible for the payment of wages to many thousands of labourers in the white industrial area of East London and in the border industries surrounding King William's Town. Every year 7,970 additional labourers come onto the job market, of whom only 37.4 per cent can be employed in the homeland itself, and 81.3 per cent in and near the homeland. This means that each year an additional 1,489 migrant workers must leave the Ciskei in order to supplement their incomes.[36] The problem was clearly stated by the Hon. Chief L. L. Sebe in 1971: 'This issue (of employment) goes beyond the purview of my Department and stretches out to the social and economic structure of a nation . . . No public service can absorb all its educated people.'[37]

In order to create employment opportununities the Ciskei government must attract industries, and in this they compete with all the other homelands. Low wages are an incentive to industries; so is the absence of recognised trade unions. The government is therefore caught in a bind. If they use what influence they have to push for higher wages and trade unions, they perhaps discourage more industry from coming to the Ciskei; if they do not, if they use their influence to persuade angry workers back to work without having received satisfaction they will be seen as 'sell-outs', as aiding and abetting white capitalists in their exploitation of the black worker. During 1974, and again 1976, the chief minister was called in to negotiate wage settlements for striking workers in the East London area.

The encapsulating white economic system thus both stimulates the aspirations of workers and frustrates them. The Chief Minister is by no means unsympathetic to their cause. He sees as the goal of his government a civilised, decent standard of living for all from wages and conditions of work which ensure that the workers will not be unjustly exploited. 'To summarise, the Government does what experience teaches is possible, and what the needs require.'[38] In this situation politics is indeed the art of the possible. And very little is possible. It comes nowhere near what the needs require. This restricts the ability of the legislature to build support for itself amongst the urban workers, who already comprise approximately 23 per cent of the Ciskeian *de facto* population.[39] This is not to postulate that the government would indeed attempt to build that kind of support, even if it had the opportunity. Even the socialist regimes in Africa have seriously neglected the building of worker and peasant support, preferring instead to build up the bureaucratic middle class, which led the nationalist revolutions of the 1960s.[40] However, it is important to note that one option is closed to the legislature in building itself a future. It is forced to be a forum for mainly 'middle-class' and bureaucratic interests.

Additional economic strain has been created because of the natural increase of the population, from 245,000 in 1936 to an estimated 602,000 in 1976.[41] The land to accommodate them has not increased; agricultural methods have not changed and productivity has maybe declined. Industrial development aimed at absorbing the unemployed is a development of the last decade: it is recent and only marginally effective. The natural increase has been augmented by those seeking resettlement in the Ciskei. Chief Jongilanga complained in the Legislative Assembly that the government was continually incurring heavy expenses as a result of people pouring into the Ciskei because they were endorsed out of places like the Karroo and the Eastern Cape and the Free State.[42] In addition many labourers displaced from white farms had come seeking land and employment in their homeland. This is the situation described at Nyaniso. Townships such as Sada and Dimbaza have been constructed to absorb such settlers. The consolidation of the Ciskei, with the consequent excision of Glen Grey and Herschel, faced the Ciskeian government with the problem of resettling 27,499 registered voters and their families in the Swart Kei area. The Republican government bears the immediate costs, but the all important problem of land scarcity and the nonavailability of employment remains unresolved. Nonviable settlements such as these must remain a drain on the slender resources of the Ciskei.

This very brief survey of the economic competence of the Ciskei government has revealed all too clearly how vulnerable the Legislative Assembly might be to pressure from the Republican government, which supplies 79 per cent of the annual expenditure. It reveals too its inability to build support among those working in South African commerce and industry, as most of its citizens do, even among those actually resident in the homeland.

The Issue of the Land

Both Sebe's and Mabandla's election manifestos in 1973 mentioned as goals the acquisition of more land for the Ciskei, and a fair and just programme of land consolidation. The extent of landlessness is considerable. In 1974 figures were quoted in the Legislative Assembly for the district of Herschel, since ceded to the Transkei, which indicated that 85.5 per cent of the population there were landless.[43] In the same year the Member for Peddie stated that between 60 and 70 per cent of the people in the homeland receive only plots, and have neither arable lands nor grazing rights.[44] Many members in the Assembly press the plight of the landless.

The provision of additional land was a point of disaffection from and criticism of the Republican government on the part of both governing party and erstwhile opposition. In 1975 Mr Sangotsha (CNP) claimed that the Ciskei stretched from the Great Fish to the Great Kei rivers.[45] Chief A. Maqoma (CNIP) claimed territory as far south as Mossel Bay.[46] As far as the Republican government is concerned these remain idle claims. The Ciskei is now one consolidated territory — achieved at the cost of excision of the two districts discussed earlier. It gained some five new farms in very good agricultural areas, and there is a promise of more. But not even the promises meet the claims being advanced in the Assembly for white occupied areas; nor will the promised land assure each rural dweller of a 10 morgen plot. There is not enough white land to meet such claims.

Thus the Ciskei government cannot in the nature of things force a 'fair and just' programme of land acquisition, and will remain unable to satisfy the claims of its impoverished citizens in this respect. Its lack of capability must be a constant cause of disaffection and alienation among the landless poor.

The Communication Problem

All important in the process of government is the communication of information. This is particularly true of a representative parliamentary system, where the decisions are made in a place distant from the people, by representatives who are in theory responsible to the people. The process of communication is even more important where institutions are new and fragile. Much of the communication in such a situation will take the form of political socialisation. It will be educative not only as to issues, but also as to modes of procedure, or the rules of the game.

The Ciskei government's communications system is partially dominated by the white press and the Republican government. It is difficult to conceive of the government being able to embark on a programme of political socialisation such as has been initiated in countries like Tanzania and Zambia. Such programmes of course have grave disadvantages according to liberal democratic theory. However, a whole set of new institutions thrust upon a people from without, and largely foreign to their own political culture and tradition, needs some such mediation. Even the educational system, almost equally important in the process of political socialisation, is not wholly under the control of the Ciskei. Syllabi in schools will tend to be influenced by the national examinations still conducted for all South Africa by the Bantu Education Department. And Fort Hare, the Xhosa-language university at Alice, is controlled by the Republican government and the Department of Bantu Education.

Problems of identity, of capability, in the sense of being unable to deliver economic goods and services particularly to certain groups in Ciskeian society, and of communication and political socialisation will certainly tend to limit the institutionalisation of the Ciskeian Legislative Assembly. These constraints are outside the control of the legislature itself. There are also internal constraints, chief among which is the structure of the legislature.

Structure of the Ciskei Legislative Assembly

In the original constitution of 1973 no less than 30 out of 50 members of the Assembly were traditional chiefs. Their numbers were increased to 33 in 1974, and to 36 in 1975; the excision of two districts in the same year reduced the number to 28, and the number of elected members to 15.

Today there are 33 official and 22 elected members. Chieftainship then is the pivotal institution in the homeland constitutional structure. The chief is a salaried officer of the Ciskeian government, approved after consultation with his tribe. The salary is small but he is also a member of the Legislative Assembly; the emolument he receives there lifts him far above the economic status of the normal rural inhabitant.

The chief fulfils a triple political role. Within his own council he is the mouthpiece of his people, bound by their customs and traditions, and by the old rule of consensus; there he acts as legislator at a local level, and with regard to district and tribal affairs. He is also an administrator, subordinate to the district official of the Ciskei government — the Bantu Affairs Commissioner — and responsible to him for the administration of a plethora of legislation emanating from either the Republic government or the Ciskei government. Here he is constrained by the bureaucratic rules and regulations governing his office, and by the fact that he is a salaried official of government, appointed by and responsible to them. He is also a judicial officer trying local cases according to African customary law. Now he also finds himself acting as legislator in a larger sphere, in the Ciskeian Legislative Assembly, constrained not only by the rules of that Assembly, but by the pressures and counter pressures of the party political game. How has this triple role reflected on the legitimacy of the chieftainship; and how does that in turn affect the legitimacy of the legislature?

The political culture of a group handed down from generation to generation in religious formulations, in myth and story of the past, is slow to amend and change. It will determine both the expectations of the people with regard to their chief and his own perception of his role. Among the Xhosa tribes, before their contact with the dominant white system, a hereditary chief exercised legislative, executive and judicial power. The chief was ideally not an authoritarian ruler; he merely articulated a consensus formulated by a group of councillors truly representative of all the people. 'Everything I say here has come from my people.'[47]

If this ideal type of a Xhosa political system is correct one would expect to find an immediate problem in the process of centralisation which drew historically disparate tribal units into intensified relationship with one another, and with a central colonial authority. Arbitrary decisions were made by the white government and handed down through the white magistrate to the chief or to his headman. Initially the latter was in a conflict situation because the bureaucratic district system was based on a geographical administrative grid and not a tribal one.[48] This had the effect of preserving the prestige and legitimacy of the chief to some extent. Now the tribal base has been restored the chief has become the man in the middle for good or for ill. He and the headman, however, are still subject to the consensual expectations of their people, which their subordinate position in the political hierarchy often leaves them powerless to fulfil.

Any supra-tribal body will disturb the delicate checks and balances inherent in the old tribal structure, first of all by passing down unpopular decisions which are not consensually legitimated, and in the second place by granting the chief the positional authority to enforce these decisions. He is no longer a 'chief for the people'. He becomes a mere mediator or broker between the central authority and the local people. Also his people are no longer free to move away and set up clientship with another chief which was once the ultimate popular sanction on the power of an unpopular ruler.

> These people have a right to choose where they would like to be ruled over because to be subject of a chief, signifies freedom. Nobody can be forced to be under a particular chief. Such is the position in our Bantu Law.[49]

In a situation of land hunger, poverty and overpopulation, the scope for such freedom is very limited indeed.

Party politics has introduced new stresses into the situation. The electoral failure of the Mabandla group in 1973 is in itself very interesting. After twelve years of 'chiefly' rule during the period of the Ciskeian Territorial Authority the party of the establishment failed to win a mandate from the people. In Hewu for instance, the verdict of the people was for the Sebe group. The chief supported the Mabandla group. The same divergence of opinion was reflected in results at Keiskammahoek, Zwelitsha, Middledrift, Peddie, Victoria East, Glen Grey and Herschel and at Mdantsane. If the chiefs of these areas still had local legitimacy it is obvious that their people did not follow their political party lead. Elections are modern, and no part of tradition or custom; maybe tribesmen will accept a chief's ruling in the *inkundla* and *imbizo*; but political party leadership would appear to be governed by principles of achieved rather than ascribed legitimacy. There is, of course, a segment of votes drawn from the urban areas in 'white' South Africa. This vote may well be anti-chief and anti-traditional. However, it is reputed to be small.[50] An analysis of the election results in 1973 and 1975 must at least raise as a working hypothesis the fact that the chiefly group lacked election appeal, even in some rural areas, and this being so, it must also throw doubt on their legitimacy as modern-style legislators and on their efficacy in a parliamentary system.

Another interesting aspect related to party politics is that the chieftainship has become in some senses a political commodity of material and strategic value both to individuals and to parties. The office carries with it a small salary; all chiefs are now automatically incorporated into the Assembly, where they draw, in addition, the same salary as ordinary members. But more important to the individual than the financial aspect is the 'political security' which such an appointment offers. Lester G. Seligman, in an interesting article on political risk in non-western countries, remarks that 'the consequences of electoral defeat and other ways of losing political office are more threatening and hazardous than in Western democracies'.[51] Frequently, in developing countries, the defeated legislator does not have a private occupation to which he can return, due to the rudimentary development of the private sector. The chieftainship in this climate of uncertainty becomes a hedge against the possibility of failure in politics. This may well explain the willingness of individuals to offer themselves as candidates for office. There has been no shortage of such candidates in past years.

The structure of the Assembly makes the chieftaincies of prime importance to contending parties, a fact which both were quick to appreciate after the election of 1973. It is not surprising that of the new chieftaincies created to date, only one is not an adherent of the ruling party, and he was in fact a Ciskei National Independence Party cabinet minister when the post was approved.

A party political role for chiefs is in conflict not only with the old tradition of consensus and tribal unanimity; it conflicts also with their role as administrator.

In 1975 opposition chiefs were accused of disloyalty to the government. On the basis of this accusation, an attempt was made to separate them from the opposition, an attempt which was to succeed in 1978 before the second general election as has been shown in the preceding chapter.

It may be concluded that the triple role of the chief puts him under considerable strain, and may well be seriously undermining his legitimacy with his people. Who can tell whether the constitutional orientation towards the traditional elite will be a political asset or a political liability; Kotze remarks on the deterioration of chiefs' relationships with their people, and its consequences: 'This deterioration tends to strengthen the chiefs' support for ruling parties upon which they are increasingly dependent. Their ability to return favours bestowed by the party with increasing recruitment for the party diminishes correspondingly.'[52] If one of the objects of incorporating the chief into the legislative process was to legitimate the Assembly, it is doubtful whether this will be achieved. The very incorporation undermines his own traditional legitimacy to a considerable extent; it may also undermine the legitimacy of the Assembly.

The socio-economic status of the elected members of the Assembly is also important, when considering the structure of the legislature and its possible effect on institutionalisation. In 1975 18 out of the 20 elected members were interviewed: nine were business men, three were pensioners, and one was a farmer. Among the six cabinet ministers, all commoners at that stage, two had been in education, there was one business man, and three were farmers. There is an interesting bias towards commerce, and there are probably good reasons for this. The salary of a member of the Assembly was lower than that for a school principal, a highly placed public servant, or a university lecturer; furthermore there is a high risk involved in laying down a profession with pension rights for a political career. Business men do not have to dispose of their businesses, nor do the higher professionals, for example, doctors and lawyers. None of the latter were represented in 1975, which may indicate their alienation from the concept of homeland government, and an unwillingness to participate in it. Whatever the reasons may be it is worthy of note that certain groups are underrepresented, namely the peasant farmers, or not represented at all, namely the working class in the urban areas, and the higher professionals. This could affect the nature of the issues raised by the elected personnel, and it could restrict the interests which are articulated by the Assembly. In the long term this will reflect adversely on its legitimacy with the groups not represented. The emergence of a one-party system could mean that the legislature will not be open to the entry of new groups into politics. It will be denied the opportunity of being arena of conflict, which could in the long run promote institutionalisation.

4. Conclusions

When we come to consider the potentiality of this legislature for wielding popular as opposed to legal authority we have noted that there are certain intrinsic difficulties. History and tradition have perhaps been on the side of a unitary concept of South Africa; there has been an African nationalist drive for participation in the central government, which controls the major economic resources. The system of local councils in the Ciskei established in the nineteenth century always languished and was not seen as a worthy goal by the newly emerged western educated elite. The traditional institution of the chieftainship, the foundation-stone of the Assembly, has suffered in the past from its incorporation in a wider political framework; there is much evidence that the erosion of the chiefs' authority is continuing in the present dispensation.

Legislatures can be seen as formulating consensus, and African society was built on that. But there is a problem, the problem of boundaries. For the consensus of traditional African society was the consensus of the small group, where each citizen could participate directly. This new set of institutions cannot be said to be sanctified by religious and moral norms within the African community.

Although the institution of the legislature has resulted in the emergence of competent political leadership, charismatic leadership is absent. Such charismatic leaders as have emerged in South Africa have had a commitment to a unitary system. The present chief minister enjoyed more support than any other leader in Mdantsane, at the time of the survey; but press presentation does not really associate the legislature with him, or with his achievements for his people. Finally we have noted that the capability of the legislature is crippled by its incorporation into the wider socio-economic system of the Republic over which it has no control, and little influence, and for whose sins of omission and commission it often has to accept the blame. It is deficient both at the level of power in that it cannot force favourable decisions from the Republican government, and at the level of 'pay off' in that it has not enough economic capacity to keep all groups moving towards the realisation of their economic aspirations which have been set by the encapsulating white society.

What empirical evidence is there of the people's relationship to the legislature? In the Mdantsane survey 75 per cent of the respondents knew that the CNIP was the governing party, the remaining 25 per cent did not know which party provided the government. When asked 'Who do you consider to be the best African leader in South Africa?', Chief L.L. Sebe was nominated by 25 per cent; Chief K.D. Matanzima by 19 per cent, although only 14 per cent of respondents were Transkeians; he obviously has his local supporters. Chief Gatsha Buthelezi was nominated by 10 per cent of respondents. Only 6 per cent nominated African nationalists of the 1950s and 1960s, namely Robert Sobukwe, Nelson Mandela and others. However 32 per cent did not respond or did not consider any present-day leader worthy of nomination. It is obvious that homeland leaders enjoy only a modicum of support in Mdantsane (Table 9.10).

Table 9.10: Who is the best leader in South Africa today?

	%	
Chief L.L. Sebe	25	
K.D. Matanzima	19	
G. Buthelezi	10	
Other	14	(6 per cent nominated Sobukwe,
None	16	Mandela or Luthuli)
Do not know	16	

When asked to mention two good things the Ciskeian government had done, 21 per cent mentioned economic activities, such as bringing industry to the Ciskei, opening up opportunities, increasing wages and salaries and improving working conditions, facilitating the opening of new businesses and the removal of restrictions on trade. Another 12 per cent mentioned improvements in the field of health and welfare, for example, increased old-age pensions, reduced hospital fees, provision of houses and clinics, and a grand new hospital. Educational improvements were mentioned by 5 per cent. However, 30 per cent maintained that the government had done nothing, and a further 23 per cent did not respond to the question (Table 9.11). Once more the responses to these questions indicate a modicum of support for the Ciskeian government. Nearly one-half had positive thoughts about its achievements but one-third remained negatively oriented, and a quarter failed to respond to the question which may indicate either alienation or apathy.

Table 9.11: Two Good Things the Ciskei has Done

	%
Economic development	21
Health and welfare improvement	12
Education improvement	5
Transport improvement	4
Some restrictions eased	1
General	4
Nothing	30
No Response	23

Tax evasion also provides some evidence of alienation from the political system. In 1974 outstanding taxes for the decade 1963 to

1973 were said to be R26,062,702.[53] Of course this was before the time of the Ciskeian Legislative Assembly. But evidence from the 1976 debates suggests that it is a continuing problem, particularly in opposition areas.[54]

Empirical evidence then shows that in a comparatively short period the Ciskeian government has managed to build some support for itself, despite the serious disadvantages under which it operates. However, it has a long way to go before it could be said to have won a place for itself in the affections of the people whom it serves.

In the long term the institutionalisation of the legislature will depend on the ability of the Ciskei to influence the encapsulating white economic system to respond to the demands of workers for a living wage, and for occupational mobility, and of the landless villager for land or a job.

Notes

1. S.P. Huntington, *Politcal Order in Changing Societies* (Yale University Press, New Haven, 1969), p. 7.
2. J.S. Mill, *Utilitarianism, Liberty and Representative Government* (Dent, London and New York, 1936), p. 239.
3. R.F. Hopkins, *Political Roles in New States* (Yale University Press, New Haven, 1971), p. 196.
4. Ciskei Legislative Assembly, Verbatim Debates, 1972, p. 43.
5. Ciskei Legislative Assembly, Verbatim Debates, 1976, p. 50.
6. Ciskei Legislative Assembly, Verbatim Debates, 1973, p. 90.
7. Ciskei Legislative Assembly, Verbatim Debates, 1974, p. 74.
8. Ciskei Legislative Assembly, Verbatim Debates, 1973, p. 73.
9. Ciskei Legislative Assembly, Verbatim Debates, 1976, p. 14.
10. M. Weber, *The Theory of Social and Economic Organization*, Talcott Parsons (ed.), (The Free Press, New York, 1964), pp. 56-7, 155ff.
11. C. Potholm, *Four African Political Systems* (Prentice Hall, Englewood Cliffs, NJ, 1970), p. 25.
12. I. Wallerstein, *Africa: The Politics of Independence.* (Random House, New York, 1961), p. 99.
13. Huntington, *Political Order*, p. 12.
14. S. Verba and L.W. Pye, *Political Culture and Political Development* (Princeton University Press, Princeton, 1965), p. 530.
15. P. Mayer, *Urban Africans and The Bantustans* (South African Institute of Race Relations, Johannesburg, 1972), p. 7.
16. Ciskei Legislative Assembly, Verbatim Debates, 1975, p. 19.
17. Charton, ' A Socio-Economic Survey'
18. Ciskei Legislative Assembly, Verbatim Debates, 1974, p. 53.
19. *Daily Dispatch*, 19 August 1977.
20. Ciskei Legislative Assembly, Verbatim Debates 1976, p. 199.
21. *Natal Witness*, 22 October 1971.
22. *Sunday Tribune*, 6 March 1977.
23. Mayer, *Urban Africans*, p. 15.

24. *Evening Post*, 23 December 1975; Ciskei Legislative Assembly, Verbatim Debates, 1976, p. 161.
25. Benbo, *Black Development in South Africa*, pp. 30, 34.
26. Ciskei Legislative Assembly, Verbatim Debates, 1975, p. 88.
27. Ibid., p. 160.
28. Benbo, *Black Development in South Africa*, p. 130.
29. Ciskei Legislative Assembly, Verbatim Debates, 1976, p. 523.
30. Ibid., p. 192.
31. Chief L.L. Sebe, ibid., p. 200.
32. Benbo, *Black Development in South Africa*, p. 191.
33. Ibid, p. 64.
34. Chief L.L. Sebe, Ciskei Legislative Assembly, Verbatim Debates, 1976, p. 61.
35. Ciskei Legislative Assembly, Verbatim Debates, 1976, p. 194.
36. Benbo, *Black Development in South Africa*, p. 105.
37. Chief L.L. Sebe, Ciskei Territorial Authority, Verbatim Debates, 1971, p. 164.
38. Chief L.L. Sebe, Ciskei Legislative Assembly, Verbatim Debates, 1974, p. 482.
39. Calculated from Benbo, *Black Development in South Africa*, p. 130.
40. I.G. Shivji, *Class Struggles in Tanzania* (Macmillan, London, 1975).
41. Benbo, *Black Development in South Africa*, p. 30.
42. Ciskei Legislative Assembly, Verbatim Debates, 1976, p. 21.
43. Ciskei Legislative Assembly, Verbatim Debates, 1974, p. 317.
44. Ibid., p. 51.
45. Ciskei Legislative Assembly, Verbatim Debates, 1975, p. 33.
46. Ciskei Legislative Assembly, Verbatim Debates, 1976, p. 235.
47. Ciskei Legislative Assembly, Verbatim Debates, 1974, p. 447.
48. Hammond-Tooke, *Command or Consensus* (D. Philip, Cape Town, 1975), p. 103.
49. Ciskei Legislative Assembly, Verbatim Debates, vol. 5, p. 23.
50. D. Kotze, *African Politics in South Africa* (Hurst, London, 1975), p. 200.
51. L.G. Seligman, 'Political Risk and Legislative Behaviour' in C.R. Boynton and C.L. Kim (eds.), *Legislative Systems in Developing Countries* (Duke University Press, Durban, NC, 1975), p. 91.
52. Kotze, *African Politics*, p. 142.
53. Ciskei Legislative Assembly, Verbatim Debates, 1974, p. 23.
54. See Ciskei Legislative Assembly, Verbatim Debates, 1976, pp. 187, 399.

10 MASS COMMUNICATION IN A TRANSITIONAL SOCIETY

L.E. Switzer

The potential role of the mass media in transitional societies has been acknowledged by most communications researchers.[1] When certain prerequisites are met — and these include functional literacy, formal education, socio-economic status, age and what has been called 'the degree to which an individual is oriented outside his social system' — mass communication can be a crucial catalyst in bringing about change.[2]

In terms of the volume of the messages transmitted, and the speed as well as the efficiency with which these are channelled directly and economically to audiences of virtually any size, mass communication would seem to have advantages over traditional word-of-mouth communication. In practice, however, the prerequisites are too often lacking in transitional societies while exposure to the mass media alone apparently is not enough to alter personal belief and behaviour.

The mass media can increase the fund of information and ideas available to the person who hitherto relied on word-of-mouth communication, and it can create desires and even needs which may not have existed previously. Mere exposure to the mass media, however, is not usually considered sufficient to bring about a change in attitude or motivate a course of action.

It would appear that mass communication is most effective when it is combined with word-of-mouth communication and, in fact, communications research in modern as well as transitional societies tends to proceed from this assumption. The two-step flow model, originally conceived in the 1940s, has been used to describe the process whereby the mass media have an *indirect* impact on their audience. This model presupposes layers of oral intermediaries who internalise mass-media messages and interpret these messages for audiences which are presumed to be unwilling or unable to absorb them directly from mass-media channels. Successful penetration of the mass media in transitional societies, then, would seem to depend on an oral elite responding to its messages and on the maintenance of a perpetual state of interaction between professional communicators, oral opinion leaders and those on and beyond the fringe of mass communication.

In reality, however, the various channels of interpersonal communication in transitional societies tend to function separately and uneasily alongside newspapers, magazines, film, radio and television. Furthermore, oral opinion leaders respond differently to the various mass-media channels. Exposure to print media, for example, may have a different impact on an oral audience than exposure to broadcast media. An oral audience may absorb *information directly* from one media channel but be *influenced indirectly* by oral opinion leaders in the interpretation of these messages.[3]

The complexity of the oral communications process is such, moreover, that the presence of the mass media may be neither an important nor even a progressive factor in promoting change. Interaction between village and city, for example, has established new frameworks of oral communication where cosmopolitan channels — sources of information and ideas outside traditional rural areas — are continually engaged with local channels inside the village community. The relationships between these oral sources of news may have more validity in explaining the role of communication in some transitional societies than attempts to relate interpersonal modes of communication with the mass media.[4]

Opinion leaders outside as well as inside the village community often do conform more closely than their followers to the prerequisites essential for the successful exploitation of the mass media in transitional societies. Consequently, they tend to be more effective users of the mass media and in villages where norms are innovative, they may be more innovative than their followers. The crucial caveat to this assumption, however, is that opinion leaders also tend to internalise village norms more effectively than their followers. This, of course, is one of the reasons why they have status in the community. In villages where traditional values prevail, opinon leaders tend to conform to the *non-innovative* patterns of their followers and, indeed, they may even reinforce this pattern should they feel it is in the interests of the community: 'opinon leaders . . . may influence their followers to reject innovations . . . The innovators in these traditional systems are separate individuals from the opinion leaders . . . [and] are viewed with suspicion and often with disrespect by the villagers'.[5]

Thus opinion leaders can discourage as well as encourage change depending on the norms of the village, rather than on their access to the mass media, and on their awareness 'that leadership is as much a property of the group as it is a characteristic of the individual'.[6]

The fact that opinion leaders are essentially *primus inter pares* in relation to their followers also suggests that the oral intermediaries are not really an elite. Indeed, their authority is measured in part by how accessible they are to their followers, how faithfully they conform to village norms and, in fact, how small the gap is between what they can do and what their followers cannot do. Too great a deviation from the norm will disrupt communication between opinion leaders and followers within the village, between village and city and, indeed, wherever messages are being transmitted through interpersonal modes of communication.

One further qualification that needs to be made before indicating how the mass media are to be evaluated in the Ciskei concerns the *credibility* of oral sources. The professional mass communicator generally adheres to a standardised code of conduct in the production and dissemination of news which is relatively independent of decision-makers and social conventions.[7] The arbiters of word-of-mouth news, however, do not operate within the constraints placed on the professional journalist. Facts and opinions are fused in messages which may be accurate or inaccurate, balanced or unbalanced, fair or unfair, true or not true. Credibility depends on the personal relationship between the individuals involved and on the status of the source in the eyes of those who are the recipients of these messages. Furthermore, despite the acknowledged role of oral intermediaries in transitional societies, little is known of the process whereby mass-media messages are accorded credibility. While these messages are diffused much more slowly when they enter oral communication networks, opinion leaders, who have no special skills in the art of mass communication, invariably operate with incomplete and inaccurate information.[8]

In the end, of course, the two-step flow model is too simplistic to explain the diffusion and interpretation of mass-media messages in transitional societies. The alternative models in vogue today, however, are based on the premise of the two-step flow model because it insists that any attempt to plot a mass-media grid in a transitional society must include relationships between interpersonal and mass communicators in the management of news.

Information for this study was obtained from four surveys conducted in two rural villages, the biggest urban area in the Ciskei and the Ciskei Legislative Assembly. The villages of Gobozana and Nyaniso were the basis of the rural surveys conducted in April-June 1976. Fifty heads of homesteads in each village, in a universe of about 500 homesteads, were selected at random. Mdantsane was chosen for the urban survey con-

ducted in December 1976. A dormitory suburb of East London, it has an unofficial population of more than 150,000 divided into ten zones.[9] The survey consisted of a multi-stage cluster sample of 300 heads of households, of which 270 were accepted for analysis in this study.[10] Forty-four of the 50 members in the Ciskei Legislative Assembly participated in a survey conducted in May 1975.
Three themes will be explored in this chapter:

1. Mass-media exposure patterns in the selected rural and urban areas of the Ciskei and in the Ciskei Legislative Assembly.
2. Attitudes towards news in newspapers and on radio with particular reference to Ciskei homeland news.
3. Some observations on the status accorded to selected oral channels of communication in the transmission and validation of political news in the Ciskei.

1. Mass-media exposure

Mass communication in the Ciskei today means newspapers, magazines and radio stations owned and controlled outside the homeland by white South Africans. Television was introduced in South Africa in January 1976 and caters almost exclusively for a white audience. The first cinema built for Africans in Mdantsane — there were none in the rural areas — was not opened until June 1976.[11] Nevertheless, the pattern of mass-media exposure was similar to what one would expect in a transitional society. Urbanites were the major mass-media consumers while rural villagers for the most part remained on the fringe of mass communication.

Household heads in the Mdantsane survey who read newspapers and magazines (85.9 per cent) and listened to the radio (87 per cent) regularly [12] compared more than favourably with urbanites elsewhere in black Africa.[13] The tendency to read English-language newspapers and magazines but listen to a radio station in the vernacular also conformed to the pattern of mass-media usage among urban blacks in South Africa.[14] Despite the relatively high proportion of respondents who claimed a reading knowledge of Afrikaans (35.6 per cent), virtually no one read publications in this language.[15]

The preference for English-language newspapers in the urban areas could be explained in part by the dominance of English speakers among whites in the Eastern Cape border region and by the fact that no

Afrikaans-language newspapers were published in East London, the principal city. The negative image blacks have of Afrikaans as the 'language of oppression' in South Africa, however, combined with the tendency of English-language newspapers to acquire a multi-racial image were probably more significant factors. East London's *Daily Dispatch* was read regularly by 76.1 per cent of the urban respondents. Of the 15 newspapers cited in the Mdantsane survey, only King William's Town's *Imvo Zabantsundu*, with 39.8 per cent of the urban respondents, appeared in the vernacular. *Imvo Zabantsundu* and *Weekend World* (33.7 per cent), published in Johannesburg, were the only newspapers aimed specifically at a black audience. The others — including Johannesburg's *Sunday Times* (25.5 per cent) and *Rand Daily Mail* (3.6 per cent) and Port Elizabeth's *Evening Post* (17.7 per cent) — were white-dominated, English-language newspapers with a multi-racial readership.

Magazines aimed at an African audience fared much better in the urban sample. *Drum* (45.3 per cent), an English-language weekly still owned by the independent entrepreneur James Bailey, was by far the most popular.[16] Lagging behind were the vernacular magazines *Bona* (17.3 per cent), a multi-lingual pictorial monthly published by Perskor, one of the two major Afrikaans publishing companies, and *Inkqubela* (12 per cent), a Xhosa monthly distributed free of charge by the South African government's Department of Information. English-language magazines like *Scope* (6.6 per cent), a glossy entertainment weekly, the South African edition of *Reader's Digest* (6.3 per cent) and *Darling* (1.2 per cent), a fortnightly women's magazine, were relatively more expensive and, unlike English-language newspapers, had made virtually no effort to appeal to blacks.

The Xhosa-language broadcasts of Radio Bantu, from studios located in King William's Town, were listened to regularly by 79.6 per cent of the urban respondents — including 21 of the 38 household heads (55.3 per cent) who did not read — and 35.9 per cent depended solely on this station. A factor which could become significant in the future was the number of radio stations for whites listened to regularly by black urbanites. Radio Good Hope (41.5 per cent), Springbok Radio (39.6 per cent) and the South African Broadcasting Corporation's English-language service (25.9 per cent) were the most popular after Radio Bantu and all projected western Christian middle-class cultural values and norms. About 5.2 per cent of the respondents apparently had access to short-wave radios and listened regularly to stations in Mozambique, Swaziland and Zambia, in addition to the BBC and Voice of

America.

The members of the Legislative Assembly (MLA) in the Ciskei Legislative Assembly apparently were less exposed to the printed media than the urbanites. Only 59 per cent read newspapers regularly while all but one legislator listened to the Xhosa-language service of Radio Bantu regularly. The vernacular *Imvo Zabantsundu* (86.4 per cent), moreover, was read more regularly than the *Daily Dispatch* (75 per cent), while *Inkqubela* (63.6 per cent) and *Bona* (40.9 per cent) were favoured by a large margin over all English-language magazines.[17]

As far as mass-media exposure was concerned, the rural areas of the Ciskei seemed to approximate the traditional non-innovative pattern outlined earlier. None of the prerequisites for exploiting mass communication were present. In fact, the proportion of *de facto* homestead heads who were 65 and above, unemployed and without formal education was probably higher than normal even for a transitional peasant society.[18] Consequently, very few of these respondents had access to the mass media: 78 per cent did not read newspapers, 95 per cent did not read magazines, 91 per cent did not have relatives, friends or acquaintances read to them, and 64 per cent did not listen to the radio. *Imvo Zabantsundu* was read occasionally by 19 per cent of the *de facto* homestead heads and 36 per cent listened to the Xhosa-language service of Radio Bantu.

As expected, then, mass communication appeared to have had a direct impact only on the urban Ciskei population. Chi-square scores suggested that education and church affiliation were significant variables up to the 0.05 level.[19] Using seven variables — education, church affiliation, income, employment, sex, age, language fluency (reading knowlege of Xhosa, English and/or Afrikaans) — a discriminant analysis showed that those who used the mass media could be correctly classified as such with a probability of 97 per cent. A discriminant analysis of those who did not use the mass media suggested a more tentative probability of 61 per cent of correct classification.

Formal education — hence functional literacy — has become available to the majority of blacks in South Africa only in the last generation. About 58.5 per cent of the household heads in the Mdantsane survey were in the 25-44 age group, for example, and 93 per cent of this age group had from 5 to 12 years (standards 3-10) of schooling. Virtually all of the urban household heads (99.6 per cent) claimed a reading knowledge of Xhosa, 84.4 per cent of English and 35.6 per cent of Afrikaans.

Church affiliation is an interesting variable in South Africa because there are more independent African Christian churches in this country than in any other on the continent, and their influence in both traditional and transitional communities has been the subject of much speculation. Mafeje's distinction between 'genuine' churches in Cape Town's Xhosa township of Langa which aspired to middle-class values and 'fake' churches which did not was used in this study to show the extent to which religion was a factor in mass-media consumption.[20]

In the urban survey, 70 per cent of the household heads belonged to 'genuine' churches which were dominated by the 'mission' tradition. Only 19.3 per cent of the urban respondents claimed to be members of a 'fake' independent African or mission church. The rural villages had not only the bulk of the traditionalists but also the highest percentage of independent church members. The historic mission churches of the Eastern Cape — led by the Methodists (28.2 per cent), Anglicans (14.7 per cent) and Presbyterians (10.7 per cent) — were dominant in the city.

About one-third of the urban household heads in the Mdantsane survey were women, and 42.6 per cent of the respondents claimed to have a household income above East London's *effective minimum level* of R193.70 for an African family of six in October 1976.[21] Most urban household heads (77.8 per cent) were employed in the white formal sector as semi-skilled production workers (18.6 per cent), messengers, counter assistants and clerks (19.5 per cent), and labourers (19.5 per cent), in manufacturing (29.5 per cent), the wholesale-retail trade (21.4 per cent) and government services (39.1 per cent). About 15.6 per cent were self-employed in the black informal sector (Appendix, n f, p. 206).

The Ciskei, then, was similar to other transitional societies in that its urbanites — conservatively estimated at 23.7 per cent of the resident homeland population in 1973[22] — were the main mass-media consumers. They showed a preference for a western oriented, English-language press but preferred to listen to an ethnic-oriented, Xhosa-language radio station. Urban blacks had easier access, moreover, to all the media channels than their rural counterparts who lacked the necessary socio-economic prerequisites.[23] Although urban blacks in the Ciskei neither owned nor controlled the mass media, they were not unlike South Africa's affluent white population in their reading and listening habits.[24]

2. Attitudes Towards Mass-media News

To determine attitudes towards mass-media news, the urban respondents were asked to select their favourite newspaper and radio station from among those which were read and listened to regularly.[25] The two newspapers most favoured by the urban household heads — East London's English-language *Daily Dispatch* (65.1 per cent) and King William's Town's Xhosa-language weekly *Imvo Zabantsundu* (20.3 per cent) — together with their favourite radio station, the Xhosa-language service of Radio Bantu (72.3 per cent) — were matched against five categories of general news.

The *Daily Dispatch* was published by Crewe Trust, an independent foundation, in 1976.[26] In keeping with many other white newspapers in South Africa, the *Daily Dispatch* includes a weekly black supplement in English and Xhosa called *Indaba*,[27] but it is also one of the few white newspapers in South Africa which tries to promote a black image in its news and opinion, sport, women's and society, business and finance pages. Firmly opposed to *apartheid* and committed to the task of 'breaking down the barriers of separation both in thinking and living' that divide the people of South Africa, the *Daily Dispatch* nevertheless accepts the 'reality of the homelands'.

At least two of the six Africans on the integrated editorial staff[28] work full time on homeland news and the Ciskei and Transkei governments strive hard to keep the newspaper informed of political, social and — particularly — economic developments. White staffers maintain that the newspaper does not present a 'negative' view of homeland news, although they feel that the Ciskei, Transkei and the white corridor in between will eventually be amalgamated into a single entity. Consequently, they were sympathetic to the Ciskeian opposition party's declared policies of non-racialism and union with the Transkei.

In 1976, however, 'homeland' news had to compete with news from those organisations created inside South Africa in the past ten years to articulate the ideology of Black Consciousness. This was why the *Daily Dispatch* — and the *Rand Daily Mail* — stood out in the white, English-language press for their coverage of black news.[29] According to the editor at the time, the *Daily Dispatch* encouraged the 'legitimation' of these dissident groups in the hope that eventually their policies would be 'incorporated into the peaceful options open to all South Africans'.

Imvo Zabantsundu, the oldest continuous newspaper founded by an African in South Africa (it was launched in November 1884 by John Tengo Jabavu), is now owned by Perskor, the Afrikaans publishing company. Prominent government ministers and members of the ruling Nationalist Party are on the board of directors of this corporation and the newspaper reflects a pro-government view on the advantages of separate development in the designated black homelands. The newspaper maintains a 'positive' image of news and opinion on the homelands focusing on the activities of the ruling party. This policy is communicated verbally to the newspaper's 16 black reporters by its white, Afrikaans-speaking editor.[30] When Ciskei and Transkei officials, for example, make speeches which are deemed to be against the interests of the South African government, the stories are rewritten. Less contentious issues raised by the speaker are highlighted or the item is simply emasculated to reflect a neutral point of view.

News generated outside the homeland agenda is not tolerated. Black Consciousness organisations still operating in 1976, for example, were not given space to air their views in *Imvo Zabantsundu* and the news generated by these groups was either ignored or reduced to the bare minimum. Although handouts and stories from contributors comprise perhaps 30 per cent of the editorial space in the newspaper, editorials, political news and commentary are written by staffers, translated into English and vetted by the editor before publication. Among other things, letters to the editor are censored for political content and, where necessary, translated for the editor's scrutiny.

Broadcasting is a government monopoly in South Africa and, as such, it offers an ideal medium for communicating the ideology of apartheid.[31] News and documentary programmes on Radio Bantu, for example, focus on ethnic topics: political, social and economic development in the homelands, personality profiles of prominent chiefs and other traditional leaders, efforts to preserve tribal identity in the urban areas, activities of the tribal universities and new developments in Bantu-language dictionaries and literatures.[32] Entertainment programmes on Radio Bantu mediate explicit informational messages as well. Virtually every feature and serial, for example, has a moral lesson, while hymns and traditional African songs are favoured musical fare. Religious broadcasts comprised about 4 per cent of Radio Bantu's total weekly transmission time of 721 hours in 1975, but all informants interviewed were of the opinion that religious themes played an indirect role in many other programmes as well. Women's and children's programmes, grouped together, stress, among other things, 'character-building stories' and include such topics as 'rules of etiquette for the Bantu'. Sports organisations which support the principle of racial separation in the selection of local, provincial and national teams are also given favourable coverage. A Bantu Programme Control Board ensures that black and white personnel responsible for programme content on Radio Bantu promote these policies.

Staff members at the Xhosa-language studios of Radio Bantu in King William's Town, like those employed by *Imvo Zabantsundu*, are expected to reflect a 'positive' view of separate development in the preparation of news programmes which are written usually in Afrikaans before being translated into Xhosa. The King William's Town studios broadcast eleven news programmes a day — seven national bulletins, two local/regional bulletins, one headline bulletin and one news commentary on national and international events. National/international news is compiled from the major domestic and foreign wire services by white staffers in Johannesburg. In addition, the King William's Town studios broadcast a summary of local/regional events twice a week.[33]

National and, of course, local/regional news on Radio Bantu gives more coverage to items of interest to black listeners than the English and Afrikaans service. Like *Imvo Zabantsundu*, however, Radio Bantu broadcasts political news outside the homelands agenda only when it cannot be ignored — as in the Soweto riots. Apart from these daily/ weekly news broadcasts, the Xhosa-language service has a special daily broadcast of parliamentary news for both Ciskei and Transkei. In fact, Radio Bantu unquestionably covers homeland parliamentary activities more rigorously than either of the two favoured newspapers.

For the purpose of the survey, news was defined as any fact or opinion channelled through the mass media concerning five specific geographical areas — Mdantsane (local township news), East London-Duncan Village-King William's Town-Berlin-Zwelitsha (regional news), Ciskei (news relating specifically to homeland activities in the rural and urban areas), national (news concerning the rest of South Africa), and international (news concerning everything outside South Africa). The respondents were given examples of recent news items and encouraged to think of other examples from personal experience. They were then asked to choose their favourite newspaper and radio station and rate each category in terms of whether or not they felt the news coverage was accurate, impartial and informative. These scores were then combined[34] to establish a credibility rating for each news category (Table 10.1). *Daily Dispatch* readers tended to give their newspaper an equally high credibility rating in all news categories while readers of *Imvo Zabantsundu* were slightly more suspicious of their newspaper's national and international news. More interesting were the credibility ratings given for Radio Bantu. Only 90 (59.6 per cent) of the 151 urban

Table 10.1: Urban Respondents' Attitudes Towards News Credibility in the *Daily Dispatch* and *Imvo Zabantsundu*, in percentages

News	Daily Dispatch (N = 151)	Imvo Zabantsundu (N = 47)
Township	69.8	78.7
Regional	77.9	85.1
Ciskei	69.8	77.3
National	74.4	69.5
International	69.1	58.9

Table 10.2: Urban Respondents' Attitudes Towards News Credibility in Radio Bantu, in percentages

News	Daily Dispatch Listeners (N = 90)	Imvo Zabantsundu Listeners (N = 39)	Other Listeners (N = 41)*
Township	72.2	65.8	65.9
Regional	78.2	78.6	67.5
Ciskei	71.1	75.2	57.7
National	73.7	58.9	42.3
International	66.3	51.3	40.7

*'Other listeners' included those who did not read and those who favoured newspapers other than the *Daily Dispatch* and *Imvo Zabantsundu*.

respondents who favoured the *Daily Dispatch* chose Radio Bantu as their favourite radio station, but Radio Bantu's credibility rating for these readers was relatively high in all news categories. *Imvo Zabantsundu* had a higher percentage of readers who favoured Radio Bantu — 39 (83 per cent) of the 47 urban respondents — but they were more critical of that station's coverage of national and international news. The most critical attitudes towards Radio Bantu news, however, were 'other listeners', that is, readers who favoured a non-local, English-language newspaper and those who did not read (Table 10.2).

The combined news credibility scores reinforce these trends (Table 10.3). *Daily Dispatch* and *Imvo Zabantsundu* readers who listened to Radio Bantu were relatively uncritical of both channels whereas those urban respondents who favoured other newspapers or did not read were more critical of Radio Bantu's news coverage. It is probable that those household heads who favoured other radio stations — SABC English (11.1 per cent), Springbok Radio (8.9 per cent), Radio Good Hope (7.2 per cent) — did so in the belief that they offered news programmes more compatible with their interests and needs.[35]

Table 10.3: Urban Respondents' Combined News Credibility Scores for Each Medium, in percentages*

	Daily Dispatch (N = 151)	Imvo Zabantsundu (N = 47)
Reading score	74.2	73.9

	Radio Bantu (N = 170)		
	Daily Dispatch (N = 90)	Imvo Zabantsundu (N = 39)	Other readers/ do not read (N = 41)
Listening score	72.3	65.9	54.8

*The combined news credibility scores were obtained by summing the multiples of the number of respondents in each category with the percentages obtained in these categories. This answer was then divided by the total number of respondents in each category.

These news credibility scores can be contrasted with the urban respondents' news priorities (Tables 10.4 and 10.5).

Table 10.4: Urban Respondents' News Priorities in the *Daily Dispatch* and *Imvo Zabantsundu* and for Those Who Do Not Read: First Preference, in percentages

News	Daily Dispatch (N = 151)	Imvo Zabantsundu (N = 47)	Those who do not read (N = 38)
Township	19.9	34.0	52.6
Regional	13.3	19.5	7.9
Ciskei	22.5	34.0	34.2
National	21.9	8.5	5.3
International	22.5	4.3	—

Imvo Zabantsundu readers showed a marked preference for local township and Ciskei homeland news which was shared by those who did not read newspapers or magazines. *Daily Dispatch* readers, on the other hand, were generally more balanced in their news priorities and more interested in national and international news. All urban respondents who selected Radio Bantu, however, were generally more interested in local township and Ciskei homeland news. There was little evidence of discrimination based on readership. Thus it would appear that *Daily Dispatch* readers, those who favoured non-local newspapers and those who did not read used Radio Bantu to *supplement* their information in

Table 10.5: Urban Respondents' News Priorities in Radio Bantu: First Preference, in percentages

News	Daily Dispatch Listeners (N = 90)	Imvo Zabantsundu Listeners (N = 39)	Other Listeners* (N = 41)
Township	21.9	33.3	34.2
Regional	14.3	23.1	0.7
Ciskei	34.1	28.2	26.8
National	15.4	12.8	19.5
International	14.3	2.6	12.2

*'Other listeners' included those who did not read and those who favoured newspapers other than the *Daily Dispatch* and *Imvo Zabantsundu*.

these areas, whereas *Imvo Zabantsundu* readers found their preferences *reinforced* by listening to Radio Bantu.

These credibility and preference ratings are useful reference points in focusing more narrowly on Ciskei news. The urban household heads generally found the news media to be credible in their coverage of homeland news, although Radio Bantu's credibility rating was considerably lower for those who favoured non-local newspapers or did not read. As expected, there was a distinct preference for Ciskei news among those who favoured the vernacular newspaper and radio station. Those who did not read also placed homeland news high on their priority list.

Roughly one-fifth (52 respondents) of the urban household heads placed Ciskei news in the top preference category. Chi-square scores for this group once again suggested that education was the most significant variable up to the 0.05 level. A discriminant analysis using the seven previously designated variables showed that those who used the mass media and preferred homeland news could be correctly classified as such with a probability of 95 per cent. Those who did not use the mass media and preferred Ciskei news showed a reasonable probability of 71 per cent of correct classification.[36] On the whole, those who favoured Ciskei news in the urban survey were less educated than the other urban respondents and less likely to read newspapers and magazines. In fact, they were more limited in their choice of media channels, being relatively more dependent, for example, on the vernacular newspaper or radio station. Urban household incomes for those who favoured Ciskei news generally were below the *effective minimum level* for East London in October 1976. In essence, those urban household heads who preferred Ciskei news appeared to have a status life more comparable with that of the rural villager.

Radio Bantu listeners in the rural villages and members of the Ciskei Legislative Assembly held views similar to urban mass-media consumers on the question of whether or not criticism of the traditional system was beneficial. More than 86 per cent of the rural homestead heads who listened to Radio Bantu felt it was not critical of the Ciskei but were satisfied with the homeland news they received from this source. More than 77 per cent of the members of the Ciskei Legislative Assembly felt that neither the print nor the broadcast media were critical of homeland affairs but agreed that this had a 'positive' influence on Ciskei development.[37] In effect, 'negative' criticism — only 9 per cent of the members of the Legislative Assembly placed the English-language press in this category — was deemed detrimental to progress.[38] In this context, legislators, rural villagers and urbanites alike associated media credibility with 'positive' news as far as the Ciskei homeland was concerned.[39]

3. Interpersonal Communication and Political News

Ciskei's rural population remained on the fringe of mass communication but this did not mean that the villagers were isolated from the outside world. Interaction between village and city, for example, was as significant in the Ciskei as in other transitional societies.

The mere existence of churches, clinics and schools in the rural areas combined with the changes wrought by agricultural innovation and resettlement schemes has produced new sources of information and opinion inside as well as outside the traditional village framework.

Increased mobility and dependence on an urban-oriented market economy has brought virtually the whole of the adult rural population — every *de facto* homestead head in the rural survey — into contact with an urban centre.[40] They may be pushed or pulled to the city as temporary or permanent migrant labourers — 89.9 per cent of the men and 31.7 per cent of the women in the rural survey were in this category — or their contact may be more ephemeral. In the process, however, new informal communications networks have been generated on the buses, taxis and trains, in the shops and beerhalls, and in the centres of work and leisure in the city.

Strong ties between relatives in village and city have also resulted in a continuous, two-way migration of information, ideas and attitudes. Gobozana and Nyaniso were typical weekend 'resort communities' for many relatives working in the cities. Evidence of the desire to maintain links with the city could be seen, moreover, in the efforts of traditional decision-makers to delay the discussion of local events until migrant labourers returned to the village.

Thus the rural villages of the Ciskei were not atypical of rural communities in other transitional societies largely independent of the mass media.[41] Interpersonal communication between village and city often worked both ways, moreover, and sometimes the village, as well as the city, initiated exchanges of information and influence.[42]

To illustrate the importance of interpersonal communication in the Ciskei, an attempt was made to establish the credibility of selected opinion leaders in the rural and urban areas who were considered potential sources of news *not* derived from the mass media. The emphasis was on formal political news offered by official governmental sources which supplemented rather than reinforced mass-media messages. Political news from official and unofficial (quantified as friends, relatives and acquaintances) sources in Mdantsane was also compared to suggest which types of political news urbanites might find most credible.

In the rural areas, most news emanating from official governmental sources was channelled through the key traditional institution at the local level, the village council. All circumcised males in a rural location were entitled to participate in the council which acted both as an administrative and legislative body (*imbizo*) and as a court of law (*inkundla*)[43] (Figure 10.1).

Messages channelled through the Nyaniso and Gobozana village councils, however, were not always validated. Evidence of problems encountered in the agricultural extension officer's attempts to introduce alternative farming methods,[44] in the birth-control programmes[45] and in efforts to influence the villagers' attitudes towards education — none wanted their children to go beyond Standard Eight and only 20 per cent would spend any extra money they might receive on their children's schooling — suggest at least indifference to those messages exhorting the villagers to make specific changes in their lifestyle. It would appear that these change agents did not have the confidence of the villagers and, in fact, only 7 per cent of the respondents felt these sources provided the most accurate and reliable news they received through the village council.

Political news, however, was a different matter. A restructuring of traditional authority in the Ciskei, as in other homelands, has led to a situation in which chiefs and headmen again play key roles in decision-making at all levels of local government. About two-thirds of the

Figure 10.1: Nyaniso

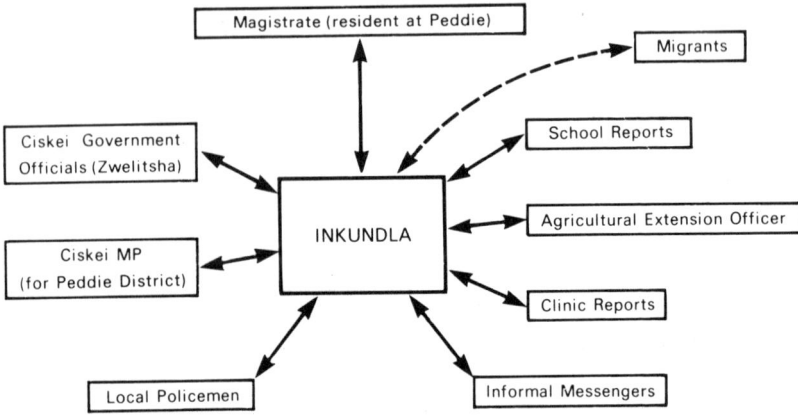

*Normally, the headman was chairman of the village council, but at Nyaniso a chief was acting in this capacity at the time of the survey. Policemen (*amapolisa*) were employed by the tribal authority to collect taxes, issue summons and inform members of the village council of forthcoming meetings. Messengers (*imisila yenkundla*) were appointed to communicate local events such as weddings, funerals and traditional rituals.

present MLA in the Ciskei Legislative Assembly are chiefs[46] and all Ciskei legislators are forced to compete for political survival within the traditional framework. Thus political news from Ciskei government officials and the MLA for Peddie, for example, was channelled mainly through the village council at Nyaniso where the authority of the chief was paramount. It was possible, of course, to subvert the system temporarily — as Manona has shown for Nyaniso where ethnic conflicts in 1973 led to political meetings being held in the local Ethiopian church[47] — but on the whole it would appear that the credibility of news received from chiefs and headmen in the rural areas was very high. At Nyaniso and Gobozana, 59 per cent of the respondents felt this source provided the most accurate and reliable news they received through the village council.

Chiefs and headmen — with the biggest stake in ensuring that the traditional system was preserved — played the major roles in communicating political news in rural Ciskei. Even the urbanites seemed to have been partially dependent on rural villagers for homeland news because it was felt that chairmen of the village councils had greater access than urban household heads to Ciskeian government officials and legislators in Zwelitsha. Above all, traditional political leaders, unlike other change agents, apparently posed no radical threat to village norms, regardless of which political party was favoured.[48]

To suggest how political news not derived from the mass media was communicated to Mdantsane, five potential oral channels were pinpointed. Four were deemed essentially official channels of homeland political news — headmen, political party leaders and town councillors (members of the Urban Bantu Council), government officials and employers who were overwhelmingly white (77.8 per cent of the urban household heads). The one designated unofficial channel — relatives, friends and acquaintances — was considered after pre-tests to be a less favourable source of homeland news.

On the surface, it would appear that official homeland sources of political news had the advantage. Mdantsane's ten zones were divided into street wards to facilitate political communication. Ciskei government officials and politicians as well as the town councillors, who were overwhelmingly CNIP men, communicated their views to the voters through this zonal grid. Many wards, moreover, contained unofficial headmen who performed much the same functions in the urban community as their official counterparts did in the rural villages.[49] The respondents' employers, overwhelmingly white, could also be expected to promote homeland politics.

The graph in Figure 10.2 suggests the credibility of the five designated sources of political news in Mdantsane.

The press in the Eastern Cape acknowledges separate homelands as legitimate outlets for African political aspirations, and Ciskei-Transkei party politics is covered extensively in both the *Daily Dispatch* and *Imvo Zabantsundu*. This might explain why newspaper/magazine readers, for example, found politicians and government officials slightly more credible than non-readers. On the whole, however, among the urbanites, relatives, friends and acquaintances were deemed the most credible oral sources of political news. Although the extent to which each of these channels was actually used as a source of political information could not be determined, the Mdantsane communications survey tended to support the view that traditional political opinion leaders were losing credibility in the black urban townships of South Africa.

In the post-Soweto riot phase evident in the rural as well as the urban areas in 1976, it was not feasible to pursue oral sources inside the informal network (relatives, friends, acquaintances). It could be pre-

Figure 10.2: Urban Respondents' Attitudes towards Oral News Credibility,[a] in percentages (N = 270)

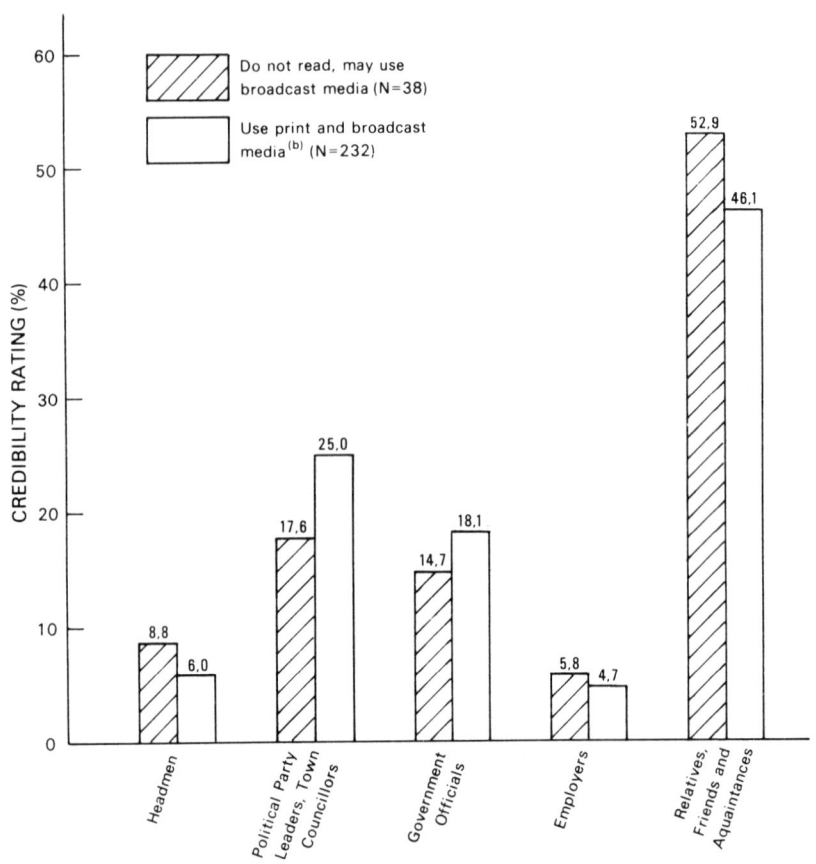

[a] Oral news credibility scores were obtained in the same manner as the mass media news credibility scores: the 'well-informed' response was given twice the weight of the 'accurate' and 'impartial' responses. The combined score is a mean per cent of the 'informed' and 'accurate-impartial' scores

[b] Those who read but for various reasons did not listen to the radio regularly (17 respondents) were included in this group.

sumed, however, that a significant proportion of the urban and rural respondents who used these sources — 34 per cent of the *de facto* rural homestead heads preferred informal contacts outside the village council — did not support the traditional political system in the Ciskei.

Conclusions

Ciskei's communications grid is roughly similar to transitional societies elsewhere in the existence of two parallel networks — one based in the rural village and dependent mainly on oral modes of communication and one based in the city where mass media reading and listening patterns were comparable to those in developed countries.

Mass communication has accentuated these differences because in the Ciskei, as elsewhere, it has mirrored the frustrations and expectations of the urban dweller. Rural villagers seemed indifferent to the urban-oriented informational messages of the mass media[50] and even resistant to change agents who were perceived as threats to their prevailing life style. On the other hand, rural villagers appeared to identify with oral opinion leaders who supported the traditional political system and presumably could be relied upon to reinforce the status quo. The *influence* of chiefs and headmen — whose status was recognised and whose interests were deemed to be in accordance with the interests of the people — still seemed to be paramount in the villages. *Information* emanating both from the mass media and from oral change agents was not accorded the same validity unless it was in harmony with traditional, hierarchical sources of information.[51]

Homeland party politics dominated the white media's view of black political news and, in practice, only English-language newspapers could be expected to criticise the politicians operating within this system or question the assumptions of separate development on which it was based.[52] Nevertheless, a negative view of Ciskei news apparently was unacceptable to urban as well as rural respondents and, of course, to the Ciskeian legislators. It was significant, therefore, that the favoured English-language newspaper, as well as the vernacular newspaper and radio station, was deemed to be a credible source of homeland news.

It was assumed that representatives of homeland parties would tend to monopolise formal oral channels of political communication. Nevertheless, a significant minority of respondents in the rural survey and a majority of those in the urban survey who preferred informal channels were not necessarily supportive of the traditional political elite.

Oral news as a whole, however, was rejected overwhelmingly by the majority of urban household heads who read newspapers *and* listened to the radio regularly (79.6 per cent). When the urban respondents were asked to designate which news source — newspapers/magazines, radio or word of mouth — they believed in or trusted the most, for example, the preference for newspapers and magazines was very pronounced.

Table 10.6: Urban Respondents' Attitudes Towards News in Newspapers/Magazines, Radio and by Word of Mouth: Belief or Trust in the News Source, in percentages (N = 215)

	Newspapers/magazines	Radio	Word of mouth
News	67.9	28.8	2.8

Interpersonal and mass media credibility scores[53] for individual news sources reflected a similar trend.

Table 10.7: Urban Respondents' Attitudes Towards News in Newspapers/Magazines, Radio and Word of Mouth: Media Credibility, in percentages (N = 215)

News	Newspapers/magazines	Radio	Word-of-mouth
Township	57.9	31.3	10.7
Regional	58.4	36.1	5.4
Ciskei	57.7	37.4	4.9
National	66.2	25.9	7.9
International	63.9	28.1	8.1
Combined credibility score	60.8	31.8	7.4

Newspapers and magazines were clearly the arbiters of news credibility. Those urban respondents with regular reading and listening habits rated print over broadcast media for Ciskei homeland news, while word-of-mouth news was rejected even at the local level. The combined media news credibility scores reinforced these trends. Newspapers and magazines were roughly twice as credible as radio and eight times as credible as word of mouth in all news categories.

It seems clear, moreover, that these attitudes have been affected by direct, rather than indirect, exposure to mass communication. In other words, the urban respondents appear to have absorbed information and ideas from the print and broadcast media without the intervening variable of oral opinion leaders. The discrimination between English-language and Xhosa-language newspapers and Radio Bantu also appears to have been based on reactions to the *content* of these media messages rather than on references to oral sources of interpretation.

There is no evidence, however, to suggest that the mass media *influenced* the urbanites in any way that would constitute a change of attitude or initiate a course of action leading to a change in the *status quo*. In fact, the cathartic effect of the mass media on its consumers that Mosel found in Thailand would appear to have some validity for the Ciskei. One suspects that even the English-language press, relatively sensitive to personalities and events outside the framework of separate development in 1976, was read more as 'an outlet for unwanted and otherwise inexpressible feelings' than as a catalyst for change.[54]

In part, this lack of influence may be an inevitable response to recurring themes in the history of the South African press: a narrow definition of news as a record of events, repressive legislation which severely limits the agenda[55] of permissible news, and an attendant acceptance of the necessity for self-censorship and sensationalism.[56]

In part, the press may lack influence among urban blacks in the Ciskei because it cannot or will not address itself to those who have influence. With few legal political alternatives outside the homeland framework,[57] urban blacks seek the legitimation of their grievances and aspirations in the only news medium willing to record them — English-language newspapers. Thus these newspapers — owned and controlled as they are by white capitalist interests — are being offered a unique role as surrogates for a genuine black press. If they accept this role, however, they will be obliged to promote the policies of those who are the credible opinion leaders. Merely recording their views — as was apparent with the *Daily Dispatch* even in 1976 — will not be enough to influence urban black readers in the Ciskei, and elsewhere in South Africa, today.

Appendix

General Profile	Rural (N = 100)	Urban (N = 270)	CLA[a] (N = 44)
Persons living in the household (average)	6.3[b]	5.2	n/a

General Profile	Rural (N = 100)	Urban (N = 270)	CLA[a] (N = 44)
Household Income (%)	n/a[c]		n/a
R 1 − 99		13.7	
100 − 149		21.1	
150 − 199		22.6	
200 − 249		15.5	
250 − 299		9.3	
300 and above		17.8	
Household Head (%)			
Sex			
Male	51.0[d]	68.8[d]	100.0
Female	49.0[d]	31.2[d]	—
Age			n/a
16 − 24	1.0	1.9	
25 − 34	11.0	31.1	
35 − 44	14.0	27.4	
45 − 49	7.0	19.6	
50 − 64	30.0	15.6	
65 and above	37.0	4.4	
Religion			
Traditional	37.0	10.7	—
Christian[e]	57.0	89.3	100.0
Mission Churches	45.6	70.0	n/a
Independent Churches	54.4	19.3	n/a
Employment			
White formal sector	10.0	77.8	11.5
Occupation:[f]			
Professional	—	20.0	4.6
Administrative/clerical/			
manager/proprietor	—	19.5	2.3
Sales worker	1.0	10.9	2.3
Farmer/forester/fisherman	—	—	—
Miner/quarryman	—	—	—
Transport worker/communication	—	11.4	2.3
Production worker/craftsman	6.0	18.6	—
Service/recreation	3.0	19.5	—
Industry:[f]			
Agriculture/forestry/fishing	—	—	—
Mining/quarrying	—	0.5	—
Manufacturing	5.0	29.5	—
Electricity/gas/water	—	—	—
Construction	—	1.5	—
Transport/storage/communication	1.0	6.2	2.3
Wholesale-retail trade/catering/			
accommodation	2.0	21.4	—
Financing/insurance/real estate/			
business services	—	3.8	2.3
Community/social/personal			
services	2.0	37.1	6.8
Black informal sector[f]	13.0	15.6	88.1
Self-employed	2.0	15.6	18.2
Subsistence farmers	11.0	—	22.7
Chiefs	—	—	43.2

Mass Communication in a Transitional Society

General Profile	Rural (N = 100)	Urban (N = 270)	CLA[a] (N = 44)
Unemployed household heads[g]	77.0	10.3	4.6
Education			n/a
No school	48.0	6.6	
Sub A – Std 2	24.0	5.9	
3 – 6	26.0	31.5	
7 – 8	2.0	34.4	
9 – 10	–	21.5	
Some university, certificate or diploma[h]	–	20.7	
Language fluency (reading only)			
Xhosa	32.0	99.6	93.2
English	5.0	84.4	75.0
Afrikaans	–	35.6	13.6
Mass-Media Exposure			
Newspapers and magazines[i]			
Newspaper –magazine readers (%)	22.0	85.9	86.4
Number of different daily/Sunday/ weekend newspapers read (in the past three months)	3	15	11
Newspapers read most regularly (%)			
Imvo Zabantsundu	100.0	39.8	86.4
Daily Dispatch	–	76.1	75.0
Number of different magazines read (in the past three months)	2	21	7
Magazines read most regularly (%)			
Inkqubela	–	12.0	63.6
Drum	–	45.3	–
Bona	–	17.3	40.9
Radio			
Daily-weekly listeners (%)	36.0	86.7	97.7
Number of different radio stations (in the past seven days)	1	8	n/a
Radio station listened to most regularly (%)			
Radio Bantu	100.0	79.6	100.0

Notes:

a. Questions concerning the number of persons living in the household, and the age and church affiliation of the household head were not included in the CLA survey. Questions relating to household income and education were included in a preliminary 1974 survey but too many legislators refused to divulge this information so these items were dropped from the final CLA questionnaire.

b. The rural survey did not include a question on the number of persons living in the household. This figure is a rough estimate based on internal evidence, including the age, marital status and job history of the household head together with the church affiliation and education of family members.

c. No estimates were made of household income in the rural survey as contributions from the migrant labourers could not be obtained.

d. Figures for the rural survey should be treated with caution. Because of the migrant labour pattern in the rural areas, most respondents were *de facto* heads of households. About 12.2% of those interviewed in the urban survey — 60.6% of whom were women — were not household heads.

e. The main mission churches are Roman Catholic, Anglican, Presbyterian, Methodist, Congregational, Dutch Reformed and Lutheran. In essence, these are the white-dominated, multiracial churches in South Africa today. Other churches, controlled by Africans but placed in this category, include the Presbyterian Church of Africa, Bantu Methodist Church, a few Ethiopian churches and Baptist churches affiliated with the Baptist Union of South Africa. White churches deemed 'not respectable' by the Xhosa in Mafeje's study — including Assemblies of God, Full Gospel, Apostolic, Jehovah's Witnesses and Seventh Day Adventists — were placed in the 'independent' church category along with most of the Ethiopian and Zionist churches described by Sundkler and Pauw. The religious persuasions of about 6% of the homestead heads in the rural survey could not be ascertained.

f. The occupation/industry profile is based on the *Standard industrial classification of all economic activities* (Department of Statistics, Pretoria, ca. August 1970). These categories provide an incomplete picture of black employment patterns since they were designed for employees in the white-controlled formal sector. Blacks with incomes derived mainly outside the formal sector have been divided into three categories. 'Self-employed' includes traders, mechanics and welders, handymen, dressmakers and seamstresses, herders, diviners and herbalists, taxi drivers, sportsmen and gamblers and a variety of illegal occupations. 'Subsistence farmers' include sheep and cattle farming and crop production as long as most of the produce is consumed by the household. 'Chiefs' either inherit or are appointed to their position. The five Ciskei cabinet ministers at the time the survey was conducted, however, have not been included in this category. They have been classified according to the occupation held immediately prior to their appointment as ministers. Two were in education, one was a government clerk, one was a self-employed businessman and one was a chief who subsequently resigned from the cabinet when he left the CNIP.

g. 'Unemployed' includes housewives, disabled persons and pensioners with no personal income. Some household heads were working in both the formal and informal sectors; hence total employment/ unemployment is more than 100%.

h. Three urban respondents actually had university degrees.

i. Photo-story magazines were not included.

Notes

1. For example, L.W. Pye (ed.), *Communication and Political Development* (Princeton University Press, Princeton, 1963); E. Katz and P.F. Lazarsfeld, *Personal Influence: The Part Played by People in the Flow of Mass Communications* (Free Press, New York, 1964); E. Rogers, 'Mass Media Exposure and Modernization among Colombian Peasants', *Public Opinion Quarterly*, 29 (1965); E. Rogers and L. Svenning, *'Modernization among Peasants: the Impact of Communication'* (Holt, Rinehart & Winston, New York, 1969), 'Mass Media and Interpersonal Communication' in Ithiel de Sola Pool (ed.), *Handbook of Communication* (Rand McNally, Chicago, 1973), J.P. Robinson, 'Interpersonal Influence in Election Campaigns: Two-step Flow Hypothesis', *Public Opinion Quarterly*, 40 (1976).

2. Rogers and Svenning, *Modernization among Peasants*, pp. 102, 104-7, 147. Religion was also found to be a variable in the Ciskei survey.

3. Rogers in 'Mass Media in Interpersonal Communication' describes this as

the 'innovation-decision process' by which one moves, in stages (a) from awareness-*knowledge* of an innovation, (b) to *persuasion* of a favourable or unfavourable attitude toward the innovation, (c) to *decision* to adopt or reject, and (d) to *confirmation* of this decision' (p. 295).

4. R. Firth, 'Rumour in a Primitive Society', *Journal of Abnormal and Social Psychology*, 53 (1955); M. Gluckman, 'Gossip and Scandal', *Current Anthropology*, 4 (1963); 'Psychological, Sociological and Anthropological Explanations of Witchcraft and Gossip: A Clarification', *Man* (NS), 3 (1968); R. Paine, 'What is Gossip About? An Alternative Hypothesis', *Man* (NS), 2 (1967); 'Informal Communication and Information Management', *Canadian Review of Sociology and Anthropology* (1970); 'Transactions as Communicative Events', Paper read at Conference of the Association of Social Anthropologists, Oxford, 1973; D. Handelman, 'Gossip in Encounters: the Transmission of Information in a Bounded Social Setting', *Man* (NS), 8 (1973); P. Harries-Jones, *Freedom and Labour: Mobilisation and Political Control on the Zambian Copperbelt* (Blackwell, Oxford, 1975), ch. 5.

5. Rogers and Svenning, *Modernization among Peasants*, p. 230.

6. Ibid, p. 231, n 25.

7. This point has been the topic of considerable controversy, but the emphasis here is on the *relative* detachment of the mass media: C. Mueller 'Note on the Repression of Communicative Behaviour' in Hans Pieter Dreitzel (ed.), *Recent Sociology No. 2 Patterns of Communicative Behaviour* (Macmillan, London, 1970); S. Cohen and J. Young (eds.) *The Manufacture of News: Social Problems, Deviance and Mass Media* (Constable, London, 1973); G. Murdock and P. Golding, 'For a Political Economy of Mass Communications' in *The Socialist Register 1973* (Merlin Press, London, 1974).

8. Mass-media messages are often disguised as rumours in interpersonal communication. By planting information derived from the mass media inside a rumour chain, and tracing the route it takes, one can suggest how the content of this 'improvised news' is distorted in the process.

9. A new zone being built in 1976 was not included in the survey, although it already had a number of illegal occupants.

10. An attempt was made to select the households at fixed-frequency intervals, but geographical factors made it difficult to adhere rigidly to this principle.

11. Prior to June, blacks could attend two 'coloured' cinemas in East London.

12. Reading frequency for each publication in the Mdantsane survey was determined by the number of issues the respondent claimed to have read in the previous three months. If the household head read at least three of the last six issues of a daily newspaper and two of the last six issues of a weekly newspaper or magazine, he/she was considered a regular reader of the print media. A regular radio listener used this channel at least three times a week.

13. D. Wilcox, *Mass Media in Black Africa: Philosophy and Control* (Praeger, New York, 1975);W.A. Hachten, *Muffled Drums: the News Media in Africa* (Iowa State University Press, Amen, 1971).

14. Market Research Africa (Pty) Ltd (MRA), *Readership*, 1975 survey report, (Johannesburg 1975), vol. 4. An independent research company, MRA has conducted national newspaper, magazine and radio audience surveys for the four designated racial groups in South Africa since the early 1960s.

15. Figures on black readership of Afrikaans-language publications for the country as a whole should be treated with caution, but it would appear that only 2.5 per cent of the adult population read newspapers and magazines in this language. MRA, 1975 survey, vol. 1, p. ix (overall summary of reading claims).

16. In the 1950s and early 1960s *Drum* was the most prominent black publica-

tion in South Africa. The 'legend' of *Drum* may account, in part, for its continued popularity among urban blacks.

17. The *Sunday Times* (59.1 per cent) and the now banned *Weekend World* (56.8 per cent) were also popular with those legislators who read newspapers regularly. Readership claims should be treated with caution, however, in view of the fact that most MLAs refused to reveal their educational backgrounds (Appendix, n *a*).

18. Appendix. P.J. Deutschmann, 'The Mass Media in an Underdeveloped Village', *Journalism Quarterly*, 40 (1963); Rogers and Svenning, *Modernization among Peasants*, pp. 226-9. Rogers noted that the ages of opinion leaders, for example, were often higher than the ages of their followers in traditional villages where this was a criterion for leadership. In 'modern' innovative villages, however, age did not have the same status and, if anything, the opinion leaders were younger than their followers; G.K. Hirabayashi and M.F. El Khatib, 'Communication and Political Awareness in the Villages of Egypt', *Public Opinion Quarterly*, 22 (1958); Rogers, 'Mass Media Exposure'; L. Nader, 'Communication between Village and City in the Modern Middle East', *Human Organization*, 24 (1965).

19. The observed value of chi-square is designated by equality with x^2 and the upper 0.05 level of the relevant chi-square distribution is given in brackets after the observed value in this study: education 13,648 (5,981), church affiliation 3,990 (3,841), age 2, 816 (3, 841), income 6,351 (11,070), employment 0,616 (3, 841), language fluency 1,811 (7,815), sex 1,420 (3,841).

20. A. Mafeje, 'Religion, Class and Ideology in South Africa' in M.G. Whisson and Martin West (eds.), *Religion and Social Change in Southern Africa* (D. Philip, Cape Town, 1975); B.A. Pauw, *Christianity and Xhosa Tradition: Belief and Ritual Among Xhosa-speaking Christians* (Oxford University Press, Cape Town, 1975), Chs. 2-5, 13; Appendix n *e*.

21. S. Gordon, *Domestic Workers: Handbook for Housewives* (South African Institute of Race Relations, Johannesburg, 1973). Estimate by the Planning Research Institute (University of Port Elizabeth) in East London. About two persons were employed per household.

The *poverty datum line* (PDL) and *effective minimum level* (MEL) are estimates of the minimum income an urban family must have each month to stay alive. PDL includes food, clothing, fuel, lighting, rent and transport to and from work. Although estimates for food and clothing, for example, are sufficient to maintain minimum health standards, this is an unrealistic measurement. There is no margin for ignorance of dietary needs, poor buying habits and inadequate budgeting; nor is there any allowance for school costs, house maintenance or the purchase of household goods, and leisure activities. Therefore, the PDL figure is increased by one-half to obtain an MEL which is an estimate of what is essential for survival. The PDL and MEL levels vary with the size and race of the urban family unit. For what is not included in these estimates, see Gordon, *Domestic Workers*.

22. Benbo, *Ciskei Economic Review*, p. 32 (based on the 1973 *de facto* population estimate of 602,000). In 1975, Benbo estimated that 173,555 Africans lived in Ciskei's urban areas. Mdantsane's population alone in 1977, however, was estimated at more than 170,000 by the University of Port Elizabeth's planning research office in East London.

23. R.R. Martin, S.T. McNelly and F. Izcaray, 'Is Media Exposure Unidimensional? A Socio-Economic Approach', *Journalism Quarterly*, 53 (1976). 'The less affluent . . . cannot afford to be selective media consumers. They tend instead to take what they can get from whatever media may be economically and intellectually accessible to them' (p. 624).

24. cf. Market Research Africa, 1975 survey, vol. 1, Whites; vol. 5, Whites,

Coloureds and Asians.

25. Each newspaper was divided into seven different categories – news, sport, women's section, leader page, letters to the editor, 'help wanted' adverts, business/finance – with one extra category for non-specified items. Radio listeners were shown twelve categories selected from the South African Broadcasting Corporation's *Radio Bantu Xhosa Service Information Guide*. The respondent picked his favourite newspaper and radio station from the number of categories he/she read or listened to regularly so long as one of these categories was news.

26. Information on the *Daily Dispatch* was obtained from interviews with the white editor, deputy editor and business manager and three black reporters.

27. *Indaba* has been published jointly by Port Elizabeth's *Eastern Province Herald* and the *Daily Dispatch* since August 1976. The launching of *Indaba*, according to the white staffers who were interviewed, not only attracted new advertising revenue and boosted circulation (from 26,418 daily in June 1976 to 28,610 daily in June 1977), it also stimulated the coverage of 'hard' black news in the *Daily Dispatch*. Sensitive to charges that black supplements created by whites perpetuated racial stereotypes and fostered a 'ghetto mentality' among blacks, the *Daily Dispatch* appointed a black editor for *Indaba* in July 1977 with 'complete control' over all editorial content. As yet, however, *Indaba* is still concerned almost exclusively with 'sensational' black news – sex, crime and sport – in the townships.

28. The *Daily Dispatch* had six black reporters, one coloured reporter and one Indian subeditor in 1976. Two black reporters – stationed in King William's Town and Umtata – focused on Ciskei and Transkei news, respectively.

29. The *Daily Dispatch* used the *Rand Daily Mail* as a guide in the selection of national and international news stories in 1976.

30. Information on *Imvo Zabantsundu* was obtained from interviews with the former white editor (August 1975 – September 1977) and four black editorial staff members, past and present. The newspaper had five editions with a weekly circulation of 55,871 in June 1977. Of particular interest was the English-language *Imvo Transkei*, allegedly launched on behalf of the Transkei government to boost its credibility rating in Southern Africa and overseas. Although *Imvo Transkei* had its own black editor and four reporters, the white editor regarded this newspaper as another edition of *Imvo Zabantsundu*.

31. The South African Broadcasting Corporation has six services – one external (Radio South Africa) and five domestic. Two national domestic channels are aimed theoretically at a white audience and are broadcast in English and Afrikaans, respectively, without advertising. Of the three domestic services which allow advertising, two are also theoretically for whites – the national bilingual English/Afrikaans service (Springbok Radio) and the regional services (Radio Good Hope for the Cape Province). Radio Bantu is the only service aimed specifically at blacks and it has seven transmissions for the various Bantu-language groups (Zulu, Sotho, Xhosa, Tswana, Pedi, Venda, Tsonga).

32. Information on Radio Bantu was obtained from the SABC annual reports for 1975, pp. 56-61, and 1976, pp. 69-73, and interviews with the white manager of the Xhosa-language studios in King William's Town and two black announcers who once worked for Radio Bantu.

33. The editorial staff at the Xhosa-language studios in King William's Town in 1976 comprised six news writers, two of whom were stationed in Umtata, the capital of Transkei. Four news writers and 18 announcers, one of whom was stationed in Johannesburg, were black. Local and regional news, in particular, was compiled with the help of 18 regular and irregular black stringers.

34. In all tables calculating the urban respondents' attitudes towards news credibility, the 'informed' score was given twice the weight of the 'accurate' and

'impartial' scores. The combined score was a mean percent of the 'informed' and 'accurate/impartial' scores.

35. There were 34 urban respondents (14.7 per cent) who favoured non-local, English-language newspapers – mainly the *Sunday Times* (6 per cent) and the *Weekend World* (5.6 per cent).

36. Chi-square scores for those who preferred Ciskei news: education 26,470 (7,815), readership 2,480 (3,841), income 4,348 (7,815), employment 0,532 (3,481), church affiliation 0,276 (3,481), age 6,258 (7,815), language fluency 1,220 (7,815).

37. Comments expressed by the MLAs on this topic were most revealing. A non-critical or neutral attitude towards 'homeland' news was 'accurate', 'fair', 'unbiased', 'true', 'encouraged' progress, gave a 'correct' reflection of events, was 'constructive' and 'without prejudice'.

38. A statement by one of the few MLAs who felt 'negative' criticism was useful: 'Pointing out weaknesses in the homeland system helps to inform the unsophisticated electorate. News media which criticize the application of separate development . . . help to dispel the *spirit of hopelessness* among the citizens of the homelands' (emphasis added).

39. This conforms to attitudes held elsewhere, however, in independent black Africa. As Wilcox puts it, a dim view is taken of any press content perceived as a negative comment on the performance of a government official or policy, Wilcox, *Mass Media in Black Africa*, p. 34. Hachten on the press in Ghana: 'The NRC (ruling council) clearly believes the press should avoid news of conflict and stress and instead emphasize unity and harmony within the society', Hachten, *Muffled Drums*, p. 462. Both the editor of *Imvo Zabantsundu* and the manager of Radio Bantu used the word 'positive' in this sense, contrasting their view of homeland news with the 'negative' criticism of the editor of the *Daily Dispatch*.

40. The nearest urban centres – for Gobozana and Nyaniso these were King William's Town and Peddie, respectively – were visited several times a week by most homestead heads. In fact, most adults living permanently in the villages had been to the major cities in the Eastern Province (Port Elizabeth, East London) and elsewhere in South Africa.

41. For example, Nader, 'Communication between Village and City'.

42. One instance of this was the death of Mxolisi Sandile, paramount chief of the Rharhabe, one of the two major ethnic groups in the Ciskei, in 1976. Rumours stemming from the villages concerning the attitude of the Ciskei government towards Sandile's funeral and the behind-the-scenes struggle to find an acceptable regent were circulating for some time in Mdantsane before they were picked up by the mass media.

43. M.E. Mills and M. Wilson, *Land Tenure*, Keiskammahoek Rural Survey (Shuter and Shuter, Pietermaritzburg, 1952), vol. 4, pp. 5-6. See Figure 10.1.

44. Nyaniso and Gobozana fieldworkers' notes. Of the 36 homestead heads who listened to the radio, only ten had ever heard an agricultural programme.

45. Ibid.

46. In 1977 there were 33 official and 20 elected members (see Chapter 5, n 16).

47. See Chapter 7.

48. Fieldworkers in both rural villages cited cases where 'tribal' office holders actually inhibited the work of change agents who were invariably younger and more educated.

49. Mdantsane survey interviews December 1976. Individuals were given the status of 'headmen' by consensus. Initially, they might offer a specific service – for example, a local shopkeeper with a phone or a self-employed car mechanic – until gradually they become *de facto* spokesmen for the street residents. As

opinion leaders, they played an important role in the wards and were normally consulted by Ciskeian party officials and town councillors.

50. Typical rural comments: 'What would I query? I know nothing and must accept what is said'; 'These modern times are not for me. All that is taking place confuses me.'

51. It has been suggested, however, that even where there is access to the mass media and the information and ideas communicated have practical relevance, it may be of little use to the peasant farmer, J.H. Fett, 'Situational Factors and Peasants' Search for Market Information', *Journalism Quarterly*, 52 (1975). This would appear to be the case in rural Ciskei where the villagers had little room to manoeuvre in deciding what to grow or in pursuing a course of action that would result in a more productive use of the available land. Relatively large family units, controlled by ageing homestead heads, subsisted on small grants of land while most of the potential labour force were working elsewhere. There were few markets available to which the farmers could sell their products and, in any event, the range of prices paid for potential cash crops was deemed to be too low. In these conditions, it is doubtful whether even an educated, literate population — with access to media which focused on useful agricultural news and with acceptable oral change agents — would believe that different attitudes could lead to a better way of life.

52. The only significant debates on the mass media in the Ciskei Legislative Assembly between 1971 and 1975, for example, concerned allegedly harmful reports on its activities in the *Daily Dispatch* (see CLA Debates, 1975, vol. 5).

53. These credibility scores were obtained in the same manner as the 'favourite' media news credibility scores in Tables 10.1 and 10.2 (footnote 34) and the combined reading and listening news credibility scores for 'favourite' media in Table 10.3.

54. Pye (ed.), *Communication*, Chapter 12; J.M. Mosel, 'Communication Patterns and Political Socialization in Transitional Thailand' in Pye, ibid., p. 226.

55. The agenda for news is important in Africa: 'While the press may not convince many people what to believe it can determine what they will talk about. The Ghanaian press serves the important function of informing the urban elites of what the major issues and problems are as perceived by the NRC. The readers may or may not support the NRC's policies, but the agenda is set', Hachten, *Muffled Drums*.

56. Vide P.B. Orlik, 'Under Damocles Sword — the South African Press', *Journalism Quarterly*, 46 (1969); T. Brown, 'Free Press Fair Game for South Africa's Government', *Journalism Quarterly*, 48 (1971); Hachten, *Muffled Drums*, Ch. 11; E. Potter, *The Press as Opposition: The Political Role of South African Newspapers* (Chatto and Windus, London, 1975).

57. As Ithiel Pool suggests, 'the effectiveness of the mass media in influencing (change) will be a direct function of the effectiveness of the politial organization to which the mass media are an adjunct', (Pye (ed.) *Communication*, ch. 14; Pool, *Handbook*, pp. 251-2).

11 MAQOMA AND CISKEIAN POLITICS TODAY

M.G. Whisson and C.W. Manona

PART 1

Maqoma Son of Ngqika 1798-1873

Before Phalo, paramount chief of the Xhosa died about 1775, his people had divided between the followers of Gcaleka, the son of his great wife, and his older son, Rharhabe of the right-hand house. The Gcaleka people stayed to the east of the Kei for the most part, while the followers of Rharhabe conquered the land between the Kei and the Buffalo rivers and exercised some control to the west of the Buffalo. Other Xhosa groups had also crossed the Buffalo, owing political allegiance to none, but recognising Gcaleka as the paramount dynasty.

Rharhabe died about 1787 after Mlawu, the eldest son of his great house. Mlawu left an infant son Ngqika (Gaika) who grew up under the regency of Ndlambe, a brother of Mlawu from the great house. Cebe, the son of Rharhabe's right-hand house died without issue, and his followers gave their allegiance to Ndlambe and his son Mdushane.

When Ngqika succeeded to the paramountcy he had an affair with a young wife of Ndlambe, Thuthula 'reputed to be the most beautiful woman in Kaffraria'.[1] The relationship was a serious breach of custom and the people were scandalised. Ndlambe used the occasion to assert the autonomy of his segment of the Rharhabe, which was centred west of modern Grahamstown, against the paramountcy of Ngqika. He went to war with Ngqika's followers and so divided the Rharhabe people into two independent segments. Ngqika was generally on the losing side in the encounters which followed and by 1809 claimed to have no more than 1,500 followers. Andries Stockenström who visited Ngqika in an embassy with Colonel Collins in that year was particularly struck by Maqoma who 'appeared to Colonel Collins a noble specimen of a savage prince capable of being moulded into a Christian hero'. Maqoma was probably no more than eleven years old at the time.[2] In 1818 Ndlambe, with the support of the Gcaleka parmount Hintsa, inflicted a crushing defeat on Ngqika's forces at Amalinde, in which Maqoma's strength and courage on behalf of the defeated side was a memorable feature.

Encouraged by the elimination of his Rharhabe opponents and urged by a diviner, Makana, Ndlambe moved against Grahamstown the following year. His forces had previously ranged as far as Uitenhage in search of stock but after 1812 had been driven back to Keiskamma. Ndlambe was defeated and the frontier moved eastward once more, this time with a neutral zone or no man's land between the Fish and Keiskamma rivers, in which all settlement was forbidden. Once more the British negotiated with Ngqika, still apparently under the illusion that he had some control over his uncle's people.

Ngqika had at least five sons. Maqoma, son of Nontoto of the right-hand house was the eldest, 'admitted by everybody to be an orator above the ordinary and a warrior unrivalled among his Xhosa comperes'.[3] Tyhali, Anta and Xoxo were born in lesser houses and Sandile, son of Sutu the great wife was born in 1821.

After the agreement in 1819, the Ngqika people were permitted to use the neutral zone and a great place was established at Burnshill, close to a newly built mission station. The neutral zone was soon occupied once more with a mixture of white and Khoi farmers as well as the Xhosa. Raids continued with the chief unable to stop them, even if he had wanted to do so. Maqoma as the dominant personality in the area was inevitably blamed by the British and in 1829 was expelled. The purpose of the raiding was as much political as economic, as the effective following that a chief obtained was largely a function of his ability to be generous to his supporters. In the contest between Ngqika and Ndlambe, the latter had doubtless gained some advantage through his successful raids into the colonial territories. In the next generation, the contest between Maqoma and the sons of Ndlambe was similar, but by this time it was Maqoma who was closer to the colonists, thanks in part to the diplomacy of Ngqika who sought to conciliate where he could not conquer. By the time that he was expelled, Maqoma was an active participant in a conflict involving Tembu leaders which brought a new group of refugees into the British sphere of influence.

Maqoma had to wait five years for a good opportunity to rally his followers to regain the land lost in 1829. In 1834 Xoxo, a young brother of Maqoma, was slightly injured in an attack upon an armed British patrol which had been sent from Fort Beaufort to drive the Xhosa across the Keiskamma river and to bring in some stolen stock. Tyala counselled peace but Maqoma demanded vengeance for the injury done to his brother, and the Sixth Frontier War began.

The Xhosa leaders could rarely match the British and settler firepower; they had scant sources of guns or ammunition beyond what

they could capture, and so conducted the wars for the most part as
guerilla campaigns, the purposes of which were to obtain stock for
their followers and to so disrupt the lives of the settlers that they would
withdraw. To these ends posses scoured the territory ceded after 1819
and the settler country far into Albany district. Stock were stolen, men
killed, wagons and farmhouses pillaged and destroyed, but for the most
part the missionaries, the women and the children were spared. To the
settlers and their families the 'war' periods involved a heightening of the
uncertainty of their lives. Such was the success of Maqoma's assault
that virtually all the colonists east of the Kowie at least, sought refuge in
Grahamstown.

By the time that it was clear that they could not succeed in their
endeavour, Maqoma and Tyahli led a substantial and disciplined force
of 4,000 men, with 400 muskets and a substantial number of horse-
men.[4] In their negotiations with the British officers, the chiefs 'instead
of being humbled and subdued, as was generally expected, appeared to
be by no means indisposed to a renewal of the contest'[5]. Even if they
had wished, however, they could not have controlled the activities of
other segments of the Rharhabe, even less the other Xhosa groups in
the region. Negotiations were hindered at every turn by the continua-
tion of raids, which the settlers saw as perfidy on the part of the Ngqika
leadership.

One important consequence of the 1834-5 war was that many Mfengu,
who had been living as clients of the Xhosa, in conditions often miser-
able and humiliating, were liberated by the British. Hintsa, the Gcaleka
paramount, together with several of his councillors, was held hostage
while the Mfengu left the lands of the Gcaleka, and the refugees were
settled by the colonial authorities in the 'neutral zone'. For this kind-
ness, the Mfengu fought for the British against the Xhosa. They
embraced Christianity and schooling on a scale far greater than that of
the Xhosa in the nineteenth century and gained extensive land rights,
including freehold.

After the war the Ngqika were allowed to return to the neutral zone,
their chiefs given magisterial authority and, in 1841, Sandile assumed the
paramountcy.

Maqoma negotiated ceaselessly with the colonial authorities, trying
to obtain more land for himself and his people. At the same time raiding
continued, Mfengu, Khoi and settler farms all suffering from time to
time. The formidable Harry Smith had gone and agents of the philan-
thropic party were in power at the Cape. Whether they thought him mad
or marvellous, the Ngqika leaders recognised Smith as a formidable

enemy, beside whom his successors were of little account. The troubles boiled over into full-scale war again in 1846 with the War of the Axe. Maqoma was opposed to the war, according to Brownlee, and would have preferred to remain at his home near Fort Beaufort. He was by this time a heavy drinker and doubtless felt unfit for another exhausting campaign. The British thought he was 'either mad or feigning madness'[6] presumably to gain information on their plans, and sent him away. The Ngqika scored one impressive success near their headquarters at Burnshill, when they captured part of the baggage train. Better armed and mounted than ever before they ravaged the frontier on a scale as great as in 1835, driving the settlers to the security of Grahamstown once more. Only after a long year of tough campaigning were they prepared to negotiate.

Sandile and Anta went to meet the British, and by either deliberate deceit or misunderstanding found themselves arrested and taken to Grahamstown jail where they spent the last two months of 1847. Sir Harry Smith, now Governor, was on his way to renew acquaintances with his old foes, which he first did by calling for Maqoma at Port Elizabeth. He ordered Maqoma to kneel, placed his foot on the chief's neck and said 'This is to teach you that I am come hither to teach Kaffirland that I am chief and master here, and this is the way I shall treat the enemies of the Queen of England'.[7] Thus by what Sandile perceived as treachery and what Maqoma experienced as a gross insult, the two brothers were united in their hatred for the British.

New conditions were imposed on the defeated people. The Ngqika were expelled from the 'neutral zone' and placed under two white commissioners who had power to review all decisions made by the chiefs. This was humiliating and costly for the chiefs as their judgments were reversed and their traditional income from fines and confiscation was cut.

By 1850 Sandile was ready to fight again and a Ndlambe prophet, Mlanjeni, believed by some to be a reincarnation of the Makana who had inspired the 1819 assault on Grahamstown, doctored the army. A drought shortened tempers and sharpened appetites for plunder. Sir Harry was summoned from Cape Town to discourage the Xhosa from revolt, but Sandile declined to meet him, saying he feared re-arrest and the treachery he had experienced in 1847. Sir Harry deposed him and ordered that business should be transacted through his mother, Sutu.

Once more the British demanded that the Ngqika should surrender some guns, following an attack on a military officer. Sandile temporised but Maqoma demanded resistance. The chiefs professed great loyalty to

Smith and the Crown, but declined to surrender any weapons. Smith put on a show of force which did not greatly impress the Ngqika forces secure in the Amatole mountains, and they ambushed another column. Maqoma, claiming that if he had been mad in 1846, it would now be seen that he was not mad,[8] took an active role in the war and directed operations from his headquarters in Waterkloof for eighteen months. The opening of the war found Sir Harry besieged at Fort Cox, his pride offended by the cheerful deception of his opponents who had solemnly kissed his boot and sworn allegiance while their military plans were maturing. African police, the Coloured Cape Mounted Rifles, Khoi and even a few whites joined the Ngqika and once more the farmers and their families fled to the security of Grahamstown. The fighting, raiding and ensuing panic spread from Colesberg to the sea. Even Sir Harry showed signs of panic when he suggested calling in Zulu help against his ubiquitous foes. Eventually it was famine, exacerbated by the British scorched earth strategy, that crushed the spirit of the Ngqika and they sued for peace. Before negotiations had proceeded very far, Sir Harry was recalled to England for failing to conquer his obstinate and elusive enemies.

The familar story was repeated. The Ngqika were ordered to leave the Amatole region and to cross the Kei, many were scattered among their former neighbours and rivals and the Grey policy of assimilation was instituted. Maqoma and Sandile appeared hostile to each other, the former claiming that he had really played no part in the war and had fled to the Waterkloof in order to escape it. There he had fought only in self-defence. The scale of the defeat, like that of the war, had been greater than ever before and there seemed no possibility of a revival of Ngqika power for another generation.

It was out of the depression so engendered that the cattle killing erupted. Another prophet, Mhlakaza, aided by his niece Nongqause began to speak of a millenium which would come in on 18 February 1857. The dead would rise and the corn and cattle flourishing beneath the earth or the sea would emerge. The white men and all who failed to participate in the killing of their cattle and the destruction of their corn would be driven into the sea. Sarili, the Gcaleka paramount, believed the prophecy in the hope that he could avenge his father Hintsa who had been killed at the end of Harry Smith's first border campaign in 1835. The combinaion of faith in the traditional style of the prophet, hope of wealth and desperation born of defeat was potent.

Under the combined onslaught of some councillors who tended to favour obedience to the prophet, others who opposed the killing and

Brownlee the commissioner to the Ngqika who pleaded and cajoled endlessly in the months before the final crisis, Sandile wavered. Maqoma threw his still formidable weight behind the prophet and Sandile obeyed, although without forcing his followers to do the same. The day of the millenium came and went. Perhaps 100,000 people died of starvation. If any leader had believed that the event could have stirred a violent revolt he could not have been more wrong.

In the aftermath of death, hunger and recrimination, Maqoma reverted to the traditional style of chiefship, having forfeited his government grant for his part in the cattle killing. He levied fines in cases brought before him for a short period but was then accused of being responsible for the death of a petty chief Vusani. He was arrested, tried and sentenced to 20 years detention on Robben Island.

Sandile, despite the apparent ill-feeling between him and his brother, pleaded for Maqoma's release and in 1866 he was released. Unrepentent and unbowed, the old man began to campaign for the return of the Ngqika and himself to the Kat river region where had had known prosperity in his youth. Once more he was detained and spent his last days on Robben Island where he died in 1873.

His final resting place at Ntaba KaNdoda is in the hills where he fought for the right to live in the plains below.

Analysis

This history of the Xhosa, from the split between the Gcaleka and the Rharhabe shows the manner in which the people are divided between the great house and the right-hand house. In each generation the division may take place and is made more probable if the heir to the great house is very much younger than the eldest son of the right-hand house.

Phalo, it is said, suffered through his proclaimed heir (Gcaleka) being an adult before his death, because Gcaleka intrigued against him. To prevent that problem, the heir was more often born to a wife married very late in the old chief's life. This meant that the right-hand house was very well established when the chief died, but that the heir was an infant. A regency made up of the mother and half-brothers of the infant paramount was one rational way to maintain the unity of the group, but as the cases of Ngqika and Sandile show, the right-hand house tended to go its own way as the young paramount gained in authority. It might divide the political chiefdom completely, as in the case of Rharhabe and Ndlambe, or continue in a state of tension as in the case of Maqoma.

The autonomy of the segments is suggested by the history. This would seem to be a matter of personalities and the ability of an individual chief to obtain a following adequate for him to defend himself from his rivals. The opportunities for exploiting the open or settled frontier and the level of reprisal to be expected from the victims of cattle raiding are relevant variables here. Seniority remains recognised as between the various autonomous chiefs — Sarili is senior to Sandile and Sandile to Maqoma and Mdushane — but that seniority is manifested in action only when the junior chief or his family concede it. Also perceptible is the operation of a segmentary principle — after the initial conflict Hintsa does not appear to have involved himself in exploiting the division between Ngqika and Ndlambe, that being an internal Rharhabe matter.

The relevance of this history for the current situation is open to much interpretation, compounded by many constitutional elements not present in the day of Maqoma, albeit foreshadowed by his suspicion of government salaries. There is a major political division between the Ciskei and Transkei, each with its own autonomous political structure based on a combination of hereditary and electoral principles rather than on a purely hereditary principle. The chiefships are analogous to medieval European bishoprics rather than to elements in the political hierarchy —chiefship at this level entitles an incumbent to participate in the legislative councils but to hold executive office *ex officio* only at local government level. Chiefs command the respect of many of their people, albeit with an increasing proportion doubting their usefulness. The *legal* authority of the paramount to decide regents for minors and to install chiefs among the chiefdoms junior to him is questionable— as is the *moral* authority of the government to do the same.

The issue of Lent Maqoma's regency — Maxhoba is his fourth cousin's son — has echoes of the investiture debate between the popes and the medieval kings. The 'pope' in this case is Xolilizwe Sigcawu — the Gcaleka paramount and close associate of Matanzima, the 'King' of the Transkei. The Ciskei 'King' is Sebe. Sebe and his cabinet obviously have the power to make the appointments, but whether they have the moral authority is a matter which lies in the hearts of the Rharhabe themselves. The dispute has a more immediate parallel in Xhosa history —the deposition of Sandile by Harry Smith, rendered ineffectual because he had no power over the hearts of the people. The results of the Ciskeian election of July 1978 would suggest that Sebe does have the authority, and the approval of the crowd at Ntaba KaNdoda underlines it.

PART II

The Reinterment of Maqoma on 13 August 1978

Ntaba KaNdoda lies high in the Amatole hills some 5 km from the Alice-Kingwilliam's Town road and is reached by dirt roads about twice that distance in length.

We approached in a convoy of vehicles which continued steadily for about two hours from 9.0 a.m. to 11.0 a.m. The cars and buses had come from all parts of the Ciskei, and from more distant parts of the Cape Province, including the Western Cape. On the top of the hill, just below a prominent rock, the road ended in a large level area, partly cleared for a car park, partly wired off around two covered platforms and partly set aside for the new 'heroes' acre' about to receive its first hero. We were directed into the car park by African traffic officers (who were also on duty at the turn off from the main road and at the turn off from the dirt road to Keiskammahoek). They appeared to be under the direction of a white officer. Space was reserved in this area for at least two South African Defence Force vehicles which brought a polyethnic guard of honour (wearing blue berets) and the military band. These elements did not arrive until the latter part of the requiem mass, when they attracted a lot of attention from the adjacent women's enclosure — entirely friendly as far as could be seen.

At the entrance of the area the women were divided from the men, with a wire fence to prevent trespassing. This was ritually prescribed, but did not prevent some well-dressed women from coming round by the back of the men's stand. The prescription did not apply to the seer, nor to a white television crew woman who seemed free to move anywhere. Guards in civilian dress, augmented with blankets and each armed with a short spear and a stick, directed the people into their appropriate areas. It was notable that a very high proportion — much more than half — of the women were dressed in distinctive Xhosa dress, of both Mfengu and Xhosa variants. Under their orange dresses several of the women, notably those on the platform for distinguished guests, wore Sebe T-shirts, or displayed some other CNIP emblem.

We established that the use of cameras and tape-recorders would not cause offence — as subsequent events showed, the intrusion of the agents of the media was positively encouraged. We then made our way to the pathway which led up to the platform. This was kept clear for the entry of the key participants and the distinguished guests by a guard made up of members of the CNIP. They wore maroon berets with plastic tags to indicate the branch of the CNIP from which they came — Uitenhage had a substantial contingent. They also wore blankets and each carried a short spear and stick. We took up a position by the entrance and listened to them singing 'Somagwaza'. This is a song or chant which celebrates the manly virtues — a traditional accompaniment to youths going to initiation or men going to war. The majority of the men in the enclosure wore dark suits, some ancient black coats, others dark but not matching jackets and trousers. There were also some elderly men in more traditional dress with a blanket over their clothes and headgear of skins. Apart from that small minority, only the active male participants, including the guards, wore distinctive 'African' dress. An African journalist, in a dasniki shirt was very conspicuous among the soberly dressed men.

The cortège arrived on time, preceded by the seer in her car. She wore a black robe with a red fabric rose, accentuating her albino features, and carried a short wand decorated with coloured beads. She endeavoured to get out of the car at the entrance but could not manage to do so. She saw that the correct ritual was followed where the coffin was unloaded and rested for a few minutes. The formal salute to the dead chief 'Aa! Jongsumsobomvu' was given and a praise poet in T-shirt and shorts with a blanket and skin hat shouted and danced around the bier. One of the mourners — a member of the Maqoma family — carried the infant son of Chief Lent Maqoma (a child of about four) and laid him on the top of the coffin. The seer apparently insisted on this as to move the bones of a man after he has been buried creates impurity which can only be removed through contact with an innocent child. Chief Lent Maqoma is a descendant of the hero and, by decree of the Ciskei government, the regent (or acting paramount) of the Rharhabe segment of the Xhosa, during the infancy of Maxhoba the heir from the great house of the time of Sandile.

The pallbearers — two local Xhosa, three Mfengu and one Xhosa of foreign origin — then carried the bier between the guard and placed it on the covered platform. The seer was driven up to the platform, helped from the car and on to the platform where she sat beside the bier next to an altar set for mass. Acolytes and servers in red cassocks and white cottas were also on the platform.

The chiefs and other distinguished guests moved on to the covered stand where they had a good view of all the proceedings. The cameramen were allowed completely free access to all aspects of the ceremonies and showed particular interest in the seer's face. South African Television, South African Broadcasting Corporation and the Department of

Information were well represented.

The opening address was given by the seer in the form of a prayer. In it she emphasised that her work was now complete and that she could now return to the Transkei. She also affirmed that since the old Chief Maqoma had now returned for proper burial in his own place, Lent Maqoma was no longer the chief of the Jingqi. 'I disrobe you,' she said, 'your robes will be returned to you by Chief Sebe in the future.' Thus she indicated what the next major ceremony at Ntaba KaNdoda was likely to be and also her view of the hierarchy of authority in the installation of chiefs.

Chief Sebe, with a leopard skin over his suit, then made the major speech in English and Xhosa. He welcomed the distinguished guests, notably official Australian and French representatives, the departmental officials (Prisons and Defence) who had co-operated in the search for the bones and in bringing the whole event to fruition, and Paramount Chief Mphephu, Chief Minister of Venda. He praised Maqoma for his leadership, wisdom, courage, strategy and diplomacy in his attempts to secure justice and a fair deal for his people when the white people were trying to take away the Xhosa's land. He quoted from a well-known poem 'Lutaba KaNdoda' by Mqhayi to enhance the significance of the site as the new heroes' acre:

> That children respect their mothers
> Their mothers respect their husbands
> The men respect their chiefs
> And chiefs respect Qamata.

Clear themes in the speech, which was delivered with great emphasis in much of the Xhosa section and well received by the crowd, were implied parallels between himself and Maqoma as the men who possessed all the qualities of true leadership, and the assertion that he is now the chief of the whole Ciskei — a strong chief to unite the people 'who like strong chiefs' to regain their rights and to deal firmly with opposition within and without. He had impressed those present at the wake at the Jingqi chief's great place the previous evening with a similar speech in which he said, 'The train has left the station and the Ciskeians are sitting comfortably in it. How can the train ever go back to the station?'

After Sebe had finished speaking the service began. This was in the form of a mass, with three of the principals robed as celebrant, deacon and subdeacon, together with a reformed church minister who assisted at certain points. The deacon, the Rev. Zantsi, preached a sermon in which he urged the people to come together like the bones in Ezekiel's vision, to be united in order to obtain their heritage. The altar and the bier were censed and holy water sprinkled liberally — including some on the seer. Communion was served to those on the stage and to the descendants of Maqoma who were sitting on the ground beside it. Choirs from schools in the Ciskei led the singing and performed individual items in the area between the platform, the dignitaries' stand and the women's enclosure. Towards the end of the service the blue-bereted South African Defence Force guard of honour marched up, led by a military band. The pallbearers then took up the bier and led the way to the graveside, followed by Maqoma's family, the senior members of the Ciskeian cabinet and senior chiefs and then the other distinguished guests. The seer was assisted from the platform and taken to the grave by car. She had taken no active part in the service, during most of which she had given the impression of being bowed in prayer.

At the graveside those not entitled to be present were sent back to the men's enclosure by the master of ceremonies and the crowd had no view of the actual interment at all. Apart from the official party round the grave, and the representatives of the media, the guard of honour stood between the grave and the crowd, with Ciskeian police in khaki uniforms available to discourage intruders. At the end of the interment the last post was sounded and the South African Defence Force contingents marched off. As their lorries drove away some of the soldiers waved cheerfully to the crowd in the car park, and a few of the crowd waved back.

The event was over, and the people dispersed to their transport or to find food.

Analysis

It is necessary to explain why the South African government should have put itself to so much trouble and expense to return Maqoma's bones to the Ciskei; why the Ciskeian government should have identified itself with the quest of the family to regain the remains of a leader who died over a century ago; and why a new 'heroes' acre' should have been instituted to accommodate the bones. It is rumoured that the site is to be developed as a major centre with a stadium, despite the difficulty of access.

Maqoma was not genealogically a very senior chief — being of a right-hand house rather than of the great house of the Rharhabe dynasty. The inauguration of a new heroes' acre for him enabled him to be celebrated in his own right, rather than as a junior to the line of Sandile whose own heroes' acre was established only a decade ago. This action also asserted the independence of Lent Maqoma and the Jingqi from the Sandile line and might be seen as a first step towards the elevation of Lent Maqoma to the Rharhabe paramountcy, of which he was currently the regent. The seer's statement that Lent Maqoma should be reinstalled as Chief by Chief Minister Sebe, went against tradition — it is Xolilizwe or a senior chief in the Rharhabe segment who should have installed him. Further, Sebe's emphasis was less upon the particularistic criterion of descent as being the basis of chiefship than upon the universalistic criteria of chiefly qualities. As the *de facto* ruler of the Ciskei, his right to overrule descent and tradition in favour of other qualities — including loyalty to himself as chief minister — was being asserted. The event thus furthered the political ambitions of Lent Maqoma within the existing Ciskeian political framework.

For Sebe, we have already observed that by his self-identification with the hero and by his implied rejection of traditional rules for the filling of chiefships he was validating the claims not only of Lent Maqoma to paramount status, but his own claims to chiefly status. That this was being done in the context of a 'traditional' ritual and with the invocation of Xhosa religious categories does not detract from the radical hypothesis being advanced. The event also celebrated the triumph of the CNIP over its political opponents in the July 1978 elections — the involvement of the CNIP as a guard of honour and the position given to and taken by the senior members of the cabinet emphasising that this was a Ciskeian event, rather than simply a Xhosa or Rharhabe matter.

The selection of Ntaba KaNoda, a mountain site said to have been a refuge and rallying point for Maqoma and his forces, as opposed to a great place of a chief (the usual resting place) may be seen as an assertion of a new tradition. Maqoma is not 'taken to his ancestors' on their land, but laid to rest in a spot chosen to symbolise Xhosa or Ciskeian nationalism, one already identified to some extent with the CNIP. Here it was that the CNIP announced its candidates for its successful election campaign and followed the announcement with a sacrifice of two goats on the mountain top, presumably to enhance its prospects.

Other parallels suggest themselves — which could have been in minds other than our own. Maqoma was a Xhosa hero who was defeated by a combination of Mfengu and British — the former have been in power, have been defeated, and partly absorbed into the CNIP; the latter have been ousted by the Afrikaners and declined to help in bringing the bones back to the Ciskei. The dealing of strength with strength is effective, weakness with weakness ineffective. Sebe was thus celebrating the triumph of Xhosa over Mfengu whilst inviting them to join him in a united effort to ensure a better future for their children.

At the broader level of South African politics, the event is consistent with government policy. The recovery of Maqoma's bones by 'traditional methods' through the seer, and the contribution of the South African Defence Force would seem to be aimed at emphasising the unity and traditions of the Ciskei as a single geo-political unit. It hastens the process towards political autonomy under a Ciskeian government willing to co-operate with South Africa.

The device of the funeral could be seen as playing anti-government bodies at their own game. The funerals of Biko and Sobukwe were attended by thousands of people – symbolising the vigour of African resistance to continued white rule. Robben Island is a symbol of both the death and rebirth of African nationalist aspirations. The return of Maqoma from Robben Island can be seen as a statement by the Ciskeian government (with South African support) that it can bring its heroes home – a symbolic, if not real, victory for the aspirations of the people through negotiation rather than through confrontation. The great crowd brought for the occasion (estimated to be 15,000 by the press) showed the popular support for Sebe.

Thus, the whole event, involving the co-operation of Maqoma's family, the Ciskeian government and the South African government (as was indicated in the procession to the grave), and the support of both traditional religious figures (the seer and the praise poet) and the Xhosa Christian bodies can be seen as a major political 'triumph' in the Roman sense, for all parties. The Maqomas have asserted their independence of and equality with the Sandiles. The CNIP has asserted its leadership of the Ciskei both internally and as the spiritual heir of those who sought to save their land from white incursion. The South African government has indicated its moral support for the Ciskei government and the aspirations of the people.

The value of ritual in this context lies in its ambiguity. It can mean, as has been suggested, different things to different people, each 'hearing' what he wants to hear in the situation. It is emotionally satisfying without being politically binding since all is open to interpretation by all the parties concerned.

Conclusion

What does an exercise of this nature prove? Certainly that the CNIP can mount a major publicity exercise and do it with panache. The presence of Mfengu chiefs as pallbearers suggests that the Mfengu are far from being united in opposition to Sebe, although the proportion of Mfengu in the crowd was low. Most of those present were rural people — a very few came from the urban centres outside the Ciskei — an indication of apathy towards the event (or unwillingness to meet the costs of coming). Makinana, a senior Rharhabe chief, was notably absent, as was Burns-Ncamashe, another Rharhabe chief of note and Mabandla, the former chief minister and a major Mfengu leader. Unity may have taken a step forward, and the important shift from genealogical to political (or universalistic) criteria as a basis for accession to chiefly office taken a step beyond that of the colonial system. But the way forward is long and it would be a true seer who could predict whether these events are totally irrelevant in the long run, whether they represent a forward, backward or sideways step in the great South African minuet.

Notes

1. C. Brownlee, *Reminiscences of Kaffir Life and History* (Lovedale Press, Alice, 1896), p. 197.
2. J. Meintjies, *Sandile* (Struik, Cape Town, 1971), p. 36.
3. Colonel Maclean quoted by Meintjies, *Sandile*, p. 63.
4. R. Godlonton, *Irruption of the Kaffir Hordes* (Struik, Cape Town, Facsimile Reprint 1965), p. 219.
5. Ibid.
6. Brownlee, *Reminiscences*, p. 314.
7. G.C. Moore Smith, *The Autobiography of Sir Harry Smith* (John Murray, London, 1901), vol. 2, p. 228.
8. Brownlee, *Reminiscences*.

12 THE ECONOMICS AND POLITICS OF DEPENDENCE

Nancy Charton

The Ciskei is an impoverished area in one of the less well developed regions of the Republic. The focal point of development within this region is the city of East London and its environs, a focal point which remains external to the borders of the Ciskei, and is itself a comparatively small seaport. The large black city of Mdantsane which has grown up 12 km away in response to industrial and urban development, lies within the Ciskei; but it is a city only in name. There is no industrial development there, and only a very rudimentary commercial sector. It is in reality a dormitory suburb of East London.

Nor can one speak of a Ciskeian urban system. There are large numbers of indigenous villages which lack any kind of urban infrastructure, or differentiation of employment and occupation. The low-level buying power in the semi-subsistence economy characteristic of the rural areas does not promote the development of an urban system. The small towns that do exist act as market centres; only at Sada and Dimbaza have a few industries been established, with government aid.

The pattern of development has conditioned the communications network. Roads run from villages and towns to the focal centre of development, promoting not interconnectedness within the system, but the outward flow of manpower and the inward flow of goods and services.

The agricultural sector is not viable. In the two village communities studied there was only one relatively large-scale commercial farmer; and every male head of household interviewed had been away from the village for some time as a migrant labourer.[1] There were few opportunities for earning a living other than on the land, and migrants did not bring back skills relevant to the economic life of the village. The impoverishment of the land has resulted in part from the natural increase of the population, and the lack of incentive which small-scale cash cropping has offered to peasants. Wage-labour on a temporary basis in the city is a more attractive alternative. In the rural survey only two out of 88 claimed that agriculture was a desirable way of life. Given the vagaries of the Ciskeian climate, the level of technical skill, and the meagre return from the small fields available, that is hardly surprising.

Investigations among workers in the factories of East London have shown that it is the young, the able bodied, and the more highly educated who are drawn to the urban centres in search of work, and higher economic returns for their labour.[2] This means that the village exports its most precious commodity, its manpower, and receives in return the cash remittances of its migrants. Such remittances are most often spent on consumer goods, which the village has had to purchase from the encapsulating white areas. It exports manpower, youth, courage and ability, and village society, having been selectively creamed of its initiative, is left to stagnate economically and politically. Headmen's and chiefs' councils are deprived of capable participants, men in their middle years, and the young who should be learning to use their political skills at local level.

Not all Ciskeians who live in the rural areas have access to fields or grazing. There are no reliable estimates of the actual number of landless people. But in two of the villages studied there are large groups of such people; their only avenue of employment is share-cropping for helpful neighbours, or contract labour in the 'white' areas of the Republic. These landless people came in from the surrounding 'white' agricultural areas where increasing mechanisation and rationalisation of the productive process had made them 'superfluous'. Influx control operating in all 'white' urban areas meant they could not seek a refuge in the cities. This movement from the 'white' farms dates back many years, as the Burnshill study shows. But considerable resettlement is also currently taking place at the insistence of the Republican government. Those living on the fringes of urban society, unemployed and unemployable for various reasons, are endorsed out of urban areas. They constitute a growing rural 'reserve army of the unemployed'. The Republican government thus adds to the pressure of population on land, which is already considerable, and the Ciskeian government is powerless to resist the repatriation of their citizens from 'white' urban areas.

An ailing rural economy is not the only problem. The population of Mdantsane lives in comparative poverty. Investigations revealed that between 40 per cent and 50 per cent lived below the poverty datum line, that there was an unemployment rate of 25 per cent and that a further 14 per cent kept body and soul together by working in the informal sector. A continuous flow of rural migrants ensure low wage levels. Job opportunities are urgently required, not merely to promote economic development and raise living standards, but to feed a rapidly burgeoning population. Industries are needed for survival.

The Republican government sees industrialisation as the answer. Industrialists were given certain inducements to locate themselves in the Berlin, King William's Town, East London triangle, that is, in the 'white' areas adjacent to the Ciskei. By March 1974, R81.3 million had been invested by the private sector and the Industrial Development Corporation, giving employment to 10,834 blacks.[3] Subsequently two industrial growth points were located in the Ciskei itself at Sada and Dimbaza, with relatively modest results. This development strategy to an extent has alleviated unemployment. However, it has increased rather than diminished the dependence of the Ciskei on South Africa. To begin with, the most important industries are located in 'white' areas, thus outside the jurisdiction of the Ciskeian government. Those located within the Ciskei require capital, technology, skilled personnel, raw material from and markets in the Republic. Ciskeians take few of the economic decisions which affect the industrial life of the territory; they cannot decide what should be produced, how to produce it or where to market the product; because markets are situated elsewhere they cannot exercise even the normal buyer's sanction in a free market. They cannot decide on the distribution of surplus on their terms, for the surplus does not belong to them. These decisions are taken by residents of the Republic, or by foreigners, and one may reasonably assume that decisions are taken in their own interests, rather than in the interests of the Ciskei. Because surplus generated during the process of production is exported to shareholders in the Republic, or further afield, and wages earned by white technicians are spent in 'white' areas, and even wages earned by Ciskeian citizens are spent in the shops of East London, rather than in the Ciskei, there is little spin-off for the Ciskei from the presence either of border industries, or from the small industries within the territory. The economy of the Ciskei remains an outward oriented economy, whose function in the total Southern African system is merely to produce cheap labour power. It lacks any interdependence, and interconnectedness. And lacking any internal autonomous dynamic it is open to all the ills of the wider system which dominates it; it cannot command the bargaining power to compel decisions in its own interests.

Another important factor in the basic structural dependence of the Ciskei is the imitative patterns of consumption set in train by its proximity to the affluent white society which encapsulates it. Many Ciskeians aspire to 'white' standards of living. Given the economic resources available, and the capital and skills to develop them, these aspirations can be satisfied only by borrowing the shortfall in capital, technology, skills and imported consumer goods.[4] Borrowing may be creative, when undertaken to improve the infrastructure and increase the production potential. But when it is ploughed into consumer spending it can only increase the degree of dependence. The mass media often contribute to this unhealthy keeping up with the Joneses, the van der Merwes and the Dumanis! Black elites aspire to white standards; and they in turn act as trend setters in consumption patterns; they also develop an interest in maintaining a standard of living which the region as a whole cannot support without incurring dependency. It must be concluded that the Ciskei does not have an autonomous economy, nor any prospect of one. It remains a poverty stricken area in one of the less well developed regions of the Republic, its economic future firmly tied to the chariot wheels of the South African economy.

The degree of structural economic dependence is matched by political dependence, built into the political institutions and exacerbated by the stratification of Ciskeian society. The Ciskei, although said to be 'self-governing', has only a subordinate legislature. The Republican Parliament remains the sovereign body. All acts passed must have the consent of the South African State President. He *may* also remove the Chief Minister at the request of the Assembly. However, there is not even a constitutional convention which might constrain the State President to remove the Chief Minister when he does not wish to do so. Thus the Chief Minister, although theoretically responsible to his own Legislature, is much more effectively tied to the Republican government by the constitution itself. Fiscally the constraints on the Ciskei are very strong. Seventy-nine per cent of the annual revenue in 1975 derived from the Republic. It would be difficult for any Ciskeian regime to carry on without a subsidy of this magnitude, unless maintained by an outside benefactor. The estimates must be approved by the Republican Minister of Finance, and all accounts are audited by the South African Controller and Auditor General. Chief Sebe indeed once complained that the Republican government actually uses these fiscal powers to ensure compliance with their wishes. The legal system remains essentially South African. No High Court has yet been constituted, and the Eastern Cape Division of the Supreme Court exercises jurisdiction there. The sweeping security powers of the Republican government have been used in the Ciskei to block the development of the Black Consciousness movement, which it saw as a threat to the homeland government. The Ciskei now has its own security police, headed by the brother of the Chief Minister, and this was used, in conjunction with the Republican security forces, to detain opposition leaders and candidates during the 1978 General Election. The communications system, road, rail, air and radio and television remain the province of the Republican government.

The administrative system is directed by seconded white officials. Key posts in all departments are still occupied by these officials, in spite of the policy of Africanisation which has been pushed ahead as rapidly as possible. The public service occupies a position of power. As in the colonial situation it still has expertise and information not shared by politicians. Parliamentarians, as elsewhere in the world, are often inexperienced and technologically ignorant. And the committee system in the legislature which could assist MLAs to gain insight into administrative problems and procedure is rudimentary, and ineffective as an instrument of control.

This checklist of overt political and administrative constraints operating on the Ciskei from the Republic is formidable. However, it can also be demonstrated that the major political actors are still tied to the Ciskeian government and through it to the Republican government. The jobs created in the public service have constituted an important element in the politics of 'pay-off', and have enabled the Chief Minister and his ruling party to build a modicum of middle-class support. Political activity among public servants is frowned upon, especially if such activity involves support for opposition parties. One might say that the black public servants are tied to the Ciskeian government and are dependant on it. They constitute another link in the chain of dependency which stretches from the Republican government into all aspects of Ciskeian life and society. Chiefs, who have a majority in the Legislative Assembly, are salaried officers of the government. A majority of the chiefs originally constituted the official opposition, but today all but three have crossed the floor to the CNIP, prised loose by promise and by threat. Teachers also constitute an important element in the Ciskeian middle class. They have grown in numbers and in status; but they too found it unrewarding to participate in opposition politics. Black entrepreneurs are now emerging as a result of the policy of Africanisation of the private commercial sector. They are dependent on a government corporation for loans to start their business, and for training. The only relatively independent sector of the elite are the lawyers and doctors. At least two are in exile in the Transkei; but as a group they have played an insignificant role in Ciskeian politics. Their absence from the legislature is remarkable; it is indicative of the estrangement of the top professionals from the homeland system.

On the whole Ciskeian middle-class elites have stood to benefit from

the homeland dispensation. Two social groups however remain out in
the cold, the landless proletariat in the rural areas and the workers in
the new factories around East London and in the Ciskei itself. Moves on
the part of the Ciskeian government to articulate their interests have
been frustrated by the South African government's land policy, and by
white agricultural, industrial and commercial interests. In the long
term then it is possible that the dependency of the Ciskei will distort
the lines of political conflict, at present drawn on ethnic lines. Where
the regional government fails to articulate the interests of the poor
peasant and of the worker, the disaffected groups will tend to focus
more and more on Pretoria, the perceived centre of power, for the resolution of their problems. And to lead them there may well be members
of an estranged professional class!

Elites are tied to the system, not by constitutional means alone, but
by bonds of common interest. This is not to deny that there is elite
competition. But the answer of the ruling party to this competition,
and to an important and growing challenge by opposition parties in
1977 was the creation of a *de facto* one-party 'state' during and after
the general election of 1978. The will of the people is said to have
accomplished this feat! But the percentage poll was low, and intimidatory tactics, especially the detention of numerous opposition personalities seems to have effectively augmented the influence of chiefs tied
to the ruling party, and of perceptions of politics as a 'winner takes all'
game, which predisposes both rural and urban Ciskeians to vote for the
party in power. The emphasis in the present 'one-party' system is on
authoritarian politics, rather than on the building of a party which
might encourage participation at the grass-roots level, and the articulation of interests across a wide spectrum. Such a party system in which
the leaders are effectively tied constitutionally, fiscally, and in terms of
personal and group interests to the Republican government can only
augment the degree of political dependence which already exists. In the
short term a one-party system and the containment of conflict could be
seen as shoring up the traditional elites, and stabilising both internal
conflict, and conflict with the South African government. But this
study has produced much evidence to show that the legitimacy of
traditional elites is suffering as a result of being incorporated in a
centralised regional structure; a chief cannot be a chief *for* the people
when he is seen to be the creature of the ruling party, and ultimately of
the Republican government. A chief minister tied to the Republic by
social, economic and constitutional bonds is similarly not free to be
chief minister *for* the people; he will be seen to be the creature of the

Republican government. Ample evidence has also been produced of alienation, particularly among certain ethnic and social groups, and in the urban areas. And it is fair to assume that in the long term, those groups excluded from political benefits, such as peasants and workers, will lack any enthusiasm for a system which consistently fails to benefit them.

Finally the mass media constitute an important link in the chains of dependence, for they mediate news to blacks either from the Afrikaner nationalist perspective, or from the white progressive or liberal perspective. Issues are judged and set forth in terms of their meaning for white, rather than in terms of their meaning for black politics. Even the traditional news network operates through chiefs and headmen, and tends to be supportive of the ruling party — thus tied to the official South African line. Whites draw up the agenda for communication of all types of news and all networks.

It must be concluded that the Ciskei is welded to the Republic by social, economic, fiscal, constitutional and political bonds. The communication system whether modern or traditional emanates from and is controlled by the dominant partner, the Republic. It would be a singular operation which could amputate the Ciskei from the body economic and politic of the Republic.

Notes

1. G.D. Sack, 'Innovation and Entrepreneurship in Two Ciskeian Villages' in Charton (ed.) 'A Socio-Economic Survey'.
2. J.B. McI. Daniel and R.W. Waxmonsky, 'East London: Study of Black Industrial Employees in Relation to Migration Characteristics' in Charton (ed.) 'A Socio-Economic Survey'.
3. Benbo, *Black Development in South Africa*.
4. G. Arrighi and J.S. Saul, *The Political Economy of Africa* (Monthly Review Press, New York, 1973).

BIBLIOGRAPHY

Ahluwalia, M.S. 'The Scope for Policy Intervention' in H. Chenery, M.S. Ahluwalia *et al. Growth with Redistribution* (Oxford University Press, London, 1974)
Annual Survey of South African Law (Juta and Co., Cape Town, 1951)
Annual Survey of South African Law (Juta and Co., Cape Town, 1963)
Apter, D.E. 'Some Reflections on the Role of a Political Opposition in New Nations' in I. Markowitz *African Politics and Society* (Free Press, New York, 1970)
Arrighi, G. and Saul, J.S. *The Political Economy of Africa* (Monthly Review Press, New York, 1973)
Ayliff, J and Whiteside, J. *History of the AbaMbo generally known as Fingos* (Struik, Cape Town, 1912, reprinted 1962)
Baran, P. *The Political Economy of Growth* (Monthly Review Press, New York, 1957)
Bekker, J.C. 'The Judicial System of Transkei' *Comparative and International Law Journal of Southern Africa* 11 (1978)
Bell, K.N. and Morrell, W.P. *Selected Documents on British Foreign Policy 1830-1860* (Clarendon Press, Oxford, 1928)
Bell, T. 'Some Aspects of Industrial Decentralisation in South Africa' *South African Journal of Economics* 41 (1973)
Benbo *Ciskei Economic Review* (Bureau for Economic Research re Bantu Development, Pretoria, 1975)
────*Black Development in South Africa* (Perskor, Johannesburg, 1976)
Black, P.A. 'An Analysis of Consumer Potential in Mdantsane' in Charton, N. (ed.) 'A Socio-Economic Survey of the Border and Ciskei Regions' (unpublished report, Institute of Social and Economic Research, Rhodes University, Grahamstown, 1978)
────'Regional Development Strategy and the Black Homelands' in M.L. Truu (ed.) *Public Policy and the South African Economy* (Oxford University Press, Cape Town, 1976)
Board, C., Davies, R.J. and Fair, T.J.D. 'The Structure of the South African Space Economy: An Integrated Approach' *Regional Studies* 4 (1970)
Borts, G.H. and Stein, J.L. *Economic Growth in a Free Market* (Columbia University Press, New York, 1964)

Brand, S. 'Agricultural and Economic Development in Southern Africa' in J. Barratt *et al.* (eds.) *Accelerated Development in Southern Africa* (Macmillan, London, 1974)

Breytenbach, W.J. *Bantoetuislande: Verkiesings en Politieke Partye*, Mededelinge van die Afrika Instituut no. 23 (Africa Institute, Pretoria, 1974)

Brookes, E.M. *The History of Native Policy in South Africa from 1830 to the Present Day* (Nasionale Pers, Pretoria, 1928)

Brookfield, H.C. 'On the Environment as Perceived' *Progress in Geography* 1 (1969)

Brown T. 'Free Press Fair Game for South Africa's Government' *Journalism Quarterly* 48 (1971)

Brownlee, C. *Reminiscences of Kaffir Life and History* (Lovedale Press, Alice, 1896)

Brutzkus, E. 'Centralised vs Decentralised Pattern of Urbanisation in Developing Countries' *Tijdschrift voor Economische en Sociale Geographie* 64 (1973)

Bundy, C. 'The Emergence and Decline of a South African Peasantry' *African Affairs* 71 (1972)

Cameron, E.D. and Cooper, B.K. *The West African Councillor* (Oxford University Press, London, 1961)

Charton, N. 'A Socio-Economic Survey of the Border and Ciskei Regions Regions' (unpublished report, Institute of Social and Economic Research, Rhodes University, Grahamstown, 1978)

Chenery, H.B. 'The Structuralist Approach to Development Policy' *American Economic Review* 65 (1975)

Cohen, A. *Custom and Politics in Urban Africa* (Routledge & Kegan Paul, London, 1969)

Cohen, S. and Young, J. (eds.) *The Manufacture of News: Social Problems, Deviance and Mass Media* (Constable, London, 1973)

Daniel, J.B. McI. 'The Swazi Rural Economy: Some thoughts on the Problems of Land Tenure' *South African Geographical Society*, Jubilee Conference Proceedings (1967).

Daniel, J.B. McI. and Waxmonsky, R.W. 'East London: Study of Black Industrial Employees in Relation to Migration Characteristics' in Charton, N. (ed.) 'A Socio-Economic Survey of the Border and Ciskei Regions' (unpublished Report, Institute for Social and Economic Research, Rhodes University, Grahamstown, 1978)

Davies, R.J. and Cook, G.P. 'Re-appraisal of the South African urban hierarchy' *South African Geographical Journal* 50 (1968)

Dean, W.H.B. 'A Citizen of Transkei' *Comparative and International*

Law Journal of Southern Africa 11 (1978)
De Lange, M. 'Some Traditional Cosmetic Practices of the Xhosa' Annals, Cape Provincial Museum (1963)
Deutschmann, P.J. 'The Mass Media in an Underdeveloped Village' *Journalism Quarterly* 40 (1963)
Dos Santos, T. 'The Structure of Dependence' *American Economic Review* 60 (1970)
Downs, D.M. 'Geographic Space Perception: Past Approaches and Future Prospects' *Progress in Geography* 2 (1970)
Du Toit, A.E. 'The Cape Frontier: A study of Native Policy with Special Reference to the Years 1847-1866' *Archives Yearbook for South African History* (1954), vol. 17, Part 1
El Shaks, 'Planning for systems of settlement in emerging nations' *Town Planning Review* 47, 2 (1976)
Fair, T.J.D. 'Some Spatial Aspects of Black Homeland Development in South Africa' (Occasional Paper 6, URRU, University of Witwatersrand, Johannesburg, 1975)
Fei, J.C. and Ranis, G. 'A Theory of Economic Development' *American Economic Review* 51 (1961)
Fett, J.H. 'Situational Factors and Peasants' Search for Market Information' *Journalism Quarterly* 52 (1975)
Finkle, J.L. and Gable, R.W. *Political Development and Social Change* (John Wiley & Sons, New York, 1971)
Firth, R. 'Rumour in a Primitive Society' *Journal of Abnormal and Social Psychology* 53 (1955)
Fisk, E.K. and Shand, R.T. 'Early Stages of Development in a Primitive Economy: The Evolution from Subsistence to Trade and Specialization' in C.R. Wharton (ed.) *Subsistence Agriculture and Economic Development* (Frank Cass, London, 1970)
Frank, A.G. *Latin America: Underdevelopment or Revolution* (Monthly Review Press, New York, 1969)
Gluckman, M. 'Gossip and Scandal' *Current Anthropology* 4 (1963)
—— 'Psychological, Sociological and Anthropological Explanations of Witchcraft and Gossip: A Clarification' *Man* (NS) 3 (1968)
Godlonton, R. *Irruption of the Kaffir Hordes* (Struik, Cape Town, Facsimile Reprint, 1965)
Gordon, S. *Domestic Workers: A Handbook for Housewives* (Institute of Race Relations, Johannesburg, 1973)
Gordon, T.J. 'The Evolution of Mdantsane' in G.P. Cook and J. Opland (eds.) *Mdantsane* (Institute for Social and Economic Research, Rhodes University, Grahamstown, forthcoming)

Gordon, T.J. 'Mdantsane: City Satellite or Suburb' (unpublished dissertation, Rhodes University, Grahamstown, 1977)

Groenewald, D.M. 'Die Administratiewe Funksionering van Bewindinstellings in die Ciskei met besondere verwysing na plaaslike bestuur' (unpublished MA thesis, Rhodes University, Grahamstown, 1976)

Hachten, W.A. *Muffled Drums: The News Media in Africa* (Iowa State University Press, Ames, 1971)

Hailey, Lord *An African Survey Revised 1956* (Oxford University Press, London, 1957)

Hammond-Tooke, W.D. *The Tribes of Willowvale District* (Department of Native Affairs, Pretoria, 1957)

—— *The Tribes of King William's Town District* (Department of Native Affairs, Pretoria, 1958)

—— 'The Present State of Cape Nguni Ethnographic Studies' in *Ethnological and Linguistic Studies in Honour of N.J. van Warmelo* (Department of Native Affairs, Pretoria, 1969)

—— *Command or Consensus* (David Philip, Cape Town, 1975)

Handelman, D. 'Gossip in Encounters: The Transmission of Information in a Bounded Social Setting' *Man* (NS) 8 (1973)

Harries-Jones, P. *Freedom and Labour: Mobilization and Political Control on the Zambian Copperbelt* (Blackwell, Oxford, 1975)

Harvey, M.E. and Hung, M.S. 'The application of a p-Median algorithm to the identification of nodal hierarchies and growth centres' *Economic Geography* 50, 3 (1974)

Heyne, J.F. 'A Transkeian Citizen of South African Nationality' *Tydskrif vir Hedendaagse Romeins-Hollandse Reg* 26 (1963)

Hirabayashi, G.K. and El Khatib, M.F. 'Communication and Political Awareness in the Villages of Egypt' *Public Opinion Quarterly* 22 (1958)

Holleman, J.F. *Experiment in Swaziland* (Oxford University Press, Cape Town, 1964)

Hopkins, R.F. *Political Roles in New States* (Yale University Press, New Haven, 1971)

Horrell, M. and Horner, D. *A Survey of Race Relations in South Africa 1973* (SAIRR, Johannesburg, 1974)

Houghton, D.H. *The South African Economy* (Oxford University Press, Cape Town, 1964)

Huntington, S.P. *Political Order in Changing Societies* (Yale University Press, New Haven, 1969)

ILO *Employment and Economic Growth* (International Labour Office, Geneva, 1964)

―― *Towards Full Employment: A Programme for Colombia* (International Labour Office, Geneva, 1970)

―― *Employment Incomes and Equity: A Strategy for Increasing Productive Employment in Kenya* (International Labour Office, Geneva, 1972)

Johnson, R.J. *Spatial Structure* (Methuen, London, 1973)

Johnstone, F.A. 'White Prosperity and White Supremacy in South Africa Today' *African Affairs* 69 (1970)

Jolly, R. 'Manpower and Education' in D. Seers and L. Joy (eds.) *Development in a Divided World* (Penguin, Harmondsworth, 1971)

Jorgenson, D.W. 'Surplus Agricultural Labour and the Development of a Dual Economy' *Oxford Economic Papers* 19 (1967)

Kahn, E. 'Native Administration' in *Annual Survey of South African Law 1951* (Juta & Co., Cape Town, 1952)

―― 'Some thoughts on the Competency of the Transkeian Legislative Assembly and the Sovereignty of the South African Parliament' *South African Law Journal* 80 (1963)

―― 'The Self-Governing Territory of the Transkei' *Annual Survey of South African Law* (Juta & Co., Cape Town, 1964)

Kantor, B.S. and Kenny, H.F. 'The Poverty of Neo-Marxism: the Case of South Africa' *Journal of Southern African Studies* 3 (1976)

Katz, E. and Lazarsfeld, P.F. *Personal Influence: The Part Played by People in the Flow of Mass Communications* (Free Press, New York, 1964)

Kay, G. *Development and Underdevelopment: A Marxist Analysis* (Macmillan, London, 1975)

Kebschull, H.G. *Politics in Transitional Societies* (Appleton-Century-Crofts, New York, 1968)

Kotze, D. *African Politics in South Africa 1964-1974* (Hurst, London, 1975)

Legassick, M. 'Legislation, Ideology and Economy in post-1948 South Africa' *Journal of Southern African Studies* 1 (1974)

Le Roux, P. 'An Analytical Approach to the Poor White Phenomenon in South Africa' Paper read at Conference of the Economic Society of South Africa, Pretoria (1977)

Leys, C. 'Interpreting African Underdevelopment Reflections on the ILO Report on Employment, Incomes and Equality in Kenya' *African Affairs* 72 (1973)

Lipton, M. 'The International Diffusion of Technology' in D. Seers and L. Joy (eds.) *Development in a Divided World* (Penguin, Harmondsworth, 1971)

—— 'The South African Census and the Bantustan Policy' *World Today* 28 (1972)

Little, I.M.D. and Mirrlees, J. *Manual of Industrial Project Analysis in Developing Countries*: vol 2, *Social Cost Benefit Analysis* (OECD, New York, 1969)

Logan, M.I. 'The Spatial System and Planning Strategies in Developing Countries' *Geographical Review* 62 (1972)

Lowenthal, D. 'Geography, Experience and Imagination: Toward a Geographical Epistomology' *Annals Association of American Geographers* 51 (1961)

Mabandla, J. Mimeographed Statement, 24 April 1973

McGee, T. *The Urbanisation Process in the Third World* (Bell, London, 1971)

Mafeje, A. 'Religion, Class and Ideology in South Africa' in M.G. Whisson and Martin West (eds.) *Religion and Social Change in Southern Africa* (Philip, Cape Town, 1975)

Malan, T. and Hattingh, P.S. (eds.) *Swart Tuislande in Suid Afrika* (Africa Institute, Pretoria, 1975)

Maree, J. and de Vos, P.J. *Underemployment, Poverty and Migrant Labour in the Transkei and Ciskei* (SA Institute of Race Relations, Johannesburg, 1975)

Market Research (Pty) Ltd *Readership* (Johannesburg, 1975) vol. 4

—— *Readership* (Johannesburg, 1975) vol. 1, 5

Martin, R.R., McNelly, S.T. and Izcaray, F. 'Is Media Exposure Unidimensional? A Socio-Economic Approach' *Journalism Quarterly* 53 (1976)

Matravers, D.R. 'It's All in the Day's Work' in Cook, G.R. and Opland, J. (eds.) *Mdantsane* (Institute for Social and Economic Research, Rhodes University, Grahamstown, forthcoming)

Mayer, P. *Townsmen or Tribesmen* (Oxford University Press, Cape Town, 1961)

—— *Urban Africans and the Bantustans* (South African Institute of Race Relations, Johannesburg, 1972)

Meintjies, J. *Sandile* (Struik, Cape Town, 1971)

Mill, J.S. *Utilitarianism, Liberty and Representative Government* (Dent, London & New York, 1936)

Miller, R.A. 'District Development Committees in Malawi' *Journal of Administration Overseas* 9 (1970)

Milles, M.E. and Wilson, M. *Land Tenure*, vol. 4 *Keiskammahoek Rural Survey* (Shuter & Shuter, Pietermaritzburg, 1952)

Moore Smith, G.C. (ed.) *The Autobiography of Sir Harry Smith* (John

Murray, London, 1901) vol. 2
Mosel, J.N. 'Communication Patterns and Political Socialisation in Transitional Thailand' in Pye, L.W. *Communication and Political Development* (Princetown University Press, Princetown, 1963)
Moyer, R.A. 'Some Current Manifestations of Early Mfengu History' in *Collected Seminar Papers on the Societies of Southern Africa in the 19th and 20th Centuries* (Institute of Commonwealth Studies, University of London, London, 1973) vol. 3
—— 'The Mfengu, Self-defence and the Cape Frontier Wars' in C. Saunders and R. Derricourt (eds.) *Beyond the Cape Frontier* (Longmans, London, 1974)
—— 'A History of the Mfengu of the Eastern Cape 1815-1865' (unpublished dissertation, University of London, 1976)
Mqhayi, S.E.K. *Ityala LamaWele* (Lovedale Press, Lovedale, 1914)
Mueller, C. 'Notes on the Repression of Communicative Behaviour' in Hans Pieter Dreitzel (ed.) *Recent Sociology No 2 Patterns of Communicative Behaviour* (Macmillan, London, 1970)
Muller, C.F.J. *Die Britse Owerheid en die Groot Trek* (Juta & Co., Cape Town, 1948)
—— *Five Hundred Years* (Academia, Pretoria, 1969)
Murdock, G. and Golding, P. 'For a Political Economy of Mass Communications' in *The Socialist Register 1973* (Merlin Press, London, 1974)
Myint, H. *Economic Theory and Underdeveloped Countries* (Oxford University Press, London, 1973)
Myrdal, G. *Economic Theory and Underdeveloped Regions* (Methuen, London, 1957)
Nader, L. 'Communication between Village and City in the Modern Middle East' *Human Organization* 24 (1965)
Omer-Cooper, J.D. *The Zulu Aftermath* (Longmans, London, 1966)
Orlik, P.B. 'Under Damocles Sword – the South African Press' *Journalism Quarterly* 46 (1969)
Paine, R. 'What is Gossip About? An Alternative Hypothesis' *Man* (NS) 2 (1967)
—— 'Informal Communication and Information Management' *Canadian Review of Sociology and Anthropology* (1970)
—— 'Transactions as Communicative Events', Paper read at Conference of the Association of Social Anthropologists, Oxford (1973)
Pauw, B.A. *Christianity and Xhosa Tradition Belief and Ritual Among Xhosa-speaking Christians* (Oxford University Press, Cape Town, 1975)
Peires, J.B. 'A History of the Xhosa 1700-1835' (unpublished dissertation,

Rhodes University, Grahamstown, 1976)
Phillips, B.D. and Renders, V. *Industrial Change in the East London/ King William's Town and Port Elizabeth/Uitenhage Metropolitan Regions: 1960-70* (Institute for Planning Research, University of Port Elizabeth, Port Elizabeth, 1976)
Pocock, D.C.D. 'Environmental, Perception Process and Product' *Tijdschrift voor Economische en Sociale Geografie* 64 (1973)
Pool, I de S. *Handbook of Communication* (Rand McNally, Chicago, 1973)
Potgieter, J.F. *The Household Subsistence Level in the Major Urban Centres of the Republic of South Africa* (Institute for Planning Research, University of Port Elizabeth, Port Elizabeth, 1975)
Potholm, C. *Four African Political Systems* (Prentice Hall, Englewood Cliffs, NJ, 1970)
Potter, E. *The Press as Opposition: The Political Role of South African Newspapers* (Chatto & Windus, London, 1975)
Prebisch, R. *The Economic Development of Latin America and its Principal Problems* (UN, Department of Economic Affairs, New York, 1950)
Prince, H.C. 'Real, Imagined and Abstract Worlds of the Past' *Progress in Geography* 3 (1971)
Pye, L.W. *Communication and Political Development* (Princeton University Press, Princeton, 1963)
Ranis, G. 'Unemployment and Factor Price Distortions' in R. Jolly, E de Kadt *et al.* (eds.) *Third World Employment* (Penguin, Harmondsworth, 1973)
Rautenbach, J. 'The Constitution of Transkei' *Tydskrif vir die Suid Afrikaanse Reg* 1 (1977)
Rhoodie, N.J. *et al., Homelands: The Role of the Corporations* (Chris van Rensburg Publications, Johannesburg, 1974)
Richings, F.G. 'The Applicability of South African Legislation in the Self-Governing Bantu Territories' in *South African Law Journal* 93 (1976)
Riddell, J.B. *The Spatial Dynamics of Modernization in Sierra Leone* (Northwestern University Press, Evanston, Ill., 1970)
Robinson, J.P. 'Interpersonal Influence in Election Campaigns: Two-step Flow Hypothesis' *Public Opinion Quarterly* 40 (1976)
Rogers, E. 'Mass Media Exposure and Modernization among Colombian Peasants' *Public Opinion Quarterly* 29 (1965)
Rogers, E. and Svenning L. *Modernization among Peasants: The Impact of Communication* (Holt, Rinehart & Winston, New York, 1969)

Rogers, E. 'Mass Media and Interpersonal Communication' in Pool, I. de S. (ed.) *Handbook of Communication* (Rand McNally, Chicago, 1973)

Rothwell, K.J. (ed.) *Administrative Issues in Developing Economies* (Lexington Books, 1972)

Sack, G.D. 'Innovation and Entrepreneurship in Two Ciskeian Villages' in Charton, N. (ed.) 'A Socio-Economic Survey of the Border and Ciskei Regions' (unpublished report, Institute of Social and Economic Research, Rhodes University, Grahamstown 1978)

Sebe, L.L. 'The Role of the Scientists in the Development of the Homelands' (unpublished paper read at 72nd Annual Congress of South African Association for the Advancement of Science, Grahamstown)

—— 'Potential Problems and Priorities of the Ciskei' *AIESEC Journal* (1975) vol. 1

Seers, D. 'Rich Countries and Poor' in D. Seers and L. Joy (eds.) *Development in a Divided World* (Penguin, Harmondsworth, 1971)

Seligman, L.G. 'Political Risk and Legislative Behaviour' in C.R. Boynton and C.L. Kim (eds.) *Legislative Systems in Developing Countries* (Duke University Press, Durham, NC 1975)

Shivji, I.G. *Class Struggles in Tanzania* (Macmillan, London, 1975)

Singer, H.W. 'Dualism Revisited: A New Approach' *Journal of Development Studies* 7 (1970-1)

Skinner, E.P. 'Competition within Ethnic Systems in Africa' in L.A. Despres *Ethnicity and Resource Competition in Plural Societies* (Mouton, The Hague, 1975)

Stewart, F. and Streeton, P.P. 'Conflicts between Output and Employment Objectives' in R. Jolly, E. de Kadt *et al.* (eds.) *Third World Employment* (Penguin, Harmondsworth, 1973)

Streek, B. 'All you need to know about Ciskei's Election' in *Daily Dispatch*, 19 August 1977

Sundkler, B.G.M. *Bantu Prophets in South Africa* 2nd edn (Oxford University Press, London, 1961)

Swerdlow, I. (ed.) *Development Administration Concepts and Problems* (Syracuse University Press, New York, 1963)

Theal, G.M. *History of South Africa Since the British Conquest* (Swan Sonnenschein, London, 1920)

Todaro, M. 'A Model of Labour Migration and Urban Unemployment in Less Developed Countries' *American Economic Review* 60 (1969-70)

Todaro, M. and Harms, J.R. 'Migration, Unemployment and Development: A Two-Sector Analysis' *American Economic Review* 60 (1969-70)

Trapido, S. 'African Divisional Politics in the Cape Colony 1884 to 1910' *Journal of African History* 9 (1968)

kaTywakadi, G.R. 'The Development of the Political Party System in the Ciskei' (unpublished dissertation, Rhodes University, Grahamstown, 1977)

University of Natal 'Workshop on Unemployment and Labour Reallocation in South Africa' (unpublished papers, Pietermaritzburg, 1977)

Van Biljon, P. *Grensbakens Tussen Blank en Swart in Suid Afrika* (Juta, Cape Town, 1947)

Van Warmelo, H.J. 'The Classification of Cultural Groups' in W.D. Hammond-Tooke (ed.) *The Bantu Speaking Tribes of Southern Africa* (Routledge & Kegan Paul, London, 1974)

Van Wyk, D.H. 'Die posisie met betrekking tot wetgewing in die Bantoe tuislande' *Tydskrif vir Hedendaagse Romeins-Hollandse Reg* 37 (1974)

Venter, F. 'Bantoe Burgerskap en Tuislandburgerskap' *Tydskrif vir Hedendaagse Romeins-Hollandse Reg* 38 (1975)

Verba, S. and Pye, L.W. *Political Culture and Political Development* (Princeton University Press, Princeton, 1965)

Vincent, J. 'The Changing Role of Small Towns in the Agrarian Structure of East Africa' *Journal of Commonwealth and Comparative Politics* 12 (1974)

Wallerstein, I. *Africa: The Politics of Independence* (Random House, New York, 1961)

Waxmonsky, R.W. 'Selected Characteristics of Bantus Employed by East London Industrial Firms' (unpublished paper, Institute of Social and Economic Research, Rhodes University, Grahamstown, 1975)

Weber, M. *The Theory of Social and Economic Organization* Talcott Parsons (ed.) (The Free Press, New York, 1964)

Weeks, J. 'Policies for Expanding Employment in the Informal Urban Sector of Developing Economies' *International Labour Review* 111 (1975)

Weisskopf, T. 'Capitalism, Underdevelopment, and the Future of Poor Countries' *Review of Radical Political Economics* (1972)

Wilcox, D. *Mass Media in Black Africa: Philosophy and Control* (Praeger, New York, 1975)

Wilson, M. 'The Early History of the Transkei and Ciskei' *African Studies* 18 (1959)

Wriggins, W.H. 'Impediments to Unity in New Nations: the Case of

Ceylon' in C.E. Welch (ed.) *Political Modernization* (Wadsworth, Belmont, 1967)

Newspapers

Daily Dispatch (East London)
World (Johannesburg)
Eastern Province Herald (Port Elizabeth)
Evening Post (Port Elizabeth)
Natal Witness (Pietermaritzburg)
Sunday Tribune (Durban)
Guardian (London)

Periodicals

To the Point (Johannesburg)

Official Reports

Tomlinson Commission Report, Union of South Africa, Department of Native Affairs, Verslag van die Kommissie vir die sosio ekonomiese ontwikkeling van die Bantoe gebiede binne die Unie Van Suid Afrika (Government Printer, Pretoria, 1956)

Department of Bantu Administration and Development, Memorandum for the Guidance of Bantu Authorities, Pretoria (Government Printer, QP 53255331-1962-73-250)

Ciskeian General Council, Proceedings and Reports of Select Committees of the Session of 1934

Ciskei Government, Official Gazettes

—— Reports of the Auditor General, 1973-6

—— Annual Report of the Ciskeian Public Service Commission, 1977; Ciskei Legislative Assembly Verbatim Reports 1971/76

NOTES ON CONTRIBUTORS

P.A. Black, M. Com. (Stellenbosch) M. Litt (Glasgow), is a Senior Lecturer in the Economics Department of Rhodes University, Grahamstown, South Africa. He contributed an article on the homelands to *Public Policy and the South African Economy* edited by M.L. Truu (Oxford University Press, London, 1976), and is the author of numerous journal articles on development economics.

Nancy Charton, BA (University of South Africa) M. Admin. (Pretoria), is a Senior Lecturer in the Department of Political Studies, Rhodes University. She is co-editor of two books, *White South African Elites* with H.W. van der Merwe, M.J. Ashley and B.J. Huber (Juta & Co.Ltd, Cape Town, 1974) and *African Perspectives on South Africa* with H.W. van der Merwe, D.A. Kotze and Ake Magnusson (David Philip, Cape Town, 1978). She has also contributed articles to numerous journals.

G.P. Cook, MA (Natal) PhD (Chicago), is a Research Assistant, Energy Research Institute, University of Cape Town. She also teaches in the Geography Department at that University. As a specialist in urban geography she has contributed an article to *Focus on Cities* edited by H. Watts (University of Natal, Durban, 1970) and to Volume 2 of *Survey of Cape Midlands and Karroo Regions* (Department of Planning, Pretoria, 1971). She is author of numerous articles in journals and of a research paper, 'Spatial Dynamics of Business Growth in the Witwatersrand' (University of Chicago, Research Paper 157, Chicago, 1974).

J.B. McI.Daniel, MA (Natal and Cantab.) PhD (Natal), is Professor and Head of Department of Geography at Rhodes University, Chairman of the Institute for Social and Economic Research at that university and President of the South African Geographical Society. He contributed to *The Swazi Rural Economy* edited by J.F. Holleman (Oxford University Press, London, 1964), to Volume 5 of *The Survey of Cape Midlands and Karroo Regions* (Department of Planning, Pretoria, 1975); he edited *Grahamstown and its Environs* (Institute for Social and Economic Research, Rhodes University, Grahamstown, 1974) and is the author of numerous journal articles.

Notes on Contributors

D.M. Groenewald, BA (Stellenbosch) MA (Rhodes), is lecturer in the Department of Development Administration, Stellenbosch University, and is the author of two papers on local government (Fore Hare Papers Volume 5, No. 6, 1973 and No. 5, 1972).

C.W. Manona, BA (Hons) (University of South Africa), is a Junior Research Officer with the Institute of Social and Economic Research, Rhodes University. He has contributed to *Culture and Morality* edited by H. Kuckertz (Lumko Missiological Institute, Lady Frere, 1979).

F.G. Richings, BA, LL.B. (Cape Town) BA (Hons.) (South Africa) is an advocate of the Supreme Court of South Africa and of the High Court of Lesotho. He has held teaching posts at the University of Natal and Rhodes University and is at present Professor of Criminal Law and Procedure in the University of South Africa. He has published a number of journal notes and articles in the field of public law.

L.E. Switzer, MA (University of California) PhD (University of Natal), is Professor in the Department of Journalism at Rhodes University. He is author of *Black Press in South Africa and Lesotho 1836-1976* (a descriptive bibliographical guide) with D. Switzer (G.K. Hall, Boston, 1979); *Politics and Communication in the Ciskei* (Institute for Social and Economic Research, Rhodes University, Grahamstown, 1979), and of numerous journal articles.

G.R. kaTywakadi, BA (University of South Africa) BA (Hons) (Fort Hare) MA (Rhodes University), was a research assistant at the Institute for Social and Economic Research and is now working as a personnel officer.

N.L. Webb, BA (Hons) (Rhodes University), teaches Geography at Lawson Brown High School, Port Elizabeth, South Africa.

M.G. Whisson, PhD (Cantab), is Professor and Head of Department of Anthropology, Rhodes University. He is author of *Change and Challenge* (Nairobi, 1964); *Under the Rug* (Hong Kong, 1965) and *Domestic Servants* with W.M. Weil (Johannesburg, 1971).

INDEX

Abraham, Hans 107, 163
administrative system 59, 66, 72, 82-95, 232
   Africanisation 92, 232
   Bantu Authority System 60, 67, 88-92; community authority 88-9; regional authority 88-9; territorial authority 60-1, 89-90, 106, 124, 126; tribal authority 60, 64, 67, 88-91, 106, 135, 199-200
   centralisation of 90, 93
   control of 66, 72-3
   departments 72
   history of 82-9
   Public service 92-5, 232; public servants 73, 92-5, 125, 137, 200; Public Service Commission 93
African National Congress 122, 132
African Nationalism 226
Afrikaans 188-90
Afrikaners 225, 234
agriculture 10, 12, 48-58, 228
   animal husbandry 50, 52, 55
   attitude towards 14, 48-58
   betterment scheme 49, 113-15
   control of 66
   development of 22-3, 54
   earnings from 10, 12, 49-50
   extension services 53-7
   farmers 125, 138
   farming: cash crop 54; mixed 52
   field size 49, 57
   party policy on 124-5
   production 23-4, 56
Apartheid or separate development 105, 119, 124, 137-9, 193-4, 203, 205
armaments 67
aspirations 230
   economic Table 9.8(a) 168-72
Auditor General 75
Ayliff, Rev. John 101

banking 68
Bantu Investment Corporation 26
Biko, S. 145, 226

Black consciousness 122, 192-3, 231
Black Peoples' Congress 122-3
Black Peoples' Convention 163
Bophuthatswana 59, 71, 76
British 215-18, 225
   government 84, 102-3, 110
   Kaffraria 84
Brownlee 217, 219
Burnshill 108-13, 215-16, 229
Burns-Ncamashe, Chief 134, 145-6, 165
Butterworth Methodist Mission 101

Cape Native Laws and Customs Commission 84
Cathcart, Sir George 84
cattle killing 103, 114, 218-19
censorship
   self 205
change 185-7, 205
chiefs 52, 222, 224-5
   chiefdoms 87, 99, 117, 220
   criteria for accession 225, 227
   in legislature 64, 124-31, 135-7, 141-7, 176-7, 232-4
   in local administration 82-91, 229
   in news communication 199-202
   Paramount Chief of AmaRharhabe 64, 106, 124, 181
   in party politics 178-9
Christianity 101-4, 217
   Xhosa Christian bodies 226
Church 190-200, 206
   affiliation: Anglican 191; Independent 191, Methodist 191; mission 191; Order of Ethiopia 104, 115-17, 200; Presbyterian 104, 110, 191
cinema 188
Ciskei
   economy 16, 29, 230-1
   geographical area 9, 61-2
   gross domestic product 49
   identity crisis 161
   per capita income 10, 14
   socio economic profile 9-15
Ciskei cabinet 61-2, 65, 72-3, 125, 130, 136

Index

Chief Minister 72-3, 142, 231-2
  Ministers 72-3, 142
Ciskei Constitution 59-81
Ciskei Constitution Proclamation 61-3, 72-3
  constitutional development 75-8
  an internally autonomous country 76-8
  a self-governing homeland 59-76, 97, 231
Ciskei Legislative Assembly 149-84, 188, 231-2
  Acts of 66
  Bills of 66-7, 77, 150-3
  chairman of 65
  committee system 158
  and communication 175-6
  and economic dependence 167-75
  ethnic rivalry in 97-8
  functions: control 156-8; law-making 150-6; political socialisation 158-9, 176
  institutionalisation 161-5
  legislation Table 9.1 152
  legitimacy of 180-4
  members of 133, 180, 190, 200, 203, 232
  parties in 123-47
  powers of 61-81, 165-7
  procedure in 65
  quorum in 65
  secretary 65
  sessions of 65
  survey of 15, 140-1, 198
Ciskei National Development Corporation 24, 38
  lending policy 26
  loans 26, 67
Ciskei political parties 72, 123-47
  attitudes towards official opposition party 138-47
  Ciskei National Independence Party (Ikhonco) 97, 108, 113, 125-33
  Ciskei National Party (Inbokotho) 97, 108, 113, 126-9, 133-5
  ethnic base of 98-108
  One Party System 139-47, 233
  policy 137-9
  in rural areas 135-6
  structure 131-5
  in townships 136-7
Ciskei Territorial Authority 60-1, 89-90, 106-7, 124, 126

Ciskei Township Board 33
citizenship 62
  Bantu Homelands Citizenship Act 62-3
  Ciskeian citizenship 61-3
  citizens 77
  SA citizenship 62
  SA Citizenship Act 63
commerce 66
Commissioner General 60, 66, 73, 107, 130
communication, interpersonal 198-203
  surveys 187
  word of mouth 185-6, 198-203
communications networks 199
  grid 203
communications system 232, 234
  postal 68, 76
  railways 68, 76
  roads 40-2, 45-6, 67, 228
community development 123
conflict 14, 97-121, 125-6, 200
  Fingo Day 104, 114
  Fingo manifesto 107
  Ntsikana Day 104
  political 233
  slavery myth 105
consensus 82
constituencies 123
consumption 230, 231
  consumer goods 22
councillors 88
council system 60
  Bantu authorities
  history of 85-7; district council 85; General Council 87; location council 85
  local councils (Iinkundla) 88-92, 229; at Burnshill 109, 113; and communication of political news 199-200; at Gobozana 135-7; regional authority 60
courts 69, 70, 73-4, 231
  Appellate Division 74
  High Court 74
  Magistrate's Court 73-4
  Regional Court 74
  Supreme Court 70, 71, 130-1
credit facilities 24, 26
customs 68

debates 142, 150-8

intervention in Table 9.5 157
issues raised in 154-6
structure of Table 9.2 153
dependence 9-11, 19, 228-34
development 16-29, 84, 87-92
  commercial 124, 138
  economic 16-29, 78
  industrial 21-7, 43-4, 48, 52, 66, 124-5, 138, 173, 229-30
  industrial decentralisation 23, 24
Dundas, Major General 83
D'Urban, Sir Benjamin 83, 102
Dwane, Rev. James 104, 115

economic analysis
  neo-classical school 16-17
  neo-Marxist school 16-19
  structuralist school 16, 18, 27
education 53-4, 66, 103, 124-5, 138
  achievement 111-13, 207
  aspirations Table 9.8(f) 169, 199
  department of 118
  and income 21-2
  and mass media 190, 197, 199, 207
  minister of 125
elections 62, 123-31, 145
  elected members of Ciskei Legislative Assembly 64, 65
  electoral divisions 64
  electoral qualifications 64
  ethnic conflict during 72, 97-108, 115
  1973: candidates 127-9; irregularities 129-31
  1974: township 137
  1978: 145-7, 220, 232-3
  of Chief Minister 72
elite
  educated elite 85, 88
  political elite 91-2, 232-4
employment 20, 22, 27, 48, 52, 57, 173, 190, 206, 208, 228, 229
English 190
entrepreneurs 232
executive 61, 72-3, 107, 124-5
extra-territoriality 69

films 186
finance 74-5, 231
  budget 92
  public expenditure 157, 175
  revenue 67, 74-5

taxation 67, 74-5, 182-3
flag 61, 62
foreign relations 68
franchise 122
  qualifications 64
  rights 62
frontier wars
  5th 83
  6th 83, 102, 216
  8th 84
  War of the Axe 217

Gcaleka 99-101, 214-20
Glen Grey 62, 123, 129
  Act 85
Gobozana 14, 50-7, 135-7, 187, 198-202
Grey, Sir George 84-5, 218
Gwali 117, 118

headman 52, 82, 84, 87, 105, 110, 125, 135-6, 199-203, 234
health
  control of 66
  personnel 125, 138
  services 138
Herschel 62
Hintsa 100, 101, 105, 214, 216, 218, 220
Hlubi 113-18
homelands 19
  Bantu Authorities System 88-91
  legislation: Bantu Administration Act 65, 69, 105; Bantu Authorities Act 60, 119, 135; Bantu Homelands Citizenship Act 62-3; Bantu Homelands Constitution Act 60-3, 66, 69, 72-5, 123; Native Affairs Act 85; promotion of Bantu Self-Government Act 60
  new deal 106-8
  news 192-9
  policy 18, 60-1

immigration 68
income distribution 11
  in Mdantsane 21, 27, 206
independence 59, 76, 78, 124, 138
influx control 229
informal sector 19, 24-5
  in Mdantsane 21
interest rates 26
international recognition 59, 78

Index

community 20
investment 172

Jabavu, J. Tengo 105, 192
justice 67, 73
  judicial powers 83-4
  Minister of Justice 73

KwaZulu 75

Laing, Rev. J. 110
land
  consolidation of Ciskei 77, 124, 138
  lack of 20, 117, 119, 124, 175, 229, 233
  rehabilitation 49
  rights 50, 91, 109-19, 217
language fluency 190, 207
law 66, 67, 69
  international 63
leadership 181-2
legislatures 149-50
  problems of new 159-61
libraries 67
literacy 190
local-level politics 50, 52-3, 109-19, 135-7

Mabandla Chief Justice 106-8, 124-31, 135, 138, 140, 163-4, 227
magazines 186-90, 204, 207
  Bona 189-90
  Drum 189, 207
  Inkqubela 189-90
  Reader's Digest 189
  readership 207
  Scope 189
magistrate(s) 84, 85, 87, 117
Maitland, Lieut. Gen. Peregrine 84
Malawi 90
Maqoma, Chief 214-26
  Lent Maqoma 220-5
mass media 144, 185-213, 234
  attitude towards 192-8
  exposure to 188-91
  influence of 205, 231
  survey 14, 188-98, 205-8
Matanzima, Chief Kaiser 165, 181
Mdushane 214, 220
Mfengu 83, 97, 99-119, 124, 126, 136, 216, 219, 221-7
migrant labour 10, 42-3, 50, 54, 124, 198-9, 228-9
military 68
missionary(ies) 101-2, 110
mobility 20, 198
Mpondo 109
multi-racialism 124, 133, 138
  non-racialism 122
Mzimba, Rev. P.J. 104

Napier, Sir George 83
national anthem 61, 63
Ndlambe 214, 219
news
  Ciskei 194-8
  credibility rating of 187, 192-204
  international 194-8
  national 194-8
  oral sources 185-7, 198-204
  political 199-200
  radio 194-8
  regional 194-8
  township 194-8
newspapers 186, 188-98, 201, 203-5, 207
  Black press 122
  Daily Dispatch 189-97, 201, 205, 207
  English-language press 188-9, 195, 203-5
  Evening Post 189
  Imvo Zabantsundu 122, 189-97, 201, 207
  Indaba 192
  Rand Daily Mail 189, 192
  readership 207
  Sunday Times 189
  Weekend World 189
Ngqika 83, 99, 102, 214-19
Nguni 100, 103
Nongqause 218
Ntaba KaNdoda 219-25
Nyaniso 14, 50-7, 109, 113-19, 174, 187, 189, 199-202

old-age pensions 118
opinion leaders 185-7, 203, 205
  credibility of 201-5
Opposition 97, 115, 139-47, 153, 158, 163, 192, 232-3

Parliament, South African 69-71, 74, 76
  Acts of 70
Perskor 189, 192

Phalo 214, 219
police 67, 200
population 9, 48-9, 174, 228-9
 growth 10, 20, 22, 27, 42
 pressure on land 12
 urban 166
poverty 10, 20, 21, 229
 datum line 20, 21, 210, 229
 minimum effective level 191, 197, 210
praise poet 222, 226
Provincial Councils 69, 70
public holidays 67
public works 67

Qwa Qwa 75

radio 68, 76, 188-98, 204-5, 207
 British Broadcasting Corporation 189
 Good Hope 189, 195
 Mozambique 189
 Radio Bantu 193-8, 207
 SABC English Language Station 189, 195
 South African Broadcasting Corporation 222
 Springbok Radio 189, 195
 Swaziland 189
 Voice of America 189
 Zambia 189
registration of births 67
relatives 201
religion 52, 54, 55
 and attitude towards agriculture 52, 54, 55
 and attitude towards mass media 190-1
re-settlement 20, 49-50, 55, 124, 139, 167, 174, 229
Rharhabe 107, 108, 125-7, 214-20, 222, 224-5, 227
Robben Island 219, 226
Rubusana, Walter 105
rural areas
 communications in 190, 198-203
 lack of development in 228-9, 233
 local level politics in 109-19, 135-6
 rural surveys 50-8, 198-203
 social occasions 52-5
 support for Sebe in 227
 villages in 39, 45, 185-7, 198-203, 228-9

Sandile 106, 110, 124, 215-17, 219-20, 222, 225-6
Sarili 218-20
school
 agency of communication 199-200
Sebe, Chief Minister L.L. 20, 48-9, 108, 125-6, 129-30, 134, 137-8, 142, 145, 164, 173, 181, 220, 223, 225-6, 231
security legislation (South African) 144-5
seer 222-6
Shrewsbury, Rev. 101
Sigwawu, Xolilizwe 220
Smith, Sir Harry 84, 216-20
Sobukwe, R. 226
Somerset, Lord Charles 83
South African Defence Force 221, 224, 226
South African State President 60-2, 65-6, 68-9, 72-7
South African Students' Organisation 122, 133, 145, 163
South African Television 186, 188, 222
Soweto 167, 194 201
stratification, social 231-3

Tanzania 90
teachers 125, 137
territorial waters 62
Thembu 107
Tomlinson Commission Report 48-51, 55, 57
towns
 in Ciskei 32-47, 124, 138, 228
 Mdantsane 9, 10, 13, 20, 24-5, 36-8, 40, 42, 43, 61, 74, 228; church affiliation in 206; educational achievement 207; elections at 14, 123-9, 136-7; household income in 206; mass media in 188-98, 201, 203-7; occupation 206-7; surveys of 15, 20, 140-5, 162-83, 188-98, 205-7
 Zwelitsha 9, 10, 13, 20, 24-5, 36-43, 61, 65, 74, 123-9, 133, 137; elections at 14
trade 100
traders 125, 138

Index

Trade Unions 138
transitional society 185-7, 198-205
Transkei 11, 59-61, 70, 75, 99, 102,
    193-4, 220, 232
  amalgamation with 124, 138-9,
    145, 163-5
  Transkei Constitution Act 60
  Transkei High Court 75
  Transkei Legislative Assembly 70
treaties 68
tribes 67
  tribal structure 177-8
Tshawe 99

underdevelopment 16, 20, 27
unemployed 229, 230
  in Mdantsane 20-1, 207
  in rural areas 20-1, 207; under-
    employed 20
urbanisation 46, 138, 142
  communications in urban areas
    185-98, 201-5
  urban Africans and legislature 166
  urban system 30-2, 41, 46, 228

voters 64, 123-9
  registration of 64
  voting 64-5

welfare 66
workers 124, 138, 173-4, 233

Xhosa 63, 83, 97-119, 124, 136,
    189-90, 214-26; Development
    Corporation 26